ADVERTISING

This Second Edition
is dedicated
with all devotion
to Jill and Adrian,
my wife and son
—the best adverisements
for life and love
I shall ever know.

ADVERTISING

its Purpose
Principles
and Practice

DAVID SHELLEY NICHOLL,
B.A. (Harv.)

 MACDONALD AND EVANS

MACDONALD AND EVANS LTD.
Estover, Plymouth PL6 7PZ

First published 1973
Second edition 1978

MACDONALD AND EVANS LIMITED
1978

ISBN: 0 7121 0166 7

Printed in Great Britain by Butler & Tanner Ltd., Frome and London

PREFACE TO THE FIRST EDITION

This book has evolved from several series of lectures prepared for students of marketing, copywriting, advertising design and photography. The classes also contained students from related fields and disciplines, most subjects being directly promotional, though not all. None of the students was taking a course in Advertising as such, for the unfortunate reason that there are no such courses to be found at any of the colleges concerned. There are indeed very few to be found anywhere, and the courses organised by the Communications Advertising and Marketing Education Foundation have yet to find wide acceptance in the industry.

Advertising is seldom treated as a subject in itself; only as the adjunct or subdivision of a "larger" subject, usually marketing. This, in my view, is looking through the wrong end of the telescope. Ten years of practical experience in a number of agencies, writing copy for a wide variety of accounts, have convinced me that Advertising should itself be the umbrella discipline under which related professions are studied—public relations, market research, media buying and so on—and that the future of good advertising lies in serious jeopardy if the contrary approach prevails.

More to the point of this book, my years of teaching have made devastatingly clear to me that no student will even begin to understand what Advertising is all about until this perspective is shown to him: that research and theory, statistics and analysis, all these are back-up resources which must recognise the paramount duty of establishing contact with a potential buyer for the purpose of making a sale, and that at the point of contact *what matters is the ad*. If the words connect and the picture inspires, you've got a customer.

Advertising, in other words, is in business to sell; the difficulty I found was to convince my classes that Advertising *was in business at all*! My first task, therefore, was to explain that the phrase "making a sale" was no meaningless cliché, that literally sales *were* made and not born . . . that it followed that advertisements were purpose-built for profit.

After an initial shock, most students accepted this and indeed welcomed the directness of the view. Student "revolts" at art schools have been substantially a result of awareness that unrealism pervades the teaching in most art courses. After three years of existing on grants, students have felt baffled resentment at graduating into a "commercial" world which did not regard itself as automatically obliged to pay them a wage for self-indulgent "creativity." One second-year design student confidently told me in detail how she planned to decorate the private office she assumed would at once be placed at her disposal by her first employer ... and her fantasy is generally shared, to some degree, by all those aiming at Advertising as a career, whether executive or creative. Alas, the fantasy is often shared even by their instructors!

If teachers of art and management courses do not, or cannot, burst this pathetic bubble at first encounter, and continue pricking it every time it blows up rosily on the horizon, I believe they are failing their duty. Most, however, do not ... some for doctrinal or political reasons, some because of sheer funk, too many from sheer massive ignorance of the commercial and industrial realities of Advertising.

As a part-time lecturer, still continuing a thriving advertising consultancy, I attempted, with like-minded colleagues, to contribute a vital dimension of actuality to classroom practice. Where I could obtain client's permission, I've even shown work-in-progress to my students, let them see the brief, read the research, and then freely comment on what I'd produced. These sessions have been as beneficial to me as to them.

This book is therefore a sort of thanks-offering to those students, and many thousands of them all over the country, who want desperately to be told the truth about what Advertising does and how Advertising works, without the frills and the egghead waffle of theoretical tomes or the expansive self-congratulatory anecdotal ramblings of retired admen. To date, all they can read are case-histories of glamorous campaigns or uninformed pontificating from dons who have never stepped inside an agency in their lives. In this country anyway, those like myself who *have* stepped inside many an agency and lived to tell the tale, haven't told it. I am telling it now. And telling it, to the best of my ability, exactly "like it is."

The whole area of Advertising is covered in these pages, but I'm not rash enough to claim the text is exhaustive. I apologise in advance for any omissions; the shape and structure of Advertising is going through an unprecedented ferment of change and my comment will inevitably lag behind some developments. Clients move from one agency to another, top men switch jobs or retire, agencies merge or are "hived off," to use a modish, rather sinister term. In trying to give an accurate and contemporary picture of my profession I would like to pay tribute to the in-depth coverage of events in my field as reported in the columns of *Campaign, AdWeekly* (now regrettably defunct), the *Daily Telegraph, The Times* and *The Financial Times*. Any errors or misinterpretation of facts, and quoted statements are my responsibility alone, however.

I would like to thank J. M. Dent & Sons Ltd. for permission to include the poems "Lather As You Go" and "Song of the Open Road" from *Family Reunion* by Ogden Nash; Little, Brown and Company of Boston, Massachusetts, for permission to include "Lather As You Go," copyright 1942, by Ogden Nash, and "Song of the Open Road," copyright 1932, by Ogden Nash (the latter poem originally appeared in *The New Yorker*); and also Longman Group Limited for permission to include extracts from *Confessions of an Advertising Man* by David Ogilvy.

I would also like to acknowledge the wide range of data and information which the Institute of Practitioners in Advertising makes available to all ... and hereby urge all students to make good use of these resources. Nor would I like it thought I was unaware of the work in teaching Advertising (with other subjects) being carried out by the Communication Advertising and Marketing Educational Foundation—generally referred to simply as C.A.M.—under the directorship first of John Dodge and now of Norman Hart. Although a number of colleges have been approved as having courses suitable for the C.A.M. Creative Diploma in Advertising, my regret is that for the major part C.A.M. trains only those already employed in the agencies, industry or the media. Thus the gap remains.

Prominent among those trying to fill the gap are Trevor Lakin-Hall and Gordon Crossley at Barking College of Technology, and Charles Sutton (in many ways the "onlie begettor" of the work my colleagues and I have tried to do) at Bournemouth and Poole College of Art. But there are others and there will be more, and my earnest hope is that this book will help them as much as their very fortunate students. Finally, I should like to thank Alan Spicer for preparing the illustrations and Chris Radley, Creative Director of Bloxhams Partnership Limited, for permission to use this material.

February 1972   D.S.N.

PREFACE TO THE SECOND EDITION

Four years having gone by since the first edition of this book was published, I have taken the opportunity to bring the contents as up to date as possible, with a thorough review of every section. Advertising as such presents a scenario which has altered little; indeed, it has altered little in essentials for several thousand years. But there are changes in media, customs and conditions and vast changes in statistics. These have all been seen to, but I have not refashioned anecdotes with new actors for their own sake since basic situations have not changed nor have the viewpoints those stories illustrate. They were true then, and remain so.

My most substantial addition has been a section on *The Theory Practitioners*, since "philosophical" works on the industry are now no longer popping up once a season and the principal theoretical tomes are now established for ritual reverence and practical disregard by succeeding generations of apprentice admen—of all ages.

All the tributes I paid in my original Preface hold good for this edition, since many of the same hands and the same sources have invaluably aided my research. I am particularly indebted to Mr. Michael Chamberlain, Editor of *Campaign*, which today is more essential to the professional and aspiring adman than even four years ago. I should also like to thank Mr. Dick Sherwood, Controller of JICTAR, and Mark Elwes, Executive Director of the Direct Mail Producers Association, both of whom obligingly made a few extremely well-educated "guestimates" for me, for which I alone, however, accept full responsibility.

The greatest change I have had to examine is the effect of commercial radio on the advertising scene. As for the Annan Report produced by the Committee of Inquiry into the Future of Broadcasting—a weighty volume of evidence scaling in at no less than twelve stone (or over seventy-two kilograms, as we must all learn to say), published on 25th March after an orchestrated series of leaks which amounted to an advertising campaign in itself—the Socialists say they will implement it in two years if *they* are in power, while the Conservatives will certainly forget the whole thing when *they* reach Downing Street. So clearly, to waste time considering its implications for readers of this book would be to stray into idle speculation if not downright fantasy. The profession thinks little of it.

The more things change, the more they stay the same. It is nowhere more true than in regard to advertising. Granted, advertisements now reach us by satellite (I refer to the placards and posters that surround arenas everywhere and often make some corner of a foreign football field forever England) and TV commercials have passed beyond kitchen-sinks to the toilet-bowl school of advertising—but the Purpose, Principles and Practice of this strange, half-mad, indispensable industry remain steady on course: to make us aware of choice and accept the responsibility of choosing, which is the basic element of a free society and the one to treasure most. The prize (and, granted, the price) is always to have liberty to be made aware of alternatives, whether by means of chimps from Chessington Zoo at the higher end of promotional achievement or Party Political Broadcasts at the lower.

1978   D.S.N.

CONTENTS

Chapter I

WHY ADVERTISE AT ALL?

Professor J. K. Galbraith, author of *The Affluent Society* (a name he coined), has described Advertising as an industry "which lends itself to competitive fraud." According to a past Labour Party discussion paper Advertising encourages "gross materialism and dissatisfaction."

These may be rough words, but they are easily countered. "Competitive fraud" is a contradiction in terms and a vindication of Advertising—the very existence of choice soon uncovers the fraud. It seems that Labour does not wish to abolish the sin, only tax it—what materialism could be grosser than that?

Nevertheless, the chorus of protests which these comments have aroused from all sides in Advertising does not come near to affecting what I consider to be the paramount requirement, that of armouring ourselves against over-emotional criticisms. This requirement will be achieved by organising and codifying the education for, and the practice of, Advertising so that it is recognised as a proper profession with a capital "P."

This aim before all else demands a wider comprehension and acceptance by the public of what Advertising really is and does, and how it developed. My hope is that this book will supply to both the student and the general reader just such a necessary introduction to a much-maligned (and let's face it, often self-destructive) way of making a living that is as honourable, and can be as distinguished, as any other in modern life.

ATTITUDES TO ADVERTISING

Even the most rabid and persistent enemies of Advertising admit the excitements and allure. Advertising has now replaced the stage as the most glamorous of the slightly disreputable—hence, not "proper"—professions, its sinister tentacles looming large and lecherous in the horrified lorgnettes of Britain's eternal Mrs. Worthingtons.

The world of entertainment which formerly beckoned their daughters to delightful perdition has, after all, its Lord Olivier, Sir Alecs and Sir Johns on the boards, its Sir Lew on the box. In

advertising agencies, however, débutantes rarely venture beyond
the reception area. When they do, one is tempted to suggest, they
are cut off with a billing.

Advertising remains both the "ponce" and the "scarlet woman"
of commerce. That this is no exaggeration was made dramatically
evident by a famous outburst from Mrs. Laura Grimond, wife of the
ex-leader of the Liberal Party, who referred to advertisers as "the
handmaidens of private enterprise at its most abandoned."

His Grace, the Archbishop of Canterbury, was fortunately more
restrained in his language. His relatively mild stricture given to the
advertising journal *Campaign* in an interview in March 1970 was
simply that Advertising had "a very dangerous power of persuasion"—a remark no doubt used often by Nero in reference to the
early Christians.

There are hopeful signs also that Advertising will soon cease being
a political football. It seems an advance that Mr. Edward Heath,
when still Tory leader, actually allowed himself to be seen and heard
at an Advertising Association conference (though admittedly while
in Opposition) where he went on record as accepting Advertising and
all its works as "an integral and essential part of modern society."
Habitual thunders from the Left, on the other hand, have tended to
be equivocal, as the Labour Party has more and more overtly made
use of agency men in election campaigns.

THE LEGISLATIVE VIEW

In the main, members of both Houses, and of all political hues
and cries, have felt, to paraphrase Oscar Wilde, that you cannot make
Advertising "good" by Act of Parliament. The *Code of Advertising Practice*, for example, was set out by the profession itself and is not a statute.
There is always a first time, however, and agency complacency on
this score is probably inadvisable. Every parliamentary session throws
up its Savonarolas, and prominent always among them are M.P.s with
Advertising in their sights, fervent folk who tend to get trigger-happy
in marginal constituencies.

A committee of enquiry on consumer protection was set up in 1959
but this did not result in legislation, and indeed the resultant Consumer Council has now been disbanded (though not without righteous howls). The Trade Descriptions Act 1968 (unlike the Indecent
Advertisements Act 1889) only indirectly concerns the profession, as
does the Consumer Credit Act 1974. While the Inertia Selling Bill
(though it brought a well-earned cold sweat to many well-known
brows, low, medium and high!) only survived to a First Reading. (*See*
Chapter XI.)

The most recent attempt to place legislative fetters on Advertising, at time of writing, was an effort by a Labour M.P. to compel advertisers to issue "corrective" ads apologising for errors of fact or description claims. This was not accepted by the Parliamentary Secretary for Trade and Industry, on the grounds that the present professional watchdogs, plus the Criminal Law are quite sufficient deterrents (*see* Appendix III).

More pertinent to these pages was the Industrial Training Act 1964, which required all facets of industry to set up organised training procedures for potential recruits. Again, this measure was not aimed especially at Advertising, though our profession remained the only major facet *which did not comply*. The first moves to correct this deplorable record are, however, at least under way (*see* Preface and p. 195).

Whether the profession has acted in time, or in the right manner, one must wait and see, but certainly the currently popular and popularised view of Advertising must be strongly countered, or the next nightingale heard by the Brahmins of Berkeley Square, the agency mammoth of J. Walter Thompson, may well be trilling a swan-song.

The practising advertising man's principal hope is that these politicians whose thinking follows Robert Louis Stevenson's line that "man is a creature who lives not upon bread alone, but ... by catchwords" will concentrate more on removing the beams from their eyes, and less on attempting to blitz out the acknowledged motes in ours.

HISTORICAL PERSPECTIVE

The current view of Advertising is over-simplified to the point of absurdity by opportunistic crusaders and other "antis." This view is that Advertising is some sort of modern blight that has come upon us as a by-product of the "sickness" of contemporary life, like the penitential sores of Job. It is unique to our society, like polio and pollution. Such propaganda would have us conveniently forget that Sir Walter Scott nearly died of polio two hundred years ago, and that London enjoyed its most exalted culture in the Augustan period of Pope, Reynolds, Swift, Gibbon and Garrick, when it was universally known as the most polluted capital on earth!

When Doctor Johnson observed in 1759 that "advertising is now so near perfection that it is not easy to propose any improvement," nearly three hundred years had passed since the first advertising poster had been printed by Caxton himself! The date was 1480; the poster industry, therefore, described in *The Times* of 28th October 1970 as the "Cinderella" of Advertising, is now in fact almost five hundred years old.

So it seems to me to be of vital importance to any study of what

Advertising is all about, before we consider the rights and wrongs of its practice and applicability, to appreciate clearly that we are not discussing an esoteric art or arcane ritual which has been newly bred in the poisoned veins of vicious modern capitalism and sponsored by the venal votaries of Big Business. Advertising may not be quite as old as sin—but it is just as unoriginal.

In The Beginning

Advertising is an indispensable, crucial form of communication, and as soon as man could grunt he began to advertise (though admittedly, as much to hide as to expose his intentions—when the former is a prime intent, we tend to call it propaganda). According to his grimace, primordial man advertised to neighbours that he was happy or angry. His warpaint advertised his tribe, the plumage of his head-dress told his rank and style.

Tombs of the Chou Dynasty, in the China of the eleventh century B.C. advertised by their grisly contents; the number of the buried chariots and the quantity of skeletons from funeral sacrifices advertised how important the entombed rulers were. Nine hundred years earlier, on the other side of the world, the Pharaohs with their Pyramids had done much the same. They advertised to earth and to heaven. They advertised to the present and to the future. They advertised to *us*!

Down on more mundane levels the ancient Egyptians circulated "lost" and "found" notices inscribed on papyrus (from which we derive our word paper)—what we would today call classified ads—and one can still see on the excavated walls of Pompeii Roman advertisements of A.D. 70 announcing the fun and games to be had at the local baths. It's a wonder some of these did not precipitate an Indecent Advertisements Act for their own time, for Frankie Howerd's "Lurcio" of TV's *Up Pompeii* would have felt right at home among them. More importantly, here in the floor-tiles can still be seen the earliest surviving example of the most familiar ad ever written: "CAVE CANEM," or "Beware of the Dog."

I think we can safely say that man (and woman) began to advertise from the moment he donned that first fig-leaf and started varying the hemline, posing indeed not much differently from many of the tableaux in the Sunday Supplements which tempt us now.

Through the ages

We encounter a more readily recognisable stage in the evolution of Advertising with the advent of the trade-mark. This manifestation of self-promotion had, of course, been around for some time in effect, taking the form of coats-of-arms, which advertised whose side you were on when shields clashed and swords bashed their way through the Dark Ages and feudalism. The Wars of the Roses might reasonably be termed, in fact, the Battle of the Trade-Marks, for a man's life could depend literally on his wearing the right advertisement of allegiance at the right time and place—to adopt a famous TV commercial, his fate depended entirely on which rose grew on him!

A trade-mark, however, is fundamentally exactly what it says, the mark of a trade (though some merchandisers tend to forget this essential fact these days), and both the barber's pole and the three balls of the pawnbroker date from as far back as the Renaissance.

Until the coming of print the town-crier was the main purveyor of ads, functioning much as our disc-jockeys do in commercial radio (*see* Chapter XII), to spread tidings of wares, wars, disasters and bargains—with about the same range of expression as a modern D.J., to judge from Hamlet's remarks to the Players. Then in 1480 along came William Caxton to print the first poster (*pace* the Archbishop) in the precincts of Westminster Abbey, of all places. He not only changed the advertising scene for ever by so doing, but gave a hint of future developments by being patronised by both York *and* Lancaster during the Battle of the Trade-Marks.

So deep and essential is the root-urge to advertise that the first press advertisements appeared as soon as there were newspapers to print them in. The very first ad for a "dentifrice" that would make the teeth "white as ivory" and sweeten the breath had to wait only till stern Cromwell was in his grave before appearing in the pages of the December issue of *Mercurius Politicus* in 1660, when London journals were already calling themselves by Latin names, in the tradition continued on our own news-stands by *Spectator* and *Tribune*, not to mention all the *Mercurys* and *Arguses* in the suburbs and provinces.

King Charles II had barely assumed the throne, in that same year of 1660, before he himself took an advertisement to ask for the return of a stolen dog, his classified ad reading, in part:

> "... Whosoever finds him may acquaint any at Whitehal, for the Dog was better known at Court than those who stole him. Will they never leave robbing His Majesty? Must he not keep a Dog? This Dogs place (though better than some imagine) is the only place which nobody offers to beg."

It would be nice if one could believe that even the highly-trained tele-ad girls of the *Evening Standard* or *The Times* could compose something half so relevant and witty.

It was not long before advertisements became so popular and

abundant that some bright spark in "Whitehal" came up with the inevitable idea of taxing them. This was imposed in 1712 (and by a Tory Government), nor was the tax removed until 1853, by which time the first advertising agencies were well established (*see* Chapter II), both here and in the United States, which is where we came in.

SO WHO NEEDS IT?

My answer to this question has by now, I hope, been made crystal clear. I would point to human nature and to history, and answer: "Who does *not* need it?"

I would urge the student to forget all his preconceptions about the profession of Advertising. The demonstrators whose placards enforest Trafalgar Square are "advertising" just as surely as the detergent tycoon—metaphorically, in fact, they are offering not dissimilar products. Wild beards, frizzed or unkempt hair are as surely advertisements as a blue rinse or a short back-and-sides. All are accomplishing the basic function of Advertising, which is simply to bring something deliberately to the notice of someone else—this is the semantic truth of the word, which comes from the French *avertir*, to notify.

Avertir also means to warn, which is fair enough comment. Advertising forces no one to make a purchase, it exerts no sinister power of hypnosis to compel anyone to part with his money. Far from being an out-of-date hangover from the days of blood-and-guts capitalism, the fact that it makes *notification of choice* freely available ensures a claim that Advertising is a cornerstone of any free society—and I make this claim.

SO WHO PAYS FOR IT?

We all do, of course, just as we pay for the research that evolved the advertised product and the package which contains the product. All are elements in the merchandising process (*see* Chapter II). If, for example, you do not cavil at paying your share of the cost of binding and printing this book in your hands, why object to the legitimate cost of advertising its publication, to the cost of the methods by which you are notified that the book exists and where it can be obtained?

Without Advertising we should not know the range of products available in any field, to buy or not, as we choose. Without Advertising we should not know what political parties stand for—or say they do—which supermarket offers the best values, what time church services are being held, when we can tune in to the news, where we can dance to our favourite music, eat our favourite food, assemble for protest . . . or how we can avoid some or all of these things and events.

The alternative of a world without Advertising would impose a dire payment on a scale far higher than any price we pay now. We should pay in a morass of drab conformity, in chains (metaphorical or otherwise), sometimes in blood, certainly always in stifling of thought. This would be the exactment if advertising techniques did not exist, even when we may feel they exist to be abused in the puffery of utterly unworthy things.

We pay for Advertising with the agony of choice. This is no robbery of self-respect or dignity; it is a gift *beyond* price. That it remains a weapon to tempt the unscrupulous in no way lessens its value. The sculptor and the burglar can use identical tools. Neither, as far as I know, is embarrassed or ashamed of the fact.

ALIBIS OR APOLOGIAS?

The late Aneurin Bevan once called Advertising "an evil thing" (perhaps because he had heard the profession described by Sir Winston Churchill as spurring "individual exertion and greater production"), yet no one advertised himself and his opinions with greater expertise. It was a very different sort of politician, as you might expect, who frankly set forth the job he believed Advertising should do and the function it served. Its value, he said, was "to create new demands, to cultivate new tastes and requirements, to promote the sale of new kinds of goods and to explain their uses to the consumer."

The most reactionary, dyed-in-the-wool, devilish capitalistic agency man would happily rest his case on that piece of stirring advocacy. Yet the phrases are those of Mr. Anastas Mikoyan, veteran among Russia's old-guard leaders, Communist of Communists.

This book is concerned with the commercial application of Advertising. However, this cannot be properly comprehended without an understanding also of the wider and deeper implications involved. It is interesting and extremely instructive, I think, that Advertising was praised by the Deputy Editor of *The Sunday Telegraph* as a useful corrective to most doom-laden editorial content. In effect, stated Mr. Worsthorne, the "vested interests" of the advertising industry "compel it to be the bearer of good tidings," so that the copywriter "revels . . . in good news."

I agree. And in the interview quoted previously in this chapter the former Archbishop of Canterbury said that *he* was selling Christianity (the term is his), "not because it is attractive" but because it was "something we sell that is good news—terribly *good news*" (author's italics).

Dr. Ramsey's words were carefully chosen. He meant what he said and therefore it is perhaps not surprising that he managed to say a great deal more than he means. The medieval original of the words "good news" is the Anglo-Saxon phrase *godspell*, which we have since contracted to "gospel." In sum, what I believe the best Advertising aims for, and is organised to achieve, is nothing more nor less than the gospel truth.

Let us now see how it is done.

Chapter II

HOW ADVERTISING IS ORGANISED

The reason why of Advertising is inextricably bound up with the rationale of *how*. The "good news" it conveys rests not only in its message but in its very existence *per se*. For Advertising, by ensuring wider markets for a product, means that product becomes more profitable to make and cheaper to buy, which in turn ensures larger turnover and expansion, which in turn increases jobs, while making a wider variety of goods and services available to the High Street. It makes experiment with new products a more worthwhile risk, development of an established product (never very tempting) a more viable and attractive economic proposition.

So the *godspell* is as much for manufacturer as for customer. Yet Advertising remains on suspicious sufferance from both its beneficiaries. Why? I think the reason is basically that Advertising forms the great communicative thread of commerce—and communication is the strongest, as well as the most tender and abused, of all the threads of humanity.

The main failing of Advertising is that humanity, in fact. One man's honest "telling it like it is" may not be his neighbour's. So the neighbour's a liar. Advertising, sure, makes all men brothers—like Cain and Abel—and the cynic cannot help wondering who wants to keep up with the Joneses when they're hoist by their own petard to the highest tree in town?

AT THE BUSINESS END

Businessmen, however, cannot afford to be cynics, and realise that Advertising is today the most essential link in the chain of activities that constitute modern merchandising. Unfortunately, the prime difficulty of determining the precise extent of its value and efficiency (*see* Chapter IV) makes Advertising an ostentatious—not to say brazen—affront to a business world more and more conditioned to believe that everything is calculable to the smallest detail. Advertising still thumbs its nose at the computer (though vice versa does not apply).

Lord Leverhulme strongly exemplified the love–hate relationship, feeling no doubt that Port Sunlight needed no artificial rays, when he bitterly remarked: "Half the money I spend on advertising is wasted, and the trouble is I don't know which half." The fact that the quotation was also attributed to John Wanamaker, the American store magnate, served to emphasise the universality of the complaint.

THE AGENCY SCENE

As I hope was made plain in Chapter I, the Advertising idea is thousands of years old. The manner in which we find it organised today, however, has a very brief history—and that history is still being shaped as I write.

The year of 1812 saw more than the start of the campaign which would burn Washington and the finish of the one which burned down Moscow; it witnessed the first campaign of the oldest advertising agency in the world, Reynell & Son, a firm of admen you can still find in Chancery Lane! Three years later, the founder of Charles Barker & Sons rushed back from Flanders with the tidings of Waterloo and was rewarded by the City with a wealth of financial and government advertising contracts, an association which remains in thriving shape today. Both agencies, you'll be glad to hear, were listed in a *Guide* of 1852 as "respectable and responsible" in distinguished contrast to a number of other "disreputable persons calling themselves Advertising Agents;" but the first British advertising agent in our full modern meaning (he didn't make the *Guide*, I regret to inform you) was probably Thomas Holloway, a self-styled "professor," who began in 1838 by marketing a cure-all pill more successfully than any rival, ending up some twenty years later with a personal fortune of £5 million, and a world-wide advertising business which extended from ads in Chinese and Peruvian newspapers to using the Great Pyramid as a poster-site! His turnover, or "billing," reached £50,000 per annum in the 1870s, and he was also running an agency in the United States where, as an American competitor noted ironically, he was better known than Napoleon. He deserved to be; he had certainly done better on the Pyramids than the Little Corporal.

In Advertising, as in most other aspects of commerce and industry, the tide now flows strongly in the opposite direction across the Atlantic. The impudent intrusion has long been avenged (the first United States agency opened in Philadelphia in 1841), now that more and more of our agencies are American-owned, the largest being J. Walter Thompson, Brahmins of Berkeley Square (they own one side of it). The second largest group is still proudly British (with expansion to Holland and Belgium) however. Called Lopex, its billing in 1976, by contrast to "Professor" Holloway's a century ago, was £42·5 million. On the other hand, its pre-tax profits were under 3 per cent—whereas the professor settled for nothing less than 100 per cent.

Agencies came into existence because of two parallel factors; (1) the rapid escalation in numbers of products after the Industrial Revolution, and (2) the vast increase in newspapers and journals as literacy became universal, if less sophisticated. The advertising agent was really an agent *for the media*, not for the manufacturer, and he was paid a commission by the newspaper-owners for selling their space. He still is.

It's extremely important for the student to realise this fact. An advertising agency—apart from its fees for specialist services—is paid by the newspaper or magazine which prints its work (the same system has been carried over into television), *not* by the advertiser whose wares it promotes. This commission varies usually from 10 per cent to 15 per cent, and gives rise to an extraordinarily ambivalent relationship. On the one hand, a newspaper can delay commission payments and force agencies out of business (Dickens, as editor of *Household Words*, did his best to scupper Holloway). On the other, newspapers cannot exist long without sufficient advertising revenue (their news-stand price covers little of their actual production cost) and will perish if it is removed, or not enough ads are forthcoming.

This mutual dependence (and, on occasion, mutual blackmail) makes for an uneasy bed-fellowship. Sometimes disaster strikes one way, sometimes another. When the John Bloom washing-machine "empire" fell it took four agencies down with it, and the scars were visible in many media. From the other side, many newspapers today are delaying commission payments to such an extent that more than one well-known agency feels seriously threatened—the clients aren't paying up either, at least not fast enough, and the extra fire-power of a new media surcharge means that guns to left and to right are boom-bang-abanging with about equal volley and thunder.

The balance of power, in the long run, is probably on the side of the Light Brigade. The number of newspapers is already decreasing—both the *News Chronicle* and the *Mirror Colour Supplement* were victims of lack of advertising—while there are still roughly three hundred agencies in Britain (the 1852 *Guide* listed only thirteen). Most of these (297) belong to the Institute of Practitioners in Advertising (called, hereinafter, the I.P.A.) and place about 90 per cent of all current advertising. It's generally conceded that there are about fifty "top" agencies, but mergers and takeovers are continually fudging this statistic. The I.P.A. is now sixty years old, and in 1976 the turnover of its member agencies exceeded £750 million.

THE I.P.A. AND THE A.A.

Everyone knows about the Automobile Association and Alcoholics Anonymous, but the third A.A. in our national life is much less familiar, although it has a much greater effect upon us all than either of the other two. The Advertising Association and the I.P.A. make up a combined aegis under which almost all British Advertising operates. Their functions frequently overlap, and they work in close partnership in many areas of the field, particularly in education.

The I.P.A. sees itself mainly as a check on the ethical standards of agency practice and has evolved from the Association of British Advertising Agents, founded during the First World War, in 1917. The avowed purpose of this organisation is to establish, "once and for all, the position of the service advertising agency, through the introduction and observance of professional standards of practice; thereby, helping to make possible as it has, both the quality and scope of the advertising and marketing services rendered to advertisers," and it admits Members (who have to pass exams), Associates and, most grand of all, Fellows. For all this grandeur and high principle, the initial impetus towards the profession's various codes of practice (*see* Chapter XV) has come from the Advertising Association.

The A.A. was formed rather later, in 1924, after a conference of the advertising clubs of the world, and it is distinguished from the I.P.A. by the fact that its membership is not restricted to agencies (clients, printers and media-owners can all belong). The A.A. is also able to conduct, through the wider spread of its membership and international affiliations, deeper research which often provides information over a more extended area of interest; its influence and prestige will undoubtedly grow with our entry into the Common Market.

We might also note here that the clients have their own parallel "closed shop" organisation, called the Incorporated Society of British Advertisers, which proudly claims that it is "the only channel in the United Kingdom through which advertisers can act and speak with unity." Though it co-operates closely with the other two bodies it antedates both, having been originally formed at the turn of the century as the Advertisers' Protection Society, and this perhaps indicates what it really regards as its prime function!

In spite of the fact that the great majority of agencies do belong to the I.P.A., which offers its three letters rather as a magic "guarantee of quality" to prospective advertisers, there is no legal compunction to belong or sit for its examinations; nor is membership, association or even fellowship at all necessary to an agency's prosperity. The 297 agencies which belong, however, handle between 85–90 per cent of all advertising placed through U.K. agencies.

Where once—and not long ago, at that—no agency considered it had properly "arrived" in the Big Time till achieving membership or election, there are today a number of non-conformist agencies who treat the I.P.A. with perhaps a slightly affected, but nevertheless effective, disdain. Both Kingsley, Manton & Palmer (who presumably feel that though "You Can Take a White Horse Anywhere," you can't make it drink) and Papert Koenig Lois (who have also flouted another sacred cow of the Adworld, *see* end of Chapter V) have snubbed what was once an I.P.A. cornerstone of principle: they dared to solicit clients away from rival outfits—during the first six months of their existence, in fact, as they themselves admitted in *Campaign*, K.M.P. attempted the offence roughly one hundred and fifty times. No sudden bolt of lightning obliterated them, rather to the profession's surprise; quite the contrary.

This particular I.P.A. official decree is now repealed, or half-repealed; you can now compete for a rival's business upon two conditions—*that the client has asked you to do so and that you don't say any rude things about the work of the agency you are attempting to supplant!* This wet and weak amendment has done little to restore the slipping prestige of the I.P.A., as David Kingsley himself said in a *Campaign* interview: "This is exactly an example of the silliness of the remaining rules because ... the client is going to want to discuss with you what he is doing at present. Do you have to pretend that you are not interested or something?" So the non-conformists stay aloof. P.K.L.'s Managing Director rubs salt in the wound by suggesting the I.P.A. should "make a pitch" to win them back; Kingsley suggests that the I.P.A. "go further in making the business competitive." At the moment, when an advertiser employs an I.P.A. member, according to that body's rather prim phraseology "they are making use of a firm which recognises that its duty is to employ properly qualified staff, to give an independent and objective judgment, and to abide by the ethical codes."

A duty which goes unmentioned and unsung, but which is possibly the advertiser's main concern, is the ability to get customers to *buy*.

THE MEDIA LABYRINTH AND THE A.B.C.

The term "media" refers not only to newspapers and other periodicals but to any means whatever of conveying the advertising message. So television, radio, posters, underground tube-cards, stamp-books, brochures, letters and neon signs—not to mention lapel-buttons and hat-ribbons or sign-writing in the sky—are all part of the general media picture. All of them fall in the lap of the media department (*see* Chapter III).

Nevertheless, it is true that (in spite of huge inroads by TV into appropriations) the largest slice of advertising tends to concern news-papers and magazines, and in selecting from among these thousands of consumer and trade publications (*British Rate and Data*, the media man's bible, lists about 4,000!) the advertiser and his agent have a formidable task. To aid them the Audit Bureau of British Advertisers was established in 1931, which publishes A.B.C. figures (Audit Bureau of Circulations) every half year. Not all journals are included, because again there is no legal compulsion to submit to A.B.C. inspection. The indispensable pages of *British Rate and Data* will, in such cases, simply state the telling phrase: "Figure in accordance with *BRAD's* requirements not received."

Have the media any tit-for-tat counter-measures of control against agencies? Oh yes, but they are far less publicised and are not easy to specify. Publishers of dailies, weeklies and monthlies have banded themselves into innumerable bodies, all of which lay down varied rules about the minimum billing an advertising agency must have before it can claim the 10–15 per cent commission, but exactly which bodies enforce which minimums on which agencies is anybody's guess.

Since this book is not in the guessing game, one can only say defi-nitely that the Newspaper Publishers' Association requires that an agency's billing totals not *less* than £100,000 per annum. For the trade press, the minimum billing required reduces by about two-thirds. It must finally be stressed, however, that more blind eyes are turned to these rulings than any media man or owner will ever admit.

DESIGN GROUPS AND "HOT-SHOPS"

The advertising agency is not an advertiser's sole recourse for expertise in the field, whatever medium he may fancy for his ads. The advertising scene is in fact fast coming full circle in its evolution.

In the beginning, as "Professor" Holloway's emulators multiplied, the advertising agent was merely, in effect if not intention, the news-paper's space-selling representative—and received a commission reckoned on the value of the space he sold, as he still does. At that time the manufacturer had concrete and fairly crude notions of what he wanted put into that space (Thomas Beecham's slogan "worth a guinea a box," which he coined in the 1850s, being an honourable exception)—rather dull repetition.

As Advertising grew more sophisticated (here we take advantage of what the logician calls presumed fact), the advertising agency took over the job of creating design and copy for the ads it placed, eventu-ally supplying other ancillary services like media selection and market research (*see* Chapter III). In time additional and separate fees were charged for these services, payment now coming from the advertiser, not the media.

At the summit of agency power, in the fifties and sixties, the advertiser simply put his product into the eager hands of the agency men and said "take it from here," waiting for ads to roll out from the other end of the sausage-machine.

All this is now changing, as the profession starts to decentralise itself (and clients begin to tire of sausages, sausages, nothing but sausages, for their money). Specially gifted copywriters and designers are setting up their own companies for the sole purpose of creating design, content and production of the ad (*see* Chapter IV), being briefed for this either by an agency or directly by the client. Some of these small firms provide copy and design, some design alone—and the latter will "farm out" the copy to freelance writers.

The more "way-out" of these creative firms were known as "hot-shops" or "boutiques." The more sensational of them run the risk of becoming fashionable, then killing the fashion dead. Some have been patronised by extremely large-spending clients—examples are Bass Charrington and the Chapman and Philips consultancy, C. & A. Modes and the design group of Alan Wagstaff & Partners Ltd., Qantas Airlines and Main Titles Ltd., the Health Education Council and the Cramer Saatchi consultancy (for anti-smoking)— and indeed I have had great good fortune in writing myself for such clients as P. & O. Lines, Scaffolding (Great Britain) Ltd., Worldmark Travel Ltd., and, through the Anglo-Yugoslav Marketing Company Ltd., for 3-MAJ Shipyards and Marine Engine Works of Rijeka and the famous Jugolinija Shipping Lines. My own "hot-shop" was home-heated in my study.

Some of these "boutiques" are producing the most stimulating ads now current, some the worst. Many go to the wall in a very short space of time. Others move on up out of adolescent flair into the "establishment," the most notable example being the Cramer Saatchi "shop"—after a 1975 merger with Compton Partners, this has metamorphosed into Saatchi and Saatchi: Garland Compton, sixth-ranking agency in the country (*see* Appendix II). However, all have given the whole business of Advertising a splendid shot in the arm, shaking cobwebs by the bale-full out of the creaking agency structure.

OTHER FREELANCE CONSULTANTS

Apart from the creative "hot-shop," the advertising scene now abounds in flourishing freelance consultants of every kind. Some of these specialise in certain types of promotion, such as direct mail or letter-box distribution—the latter firms will undertake to slip a given piece of literature through X-thousand letter-boxes in the southern part of X-county or in certain streets of X-city, at a cost scaled at per thousand deliveries.

There are outfits which confine themselves to designing and printing trading stamps or vouchers. Others produce buttons which sport slogans of all descriptions and every possible innuendo. Other firms concentrate on exhibitions or packaging. There are research and marketing firms, and consultants in public relations (*see* Chapter IV).

The most revolutionary (or reactionary, according to one's viewpoint) of all these consultants is the media broker, who has only recently risen above the rash. Looked upon with extreme suspicion by his fellow professionals, this specialist, as his title implies, offers expertise in the field of placing ads where they will do the most good. As with most modern business practice, this "new" branch of the advertising profession has enjoyed a preliminary canter down New York's "Ulcer Gulch" proving-ground of Madison Avenue. No one seems to notice that he is merely doing what "Professor" Holloway did, one hundred and thirty years ago. But *plus ça change, plus c'est la même chose* could well be the most endurable motto of Advertising, and some may think it apt that the saying first appeared in a Paris journal called *The Wasps*.

Companies which produce cinema and television commercials are in a class of their own, of course, and their specialist contribution is considered with others in Chapter IV.

Latest newcomer on to the advertising scene is the so-called "marriage broker." What this specialist does is to supply an advertiser with precisely the type of advertising service he needs—and no more. The client may require copy and design alone, or packaging, or media buying, or perhaps just some market research to tranquillise or exacerbate his doubts, or a TV commercial or a poster campaign. In whichever combination these services are required the marriage broker will contract for them on client's behalf, co-ordinate their efforts, obtaining his specialists from what seems the most appropriate source suitable to the product and financial resources offered.

Nor will the marriage broker obtain these distinct services from independent consultants or freelances alone. Agencies themselves are expected to hire out the services of their various departments on an *à la carte* basis to the broker. (This will in fact extend the practice already current by which agencies get "outside" experts to do certain jobs, though without telling the client!)

The advantage is obvious. The client will no longer worry—as indeed he is increasingly now doing—about paying, through inflated agency fees, for services he either doesn't want or doesn't adequately receive. To put it another way, he won't have the gnawing fear that the big-agency costs he is incurring will be outrageously surcharged to subsidise overheads on departments he will never use. The disadvantage? This is obvious, too, on a moment's reflection. The client, in paying the broker's commission, will soon be racked by doubts as to whether the broker and agency have conspired to "put one over" on him.

This is not cynicism: it's business. Advertising is a business profession whose development seems often to go in circles. The original agencies which succeeded Holloway were nothing more nor less than media brokers. Who can deny that the marriage broker is simply the agency of tomorrow, in slightly different guise?

What the over-cautious client must beware of is being scared off the best professionals because of the imitations and proliferations among these firms. Even their cannibalistic attitude to talent is sometimes more apparent than real. By crying wolf once too often the client may end up with a flock of sheep on his doorstep. These will waste his money more than the wolves. Quality is the criterion he must look for; quality *and results*.

ANGLO-AMERICA OVER EUROPE

Undeniably, United States control and influence over the British agency scene is continually growing, and has been doing so since the war. It's idle to speculate whether this is "good" or "bad." It's happening, and must be understood.

Only one British practitioner has had much direct effect on American advertising methods since "Professor" Holloway in the 1870s, and that is David Ogilvy, who once stated, quite truthfully, that the combined revenues of his nineteen clients was "greater than the revenue of Her Majesty's Government."

Mr. Ogilvy's well-known career is highly and significantly illustrative. He began with a London agency, Mather and Crowther, who put up the money, in partnership with another famous London firm, S. H. Benson Ltd. (setting of Dorothy Sayer's whodunit *Murder Must Advertise*, written in 1933) to open a New York office called Ogilvy, Benson and Mather.

In the past few years, Mr. Ogilvy has not merely bitten the hand which fed him, but swallowed it whole—to the hand's intense delight, it must be added. Mather and Crowther has disappeared under the Madison Avenue umbrella on a new world-wide structure called Ogilvy and Mather International, of which it is now the London office—and that office is now called Ogilvy, Benson and Mather Ltd., having swallowed Bensons to become, next to J. Walter Thompson, our largest agency. So S. H. Benson's old firm, which helped start

Ogilvy abroad, has duly been consumed by its young. The young man who opened his doors on Madison Avenue in 1948 (just about one hundred years after Holloway had done the same), without a single client on his books, became Chairman of a huge global organisation, with offices in New York, Chicago, Los Angeles and San Francisco in the States, Toronto in Canada, London and sixteen other countries in Europe, South America and South Africa. Later, returning to his first love, the *creating* of ads, David Ogilvy demoted himself to Creative Director, and last year became the first non-American to win election to the *Advertising Hall of Fame*.

Today, three-quarters of the top twelve London agencies are American-owned, the exceptions being Lintas, Dorlands and Masius Wynne-Williams.

The giants set the trend, however, and American influence is twice as real as apparent, since more and more key positions in small, medium and large agencies are being filled from the other side of the water. Dorlands, we may note, long had an American as Creative Director. There is small comfort in considering the situation in the light of a brain-drain in reverse.

Yet it is not so much "America over England" as "Anglo-America over Europe." Advertising is becoming *internationalised* rather than *Americanised*—the only trouble is in telling the two adjectives apart. This will become, I believe, increasingly more the case in today's new era of *Concorde* and the Common Market.

Clients, especially the bigger ones, require agencies which can offer a *global* service. The £400,000 Max Factor account was moved from Alexander, Butterfield & Ayer Ltd. in June 1969, simply to achieve a "one-world" agency approach; the account was taken over by Hobson Bates Ltd., whose Californian agency is used by Factor. But isn't that the home of the cosmetic giant? Indeed it is. Yet A.B. & Ayer is an American-owned outfit, while Hobson Bates is not ... and yet ... and yet ... the Creative Director, at time of writing, at Hobson Bates is also an American.

The moral seems plain enough. Internationalised does mean Americanised at present, but this needn't always be so. After all, to pluck crumbs of hope from below the salt, who would have dreamed that the United States pop-music scene would one day be dominated in the mid-1960s by British influence?

THE "HOUSE" AGENCY

This is a phenomenon that is fast disappearing from the London scene, but its influence on the development of Advertising has been such that we cannot omit a brief examination of some famous names among "house" agencies. The term means simply an agency that confines its efforts to promoting the products of one client company only, and is itself owned by that company.

Charles Barker & Sons belonged to this category for many years, since they advertised only government business (work of a very prosaic, but extremely lucrative kind). Today, of course, they are renowned for their Midland Bank TV and cinema commercials and are starting to accumulate "West End" accounts.

When Lord Thomson consolidated his newspaper empire behind the copper-ribboned façade of Thomson House on Grays Inn Road—building over Kemsley House like Ilium over Troy—he installed on the second floor what he called the Thomson Marketing Division, the "house" agency for all his properties and interests. The division handled not only his newspapers and magazines, but promoted his other companies, like Speedwriting, Scottish Television and Thomson Television International—whose ads proudly announced their African customers, and whose brochures proclaimed the students from these countries.

The most well-known "house" agency is without doubt the firm of Lintas. The name derives from self-explanatory initials—Lever International Advertising Services. In 1970 the great institution, whose founder so long ago declared his love–hate attitude towards Advertising, took the major step also of taking on its first client outside of the Unilever fold.

What with takeovers and diversifications pulling in opposite directions, the organisation of Advertising seems headed either for fragmentation, ossification, or maybe a bit of both. Whatever happens, the advertising agency is likely to remain at the dynamic centre of most promotional activity for a long time to come. So we had best take a good look at the parts which make the whole.

Chapter III

ANATOMY OF AN AGENCY

It is not hard to understand why the advertising agency should be so misunderstood, its function so misinterpreted by the general public. Like the old Wild West, Adland into Badland, it lends itself to myth-making—a natural hazard of the genre. The result is that whenever a novelist or film-maker or TV producer requires a character who can be both "with it" and, at the same time, a member of the established business community, he puts him into Advertising, usually as an Account Executive.

Any connection with real-life advertising (if that does not seem too much a contradiction in terms) is tenuous, at best. Admen seem the pillars of suburbia to fiction-mongers, their slogans lurking round every conifer, the stockbroker belt being lapped by the agency truss on every corner.

The husband of the heroine in the successful TV comedy series *Bewitched* was just such an Account Executive. He appeared to spend most of his time being copywriter and designer as well, while client-contact went to the wall. We saw him sitting up all night, agonising over headlines, which he scribbled in giant letters on art-sheets pinned to every stick of furniture in the place. In short, he behaved like no Account Executive would ever dream of behaving, and like only the emptier show-offs among the creative staff, for that matter. No wonder his wife felt not just bewitched, but bothered and bewildered as well.

In his superb book on American admen, *Madison Avenue, U.S.A.*, Martin Mayer quotes the Executive Vice-President of one agency as saying he entered the profession thinking "Advertising will use my virtues and support my vices." Presumably he was not disappointed. However, Mr. Mayer also cites the sobering statistic that the average advertising man in the States has a life-expectancy ten years shorter than anyone else. Whether acting up to the first quote leads inexorably to the second is for you to decide.

AGENCY "FRONT" AND LAYOUT

We must acknowledge right away, I think, the difficulty of precisely defining departments and personnel in advertising agencies.

Not only is the function and form of various staff titles constantly changing, but the man behind the title is changing constantly, too. Distinctions are extremely blurred—often quite intentionally—and in this chapter and the two following I shall put forward definitions and delineations which must be taken only as a reliable *pro tem.* guide to aid the student in taking initial bearings on his first job.

You will soon discover, as you tramp the corridors of agency power, that in no other business is "face-value" so prized, and disprized, a possession. The Chairman of one of London's most image-conscious agencies, K.M.P., referred to in the last chapter, has stated in *Campaign* that "there are three basic ways of keeping your key people happy—money, love and fitted carpets." Nevertheless, K.M.P. has preferred to forsake this for an open-plan office for reasons of internal efficiency. In the words of his partner, David Kingsley, the firm is deliberately not "formally structured ... even things like working to an open-plan ... add to the speed with which we can do things, the simplicity with which we can have meetings ... Merchant Bank Partners worked together in one room for many years." K.M.P.'s staff may feel, however, that Kingsley's remark in *Campaign* about the value of obtaining "the total pool of advice" is at variance with his partner's assertion to *The Financial Times* that "the number of people ... whose absence or presence will actually make a difference to the quality of the company's work ... is unlikely to be more than 20 per cent."

LIKE ANY OTHER BUSINESS?

The answer to this question is both yes and no. In outward manifestation the similarities are there, from Chairman to office-boy, from luncheon-vouchers to company reports (in the case of those agencies which have "gone public," a modern trend), from expense-account lunches to office parties. Yet we must also recognise that there is no business like show-business, except for Advertising—one reason, perhaps, why the show-biz world is so bad at portraying it ... the Ad world is strictly Ad lib.

In fact, as the modern agency has evolved from its beginnings as a media commission-merchant (*see* Chapter II), so it has steadily frayed the moorings which anchored it, perhaps precariously, to the conventional business world. Or one can more accurately say that the advertising agency is the one sector of business which has retained the buccaneering traditions of the nineteenth-century firms.

Kingsley, in the interview already quoted, stated that, to his mind, most agencies "seemed badly managed and inefficient" and failed to keep abreast of modern business trends. While across the Atlantic the

retired chairman of Foote, Cone & Belding recently confessed that
all too many clients still believed "agency people are inherently slip-
pery to deal with."

Before too rash a judgment overtakes us, however, let us consider
the case of the Kirkwood Company. This agency, one of London's
newest, was named in that stark fashion simply because, when set up
in October 1969, the firm consisted solely of one extremely well-
known and highly esteemed Creative Director, Ronnie Kirkwood
(who once happily posed for a double-page ad stating "Ronnie Kirkwood Never Uses Makeup"). He had no offices, no staff, no clients
even. Moreover, six months were to pass before any clients could be
announced. Nevertheless, Mr. Kirkwood was not only able to garner
prompt financial support from the Gresham Trust, the famous merchant bankers, but had to turn down several competing offers of City
capital. His firm is now a stellar attraction of the giant Lopex Group,
who bought it for £800,000.

Perhaps the financiers remembered how, back in 1893, one Samuel
Herbert Benson also set up on his own, at 100 Fleet Street, with only
one client—Bovril. When Bensons "went public," one month before
Kirkwood hung out his camp shingle, the shares were over-subscribed
sixteen times!

So we may safely take our lead from the City, which never throws
money away on mere glamour, as any film-maker, trying to raise the
wind, will tell you. The plain truth is that, behind the show-biz razz-
matazz, the 1967 Companies Act now forces *all* advertising agencies,
both public and private, to file comprehensive financial details with
the Department of Trade and Industry. More and more, then, they
are compelled to conduct themselves *and to be seen to be conducting themselves* in a proper businesslike manner. As the last chairman of Bensons
(before merger with Ogilvy and Mather) is quoted as saying, "the
Stock Exchange is one of the hardest taskmasters you can have."

THE EXECUTIVE STRUCTURE

Only an approximate indication can be given here (*see* Fig. 1), since
practice and responsibilities vary immensely from firm to firm, and
on occasion, from day to day. Also, the internal structure of work-
loads varies, so that even where tasks are similar the *degrees* of output
expected can differ, not just from one agency to another, but from
one year to another, as partners come and go in a sort of "lobster
quadrille" (as described by Lewis Carroll's "Mock Turtle") and executives, having "cleared all the jelly-fish out of the way," proceed
to "change lobsters" and "turn a somersault in the sea" before returning to land ... after a further change of partners, of course.

This is not to say that agencies, for all their reshuffles and "rationalisations," are unconventional in their executive structure. However, they are certainly unconventional in the way these conventions are treated. The ladder you set out to climb resembles the ladders available in other business activities and most of the rungs have similar

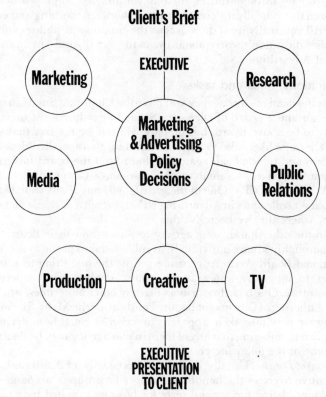

Fig. 1.—The operational structure of a typical advertising agency. Depending on size—and past or future mergers—there would be more or less stratification.

labels. In Advertising, however, people are more likely to move the ladder while you're looking the other way, so that it rests against a strange window the next time you climb, or maybe rests against nothing at all.

There are more Cheshire Cat grins in Advertising. For instance, the man who is introduced as your Chairman one week, may be your Managing Director the next (or later the same afternoon), and vice versa. As agencies merge, break off and re-form in the lobster quadrille (red-faced and boiling), you may also find that the man you meet as Design Supervisor on one product campaign, will suffer his sea-change into something as rich and strange as an "Account Group Director" in regard to another product. Depending on how many jobs you get through during the day you may be employed by half a dozen theoretically different companies between morning and evening. All you really need do is accept the situation as philosophically as Alice did—don't worry about the matter at all, and just enjoy the job of Advertising.

Definitions, titles and tasks

At the head of your agency you have the Chairman, his Managing Director and a Board of Directors. So far so good, most of them are likely to be above-Board, but prepare yourself for the fact that your M.D. is quite likely also to appear behind his vast metalled desk clad in jeans and trendy head-gear, and that round the board-table may conjoin a Quaker, an unabashed Con-man, a Communist, and an M.A. with the D.T.s. One of the greatest charms about your betters and closer colleagues in Advertising is that, to coin a phrase, you never know where they've been. Neither, always, do they.

On the other hand, your agency top-brass and their Board may be thoroughly square individuals, as rubber-stamp prone as any conventional Board. With Advertising people the first thing to learn is never to judge by appearances—you're dealing with experts in appearance. One boardroom looks like any other most times, whether its a gathering of City magnates, the Politburo or the Mafia. In Advertising we may take their apparent function as roughly understood, simply remembering that any of them in *your* agency may be doubling in some of the following posts.

Account Director. Usually, though not necessarily, of Board rank, this executive oversees the handling of a specific group of accounts—an "account" being the general term for business supplied by a client, whatever its size and commercial value—and he is held responsible for those accounts at the highest level. He also settles fees and budgets with clients and often has a "wining and dining" relationship with them. (To clear up a popular misconception of this aspect of an adman's day, however, the prosaic fact is that, answering an I.P.A. Survey in 1975, no agency admitted to spending more than 1·9 per cent of its income on client entertainment.)

Account Executive. He is deputy for the above A.D., on the same accounts, with the difference that he liaises with the grit and sweat of Advertising. Account Directors are broad policy decision-makers; their Account Executives are carry-outers of those decisions, testing their practicability. An Account Executive organises the market research, briefs the copywriter and designer, sees space is bought for the advertisements in decided media and puts in hand the production and printing. Usually, he sells the agency work to the client, aided or hampered by his A.D., according to the respective calibre of the executives concerned. On the day-to-day level, he is the link between agency and client.

Media Director/Media Executive or Planner. With status and responsibilities divided and shared as above, these two gentlemen purvey the agency's expertise in the placing of advertising, whether it is how many millimetres shall be taken in which newspaper, or what poster sites are available for certain months at the right price, or how many seconds or minutes should be bought on radio or TV. After their advice is taken, rejected or modified, they are responsible for booking space and time and negotiating the best prices of "deals" from media. This they do in person, or through a staff-member called the Space-Buyer who occupies the lowest rung on the media department ladder.

Depending on the size of their department, Media Executives have on tap extensive files of periodicals (called "voucher copies"). They are responsible for seeing that all copy-dates are met, are correct, and, if necessary, amended or extended to meet sudden "panics"—a copy-date being the last date before publication on which a given medium will accept an ad for insertion and guarantee its appearance. How a client's budget is spent depends a great deal on the knowledge, contacts and intuition of the media man. The Media Executive is the link between client and media-owner.

The creative side

Creative Director. Not usually found on the Board, this gentleman (or it can be a woman, of course, as can any of these executives; women will find that in Advertising their sex is less discriminated against than in any profession) is responsible for all the creative output of an agency. He tends to "float" a lot—during one December week in 1969 three London agencies announced switches in this crucial post. Sometimes you will find him called a Creative Supervisor to forestall him getting ideas above his station. He is the link between the Account Executive and the writers and artists.

Copy Chief. He hires and fires all writers and oversees their work, often choosing to do the writing himself on the more plum accounts. His direct responsibility is to the Creative Director for all writing assignments, but often combines the two posts in himself.

Art Director. This gentleman may be called the Art Supervisor, for similar motives as above, but he is the design equivalent of the Copy Chief—like him also, but much less frequently, he may also double as Creative Director. He is in charge of the artists.

Whether called Art Directors, Visualisers or Designers, these artists all produce the illustrative side of an agency's work. Their titles may be compared to sergeant, corporal or other non-commissioned officers (though income does not always correlate—agencies seldom follow Humpty-Dumpty's precept, "When I make a word do a lot of work like that, I always pay it extra.").

Production Manager. This gentleman is in charge of the production of the actual printed end-product of the agency's assorted skills. The block for the press advertisement, the printing of the poster or brochure, the two- or three-dimensional reality of all the speculation, compromise, theorising and other hot air and heavy breathing, all depend on him. He ensures delivery, first of proofs and then the finished artwork, on time and in the right place—and "on time" means in time for the client to see and approve before work is irretrievably published.

Under this executive the Print Buyer operates, who (like the Space Buyer in *his* department) negotiates with printers the best deal possible under the available client-budget. It follows that he owns, or soon collects, an intimate and detailed knowledge of printing-methods and printers themselves; the latter can come in widely assorted sizes and species, and so can the prices they charge.

When an agency's creative department is overloaded with work—resulting from most agencies' tendency to underman on the creative side (writers and artists represent, in most cases, only about 18 per cent of the agency payroll)—"outside" talent (*see* Chapter IV) is bought in by the agency's Art Buyer.

Oiling the wheels within deals

Traffic Manager. This may at first sight seem an unromantic post amidst all the other glamorous dazzle on hand, but in fact it's one of the most essential in any agency. Sometimes this executive is entitled Traffic-Controller. Sometimes his work is done by an under-paid, but dedicated, secretary-cum-typist-cum-assistant, a woman worth a fortune (which she never gets, in any business) who organises the milling blowhards like the recalcitrant boys they are. However, acknowledged by title or not, the duty of a Traffic Manager is so to organise the agency schedules that every stage of business is accomplished as speedily and smoothly as possible. He is both the logistics expert and the quartermaster-general of the agency.

In theory, his index-cards, his board-plans covered with coloured tags, dotted with pertinent pins (on dull days, pin-ups) should inform his eye instantly what every executive, writer, artist and production team is doing each hour of the working day. He is the *first* person who should be told by the Account Executive when a new job is ready to go into the pipe-line, or when "the panic-button is pressed." He is often the last.

Progress Chaser. Under the Traffic Manager serves a lowly being who is every agency's "man you love to hate." He is about as welcome round the premises as that other P.C. is to a street-vendor selling pearls for sixpence in the rush-hour. He receives the dubious hospitality given a bum-bailiff who squats in your neighbourhood till "obligations" are paid-up (see Ngaio Marsh's *Surfeit of Lampreys* for a vivid illustration of the term). The name describes the task: he "chases progress"—impedes it, his victims would claim—and hounds everyone, of high and low estate, till their work is done and handed in on the time specified by traffic shedules.

Ideally, no personage is too mighty for his brusque or suave attentions, and to one and all he is a "damned, smiling villain." Yet, being the very needful goad of the profession, he is never paid enough, since his unattractive talents should combine those of turnkey, turncoat, psychologist and expert nag. Advertising is full of self-styled matadors. The traffic department provides the unsung picadors.

Efficiency extras

We cannot leave this examination of Agency anatomy without reference to the art studio. Here is conducted by usually brilliant technicians the art of the possible, as distinct from the creative department, from which emerges the art of the plausible. To transmute the second into the first, or into the nearest feasible facsimile, is the studio's job.

Here are found typographers, illustrators and finished artists of various specialities. It is they who turn the approved design-and-copy into a workable proposition by preparing it for printing. It is their expertise which enables the creative ideas that are the life-blood of Advertising to be realised in print with the least possible alteration, however seemingly outrageous the type-size asked for, the colours specified. From them comes, in other words, the artwork.

Please understand that this survey of the anatomy has not included every single link-bone of the skeleton, nor has it discussed all known ways of assembling the bones. Some agencies use an all-in system which allots jobs to individuals as they occur, from whatever account. Others use a group system, self-contained cells of executives and creative people who operate exclusively on certain products, and no other. A few agencies are big enough for the indulgence of maintaining "think-tanks" of creative "trouble-shooters," who roam round helping out on many different accounts. Some have experts who work for them only part of the year, but on regular retainer.

YOUR PLACE IN THE SUM

The permutations and combinations are almost infinite, and time alone will show where *you* will fit into this skeleton. The framework will often require knobs and joints for temporary attachment, which must come from outside independents (*see* Chapter IV). Some agencies have a great deal more bone-structure than I have so far covered, with departments for research, public relations, marketing and television. Some boast one strong head, take it or leave it—others are hydra-headed and boast equally about it. The sum of the parts, public and private, never add twice to the same total.

SPECIALIST SERVICES

It has been estimated that by 1980 nearly half the advertising agencies of Europe will have disappeared. This is the prediction of Jean-Max Lenormand, Vice-President of McCann–Erickson Europe, and in so saying he presumes about 2,000 agencies into the dust. He suggests that the agency scene will be dominated by twenty multinational groups—which means, though he doesn't add this fact, American-dominated—no medium-sized agencies at all, but a lot of small local agencies for handling accounts of strictly parochial or national appeal.

This accords entirely with my own reading of the scene, and this chapter will consider both some of the causes for this (other than those already touched on) and the resultant importance of the small, special-ised consultancy.

In Chapter II we noted that already the trend among advertisers of all sizes is to turn from big agencies and to patronise small firms specialising in particular branches of advertising and promotion, or marketing, public relations or research. We shall consider this aspect of the total advertising scene in more detail now, since your entry into the profession may well be more likely through one of these "side" doors than through the main agency concourse. You may indeed find it more than satisfying to stay happily and fruitfully "side-tracked" on what can well prove to be one of the main-lines of Advertising in the rupturing seventies so confidently forecast, even though, in the words of David Abbott of the French Gold Abbott Partnership (now transmuted into the French Gold Abbott Kenyon and Eckhardt agency) : "A strong London agency will be the pivot of most E.E.C. operations."

What we shall be talking about here are the big areas of expertise, of course, not the myriad small companies that supply Advertising with its purely technical services, like artwork, slide-reference libraries, lettering (which Letraset has completely revolutionised), taped sound-effects and so on. I shall divide the causes (or the causa-tion, as the dons would say) for the emergence of consultancies into the client viewpoint and the agency viewpoint—diametrically opposed, granted, but by no means dissimilar.

THE CLIENT VIEWPOINT

Dealing through a large "name" agency has, many clients feel,
become simply very uneconomic—also impracticable, from a control
standpoint. Overheads of big agencies have risen enormously in recent
years, the jeopardy of perennially low profit-margins made more pre-
carious for a time by the burden of Selective Employment Tax which,
in the biggest outfits, added £100,000 annually to costs. Many firms
(on I.P.A. advice) passed S.E.T. on as a surcharge to clients. Clients
also believe, with some justice, that agencies' fees for, say, creative service alone, undergo rather violent "mark-ups" to help support other
agency departments, like research of public relations, which they
never use.

This has two consequences, in the client's view. First, he suspects
that the cost of his advertising may be unnecessarily high. Secondly,
he believes he is not spending sufficiently with the agency to keep
the proper solicitude and respect which he reckons are his due. In
other words, he is losing control. In both cases he is entirely correct.

Remedy for the small advertiser is to turn to specialist consultancies
which will provide him with precisely what he needs and no more.
He gets what he is paying for, and can obtain a much better running
check (though not foolproof) that he is indeed paying only for what
he is given.

Another factor for many firms in making their decision to withdraw
from large agencies is that they themselves are being driven by high
city rentals to relocate their offices in the countryside. This brings
not only a boom to local consultancies but to provincial agencies, of
course.

THE AGENCY VIEWPOINT

As you would expect, the economics of Advertising dictate a rather
different outlook on the agency side. In 1975, I.P.A. agencies were
saddled with £1,014,000 in bad debts from clients—and the law puts
the burden on *them* not the media (hence the saying that the media
may carry the advertising but the agencies carry the can). But, even
before, the S.E.T. burden (which in 1970 cost the advertising world
well over £1½ million in total!) meant a choice for them of the following consequences, depending on particular client–agency relationships.

1. Agencies have increased their servicing fees. The 15 per cent
commission from media-owners has long scarcely sufficed for overheads, much less for minimal profits. The client has been "surcharged" for benefiting from the agency's expertise in media-buying,

creative work, market research or whatever—these services previously having been taken for granted—and for nothing, or next to nothing. Newer agencies have accelerated the switch. K.M.P., for example, operates roughly half-and-half on fees and commission. On average, however, nowadays £37 in every £100 of agency income derives from fees.

2. The client's work is "farmed out," sometimes with his knowledge and consent, more often without either. That is to say, if a particular campaign cannot be fitted into the agency's work-schedule on time, or if it is too small to warrant the best (and most expensive) creative brains in the agency being lavished upon it, then the jobs are given to freelance copywriters and designers, the result of their labours being, however, presented to client as the agency's own work. Whatever charge the freelance suppliers make to the agency is then passed on to the client suitably embellished, sometimes doubled.

Some extremely well-known national manufacturers would be mightily amazed did they discover who actually created the campaigns, and did the public relations, publicity and marketing, which have been sold to them as agency work—and not infrequently accepted only because of that agency's sacred name! Of course, where this "farming out" is known and agreed by client, the reverse can be true: the agency-presented work is often accepted because of a famous freelance's "sacred" name and repute.

3. The agency resigns the account, sometimes to the stunned amazement of the client, who has been for so many decades accustomed to dealing out the "no longer in need of your services" letter. Thus, in the past few years, the MacLaren Dunkley Friedlander Agency resigned the £250,000 billing of Personna razor-blades (partly, please note, because the Personna management had flirted with "outside" consultancies, anyway). Thus did Foote, Cone & Belding resign its "unprofitable" £131,000 share of the Bristol–Myers product stable (Clairol and Vitalis) while, at the same time B.-M.'s other agency, Greys Advertising, resigned their £200,000 billing for Mum and Fresh 'n' Dry.

London Progressive Advertising decided that a £20,000 billing was not progressive enough and showed the door to Lillywhites, while the David Williams Agency had no sooner devised their "Come Over to Kent" campaign than it rejected its own advice and suggested the cigarette firm go elsewhere, Kent having cut the appropriation.

Perhaps the most famous recent instance of this trend was Ogilvy and Mather's resignation from the Hathaway Shirt account—their ads made David Ogilvy famous many years ago though it was even then, he tells us, only a "relatively small" account. Let me close this by pointing out that even the prestigious Cunard account has under-

gone the humiliation of being resigned by an agency on the grounds
of "unprofitability."

ENTER THE SPECIALISTS

These examples all help to show the deep-seated dissatisfactions
which are now bubbling and babbling through traditional advertising
agency patterns, and how they got there, and grew. One moment
we have too many agencies chasing too few products; the next we
have too many products chasing too few agents. Everyone bemoans
the 15 per cent commission system, but instead of doing anything
about it the media-owners, the agencies and the clients conduct a per-
petual "we never closed" three-ring circus to circumvent the rules,
such as they are.

Commissions are split two or three ways—not always with the
knowledge of all parties. Service fees are grossly inflated when not
invented altogether. Fictional "departments" are paraded to lure
accounts from rivals who possess either more scruple or less imagination. All of which adds to the price the customer will finally be asked
to pay, making the task of selling to him that much more needlessly
difficult.

The profession of Advertising spends far too much time making
booby-traps for itself, and, by falling into them every time, brings itself
again and again to a *reductio ad absurdum* situation. Let one instance
suffice. In its prime, the Thomson Marketing Division (a virtual self-
contained agency) was placing its ads (for Thomson products) in, say,
The Scotsman (a Thomson paper) or on Scottish TV (owned by Thomson) through an "outside" agency (also owned by Thomson), so that
the 15 per cent commission rebate could be legitimately claimed back
from Thomson's right hand by his left.

So indeed, it is very much time for the advent of the media and
marriage brokers (*see* Chapter II). It is time for the big agency groupings to serve limited, clearly-defined purposes and be serviced by
specialist independents, who also have *their* own clients and are therefore satellites of no one, owing fief to none.

We can look to Germany, where huge accounts like Coca-Cola,
Mattel toys, Nestlés and Ronson lighters have all moved their business
over into the new small compact creative outfits. We can look to
America, where the vast Magnavox TV and radio empire has placed
its whopping $4 million billing into freelance hands, where even the
fabled Doyle Dane Bernbach Agency last year had a giant shoe-
account taken from them and passed over to consultancies. *Sic transit
gloria*, but there the situation is, and there's better to be made of it.
The chance is *yours*.

THE CREATIVE SPECIALISTS

The more self-evident "hot-shops" and "boutiques" have already been considered (in Chapter II), but there is another related, though rather different, category of freelance firm. This is the creative group which, while dealing directly with advertisers on its own account, also produces "sub-contract" work for established agencies. The fondly-recalled "Cynthia" ads, which showed a very classy lady displaying a generous amount of thigh in the back of a limousine as richly upholstered as herself, over the copy-line "Cynthia isn't wearing panties," cool and hot at once, were produced by just such an arrangement. Though the agency was Vernon Stratton, the debby Delilah actually did her thing for the consultancy of Aalders Marchant Weinreich, who, in their own right as an independent outfit, were also responsible for the Mary Quant "Make-up To Make Love In" campaign, this time commissioned directly by client.

Television production companies are the outstanding examples of small independent advertising units—some have been known to operate from a phone-box! There are big agencies which maintain their own TV departments, but most employ outside companies, co-ordinated by a TV expert from within the agency. This latter executive often doesn't know a cathode ray from a laser beam, but his post is, where possible, strictly administrative.

Though they come and go like yo-yos, there are at any one time roughly two hundred independent TV production companies in Great Britain (the J. Walter Thompson agency alone makes use of fifty of them!), their size varying from the "two or three gathered together" type, operating costs supplied by someone else's shoe-string, to the largest of the lot, the James Garrett Organisation, located in a converted Jesuit library on Farm Street, in London—and perhaps there is significance in the fact that from these erstwhile premises of the "spearhead of the Counter-Reformation" should come the triumphant Tory TV programmes of the General Election of 1970.

THE TV BOOM ... AND BOOMERANG

The television-commercial industry is always in a state of flux, with personnel as with firms, since each new assignment sets a different package of talents working together, spending anything between £5,000 and £19,000 to produce just 30 seconds of advertising. And the cost of the time of showing on the small screen comes on top of that, ranging up to something under £7,000 for sixty seconds between the peak Sunday hours of 7 p.m. and 11 p.m.

This cost factor is so variable because of the range of requirements, either of client or agency. The commercial may require location trips with "Alf Garnett" to Australia, it may require following an expert girl-balloonist being Nimble in the sky, some complicated animation, or perhaps only a table and chair. One of the best commercials ever made simply shows you a tomato-ketchup bottle being thumped in vain—an exasperated "voice over" soundtrack does the rest of the selling.

You may be paying Olivia Newton-John £10,000 or a famous director, like Dick Lester, £500 a day. You may have George Best extolling eggs, James Robertson Justice grumpily spearing cheddar—or that much prettier relative of his helping to put sex into Schweppes. The voice may be that of someone imitating James Mason (who threatened to sue) or Orson Welles imitating Orson Welles on behalf of frozen food.

This is an exciting field where the future is wide open. True, the initial boom that began when the first British commercial ever screened, for Gibbs-S.R. toothpaste "cool as a mountain stream," went out in 1955, has lost its first fine flush of frenzy (especially since colour now adds 25 per cent to the cost) and TV's share of total advertising revenue dropped in 1969 from 27 per cent to 24 per cent ... though today it still garners over £250 million through the box.

Several TV production companies have spectacularly collapsed, like Augusta Productions, veteran of over 1,200 TV spots, including the "Katie" commercials for Oxo. However, confidence cannot help bounding high in a medium which can reach so many housekeeping budgets where it hurts least (programmes like *Coronation Street* regularly reach over 9 million homes), even though its specific effects are little known (*see* Chapter XII, however, for more detail).

You may not realise that most of the new commercials are on parade every Monday morning (except Bank Holidays) at 9 a.m. on Channel 9. The programme is called *Monday's Newcomers*, which sounds, and occasionally looks, like a regular soft-soap opera, except for the fact that it's the one programme on Independent Television which is *not* advertised.

PUBLIC RELATIONS

To professionals and the lay-public alike the people employed by and for what is called public relations are known as P.R. men, so we'll stick to that. The "P.R. man" is an attractive target to those who dislike all forms of Advertising, and he is probably the man most in the mind of journalist Molly Parkin when she included in a *Campaign* tirade these remarks:

"They excel ... at ordering from the right menus but the food never makes them fat. They are good at getting drunk yet remain as boringly the same as when sober ... They are obsessed with getting old, bald, impotent and overweight ... obsessed with all these things and of course their earnings. Little wonder then that a group such as this produces what it does produce."

She adds, for good (or bad) measure, that their sex lives bring them no satisfaction. The P.R. brigade are regarded far and wide as the "quacks" of Advertising.

I am introducing them here in their guise of independent consultancies, but there are three ways in which P.R. men can function; (1) as a firm of "outside" consultants; (2) as an advertising agency department; or (3) as a client's department. As with creative consultancies, P.R. men can be more than one of these alternatives at once, acting (and "acting" is the operative word) as an agency department when, in fact, that agency has no such permanent animal on the roster but wishes to pretend it has. P.R. men can perform this charade for a client also.

The job of public relations not so much defies definition as *dares* it. My own answer to the dare is to define its task as to influence the climate of public opinion—or a given segment of it—so that an increasingly favourable view of the client is nourished and acted upon. Public relations can be applied to a product, a person or a policy. How many people are working in public relations firms is anybody's guess—they are a law unto themselves, like real-estate men—but as a group in this country they get through about £80 million worth of business a year.

Press and publicity

Public relations men are infinitely adaptable and work in countless numbers of ways their wonders to perform. They use the Press, via handouts and press-releases or inspired gossip and the staged "news" event, and spread their efforts to all acts of publicity which can be managed within the limits of taste and available expenses. Their activities are in theory overseen by the Institute of Public Relations, founded in 1948 and duly incorporated into respectability in 1964, with a written constitution and code of conduct. However, membership of this body is not compulsory and does not carry even the hypothetical *cachet* of belonging to the I.P.A.

Despite very hard criticism from public relations consultancies themselves, the I.P.R. is a sincere and earnest organisation, which, a few years ago, claimed 1,875 Fellows, Members and Associates. But since this is 1,000 *less* than the membership announced by the I.P.R. president in the previous year, one retains a strong impression that

someone somewhere is taking the P.R. out of someone else. Hard
words perhaps, but when we consider that it was not until the
November of 1969 that the I.P.R., of all organisations, agreed to open
a few of its meetings to the Press "as an experiment," the scepticism
seems justified.

One Managing Director of a public relations consultancy has
summed up his work-philosophy as: "a punch is most effective if delivered with the whole weight of the body behind it"—public relations
providing that weight, of course. I would liken its techniques more
to the methods of judo and karate, i.e. the judicious deployment of
weight for optimum effect in a given place at the right moment of
time.

Handouts and hoke

Public relations consultancies are at the service of anyone or any
organisation with a special interest to promote, a viewpoint to dissemi-
nate. "You gotta give the people hoke" runs the song, but hocus-pocus
is only a small part of the game (and to succeed, you must play it
as a game, albeit a serious one). The man who drafts an inter-office
memo for the boss and the man who lobbies M.P.s into legalising pot
or the latest junta, are both in public relations.

P.R. men see that their clients, or the products of those clients, are
mentioned in the paper, talked about on the air, photographed at
premières (or with premiers) and featured on *Nationwide*. They are
Vance Packard's notorious *Hidden Persuaders*, the originals of the *Man
in the Grey Flannel Suit*.

However, the suits in which they mainly specialise are the
Emperor's New Clothes.

One of the most important goals of public relations is the achievement of a non-happening—the apple that never fell on Newton's
head, the rag-queen who was never really kidnapped, the film-star's
jewels which were never really stolen (and were probably never
jewels). As so often, Oscar Wilde, one of nature's P.R. men—though
not always to his own advantage—summed it up best: when asked
if it was true that he had once walked down Piccadilly "with a poppy
or a lily in his medieval hand" as suggested in Gilbert and Sullivan's
Patience, he replied with the scorn of the true professional: "Anyone
could have done that. The great and difficult thing was what *I*
achieved—to make the whole world *believe* I had done it." What he
actually did was to get himself written up in *Punch* and other periodicals by "rescuing" violets from a florist's window (after making sure
he had a large audience of passers-by) and to be overheard, as he
reverently inspected Frith's enormous canvas *Derby Day*, just purchased for the nation, to comment "Is it really *all* done by hand?"

For the acres of news-coverage this sort of antic brought him here and in the United States, he of course paid nothing.

MARKETING AND RESEARCH

In 1965, the Confederation of British Industry decided to set up an eighteen-member Standing Committee on Marketing. By November 1970, one name had been announced—the Chairman's. Whether every member's selection would take five years was not made clear, but what was clearly evident was that marketing is not far behind public relations in regularising itself.

An *AdWeekly* Special Supplement of March 1967 carried this daunting definition: "Marketing is the management function which organises and directs all those business activities involved in assessing and converting customer purchasing power into effective demand for a specific product or service, and in moving the product or service to the final consumer or user so as to achieve the profit target or other objectives set by a company."

Now you know what marketing is—or do you? I can only comment that this sort of definition will certainly be much fancied by those who like such descriptions. The author is not of their number and this type of definition will be looked for vainly in these pages. It is readily on tap elsewhere. The literature—if that's the word—on this field is so prolix and prolific, not to say prodigal, that I feel no need to dwell on it.

Students among the readers of this book are more than likely to find a hefty marketing department attached to their college, and they will find a number of books on the subject in the recommended reading lists in Appendix I. The profession also has its own powerful governing body in the Institute of Marketing and Sales Management which claims over 15,000 members, and, interestingly enough, has a name whose second half is hardly ever used, though it is far more effective in clarifying the functions of its membership than the first half.

If you run an independent marketing firm your specialist job is precisely that, to *manage* sales, i.e. to make them first possible, then practicable, then profitable. Marketing sees itself as a science which covers every area of the consumer society. In theory, marketing techniques include programming research and development of a product, followed closely by the research and development of customers for that product. The professors (it has a plethora of dons, alas!) of this "science" try to bedazzle us with awesome phrases like "distribution patterns," "demographic trends," "socio-economic change," "evaluation concepts," "brand strategy," "budgetary control" and there are plenty more where they came from! Under this generous umbrella the "theory practitioners" flourish (*see* Chapter VIII).

While it is tempting to add to the waffle, to the dinning of dons, I shall try to resist. I am aided in this resolve by recalling the big bakery chain which spent £5,000 on a market research project which duly reported, with the aid of an inch-thick expensively-bound dossier and the obligatory wall-charts and graphs, that British housewives preferred fresh bread to stale. Ruefully, I recall personal experience of a marketing computer which gave Oxfam completely contradictory feedbacks at different times in response to identical information. I recall the magnificent and painstaking efforts of the British Market Research Bureau which "discovered," to its intense embarrassment, that one in every five rugger players was a woman.

In *The Times'* City News of 18th November 1970 was the delicious report of a government inquiry into investment grants which boasted of having saved the taxpayer £12,000 ... the unfortunate catch, as *The Times* gently pointed out, was that the inquiry itself had cost £16,000! This can now serve us as the perfect parable for much of modern marketing that uses sledgehammers of research on the nuts of us poor consumers and (like Whitehall) makes us pay for it through the price-tag.

What marketing does

People in the marketing field are split up in their sphere of activities much as P.R. men are split up; they operate either in a client's own department, an agency's department, or as an independent consultancy. Some mammoths among agencies, like J.W.T., have huge marketing departments, staffing over a hundred. Other grey-templed eminences, like Ogilvy and Bernbach, distrust such over-emphasis. "Advertising," simplifies Ogilvy, "is a place where the selfish interest of the manufacturer coincides with the interests of society." I find this begs too many questions. Bernbach goes farther and more bluntly has no use for marketing plans at all, stating that "the best plan in the world isn't going to make an ad that sells merchandise."

As for market research, the dangers of over-amplifying the utility of this branch of marketing was admirably put by the head of a big research organisation in the States, when he confessed to Martin Mayer: "If you ask people what they think of the Trade Metallics Act, you'll find they all have an opinion—and there isn't any such Act."

Taking time off from swapping ripostes with Dorothy Parker at the Algonquin Round Table, the acerbic Alexander Woolcott (original of *The Man Who Came To Dinner*) once remarked: "You don't have to be a chicken to tell a rotten egg," a comment which well summarises much of the opposition view to marketing and research. Where Advertising is concerned (this book's concern, in fact) no statistics can ever replace the promotional flair born of experience and technique. If Beethoven had studied contemporary research on what range the human voice was capable of he would never have written the Choral Symphony. And, of course, there were centuries of available and respectable research tomes to assure Columbus he would take a header off the edge of the world, *Santa Maria* and all.

As often as not, it is the client's demand for research—which he uses as a status symbol—which increases its volume far beyond need. There is a prevailing mystique about marketing which helps convince the client that the ads he is given are right and reassures him about the potential of his product. It was indeed research marketing which proved the effective appeal of the slogan "Cleans Your Breath While It Cleans Your Teeth"—but it was hired to do so sixteen years *after* the slogan got sales going like a bomb for Colgate. The original copywriter hadn't needed it, but Colgate wanted the reassurance of hindsight.

Very few clients have the courage to "defy augury" like Hamlet and to know the ready-cash is all. Marketing gimmicks are the goose-entrails of modern merchandising, literally the guts.

Ideally, marketing should delineate the whole environment of selling within which you exercise your talents in Advertising. Regard it, by all means, as a source of information for briefing—but never forget that other fallible hands have fed in the initial stimulus from which the information derives. Could it be found in perfected form, marketing consultancy should function as the quantity surveyor of the market-place, enabling a manufacturer to develop a product for which demand already exists *or can be inspired into existence*, should help him determine presentation, packaging, distribution, and calculate for him where and to whom it will sell, and at what price.

Pros and cons

Against Bernbach's criticism that he has no need to commission a survey to tell him that "there appears to be salt in the sea" remains the argument that a research survey, and one very much in-depth, certainly would be required to tell him exactly how much salt was in which particular sea, where salinity was under 35 per cent, where it was over 40 per cent, and what was in-between. This is what marketing sets out to do.

Does it succeed, though, even with Gallup, Harris and Nielsen Polls to aid it (a Harris Poll conducted in May 1970 somehow proved that more people believed in God than in life after death!), with Sampling Panels, National Readership Surveys, Marplan, MEAL, and TV data supplied by Audits of Great Britain (whose audience measurements for JICTAR, the Joint Industry Committee for Television Advertising Research, replace today the once-famous TAM ratings provided by Television Audience Measurement Ltd.)—on all of which polling, sampling and testing we spend over £40 million per year? I say "we" not just as advertising people but as consumers, because that cost is part of the price-structure; it all comes home to roost at the check-out point.

The opportunity to succeed has certainly been present in our economy as never before, since 1964 when the scourge of Resale Price Maintenance was at last abolished. This brought price and demand at last into their most direct causal relationship ever. The marketing profession seemed poised to inherit the earth, but (apart from splendid exceptions like Marks & Spencer) it hasn't happened. On the contrary, the National Marketing Council, set up by Labour in 1965, has had very little impact either on management or public consciousness, and a Tory Parliamentary Secretary to the Board of Trade had to announce in the Commons the Conservative view that there exists "a need to promote this awareness [of marketing] and an acceptance of modern marketing techniques."

We have heard such noises before from the other side. Let us hope that more than just another resounding echo results on this occasion. Let us leave the politicians and marketing mandarins to ponder away at their imponderables and return to the essence of Advertising—the progress of an advertising campaign. Paraphrasing Roy Campbell's poem "On Some South African Novelists," let us now leave our chat about "the snaffle and the curb" and get down to "where's the bloody horse?" Indeed, these snaffles and curbs can only urge the horse to gallop off in all directions at once, without the proper harness of a solidly-planned campaign.

For here is the only reliable touchstone of success—whether our advertisement brings a sale, or not. The cash-register is the ultimate marketing factor, from which there is no refuge or appeal.

Derek Bloom, Marketing Services Director of Beecham Products, was forced to confess wryly, after the Market Research Society's 20th Annual Conference this year, that "the development of a market research industry, the provision of more and more exploratory and analytic services ... has itself thrown up more problems of reconciliation and interpretation." In other words, it's still all mostly mirror-talk.

We can leave marketing and market research safely in their new-found, if suspect, respectability, which can only be compounded (or complicated perhaps) by the growing use of their techniques in, of all places, the Soviet Union, where these ultra-capitalist (or so we have preened ourselves) tools of modern Advertising in the affluent society are now in regular deployment by the "Comrades of the All-Union Scientific Research Institution of Consumer Complaints," who report to the K.G.B. no doubt.

Chapter V

PLANNING A CAMPAIGN—1

In reviewing just how an advertising campaign evolves I ask first that students school themselves to accept and understand from the start that the variables are infinite, and I assure them that this is not a "cop out." Here immediately, of course, we part company with our flight of fancy of the K.G.B. as Klient, since—apart from the legions of the blind who lead the blind—the Lubyanka's terms of market research are utterly and depressingly predictable. No mere coincidence decreed that the apostle of conditioned reflexes was a Russian!

Critics of Advertising like to pretend that the Admass World (the marvellous noun was coined by J. B. Priestley) is one of absolutely conditioned response, with admen throwing bucketfuls of conditioning powder in everyone else's eyes; that it produces a people which cannot distinguish Hollywood from the trees, that our God is One Who thunderbolts with Flash, our only sin to be castigated with Brand-X certificates. If this were true there would be no need for advertising campaigns at all—the Consumer Society would buy to rigid predetermined patterns, and the whole "persuasion industry" junked as irrelevant.

It is not true, however, and it is these same critics who are the more blinded by Hollywood's silver-screen lining on our cloudy profession, by the unreal notions of Advertising propagated by such films as *The Hucksters*.

The profession does not help its claims to respectability and legitimacy, however, by often seeming to accept this "predetermined" premise as true. Bernard Shaw said that all professions were conspiracies against the laity, but we are worse—we are a conspiracy against ourselves. Many media and research departments believe they have a vested interest in asserting that all "C" housewives in Newcastle upon Tyne (*see* Chapter VI) will behave in the same way always. Their blandly hysterical assumptions (real or pretended) that the reactions of Mr. and Mrs. Admass to given stimuli can always be scientifically measured and forecast (there are fads in the "science"—not too long ago, all Account Executives would earnestly assure me that blue "was not a selling colour") have resulted in some of the most appalling advertising ever seen.

VARIETY IS THE SPICE

The best in Advertising makes only one basic assumption: it predicates humanity—and for this "failing" I would defend it unceasingly. Your true professional adman knows down to his bootlaces or slip-ons that in taking aim at the virtues, follies, vices, vanities and impulses to self-betterment and self-improvement that are packaged inside these great untidy heaps which make up humanity, he is trying to hit a moving target. Advertising which assumes the fact despairingly may also fail, but fail honourably.

The chronicle of a campaign you will read in this chapter and the two which follow can give, at the most, only a limited perspective on the big guns, and show only a portion of the target area. The events described, and their sequences, can't possibly be exactly similar to your happenings in the adworld. But the right outline *will* be there in whatever campaign you may meet in the future. It may include more or less of the ingredients on these pages, but you will know where you fit into the jigsaw. Whether they call themselves by different titles or not these are the men you will meet.

Let them pick your brains, if you must—don't let them pickle them in a jar of non-commitment.

THE "CLIENT SIDE"

Let us know the "enemy," because much of the time your target will be the client as well as the customer. If we assume that the client is a sizeable concern, one which has several brands on the market, then it will be an overall Advertising Manager, responsible directly to his boss (whom we shall envisage as a looming, formidable presence called the Managing Director) for the total advertising programme of the company; he may also be the firm's Publicity Director, though publicity may be a subdivision of his department. He will naturally work in close collaboration with the Sales Manager, and will sometimes be the same person; indeed, the M.D. himself may wear all these hats at once, but there's no point in confusing you by assuming so.

What you must remember is that none of these executives will necessarily know much about Advertising, but all will have the company's accountants on their backs, and the Sales Manager is held responsible by the Board of Directors for disappointing results. The handiest person for him to pass on the buck to is the Advertising Manager—and from him the buck starts inexorably on its way to you. It may be swelled to a buck-and-a-half by the time it lands on your plate, because Advertising Managers have come in for a lot of stick lately, not least from their own body, the Incorporated Advertising Managers' Association, which has sternly warned all members that they may be rapidly falling behind in new techniques.

Their main threat comes from what the retiring Chairman of the I.A.M.A. in 1972 bitterly called the "great god" of marketing (*see* Chapter IV). Whatever the actual or specious values of marketing, there is no doubt that the Marketing Manager in many big industrial and manufacturing groups is fast superseding his advertising colleague in rank and status, when not obliterating him altogether. In an average-sized client set-up, however, it is the Ad Manager who will hold ultimate sanctions over you, who will pass or reject your work, will fire and hire agencies.

He will also administer, and help determine, the appropriation for a product, i.e. the amount of money which your agency is authorised to spend on client's behalf in the course of a year. It is all these client appropriations added together which give your agency its *billing*.

THE KEY CLIENT EXECUTIVE

Under the overall (and overriding) authority of a large firm's Advertising Manager are the Brand Managers, who have one or more specific brands of the company under their charge. The Brand Manager is therefore the executive who deals most intimately with the advertising agency, his company's main contact-point in the client–agency relationship—as his opposite number, the Account Executive, is for the agency side. If these two men don't hit it off you may as well wash your hands of the account. Whether or not you consciously employ what American admen like to call the "client relations maintenance system," that relationship certainly does need constant supervision and repair, liquid or otherwise.

Specifically it needs this because the Brand Manager occupies a highly vulnerable position. If the advertisements fail the dreaded M.D. will be down on *him*. The fact that the advertising agency will also suffer, and perhaps lose the account is small consolation. His breed was sharply characterised, in a *Campaign* article of July 1969 by Rex Winsbury, as "bright young men in search of an identity"—because his is hemmed in by client pressures, from his obvious superiors and from the marketing and research departments of his firm. However, whether he is a needle-bright graduate on the make, or on sufferance from "relative" reasons, or a canny old stager on the cadge, it is greatly to your interest to bolster and qualify an "identity" for him, with profitable advertising.

Let us stress here that while I shall keep calling him the Brand Manager for convenience, this executive may be very different from the *Campaign* archetype. In a small firm it may be the Managing Director himself. In a larger company it may be a young chap on £3,000 a year. In some instances it may be the Publicity Director, if that should be the only branch of creative service which is sought.

On more excruciating occasions the Brand Manager you have to persuade can be one of *your own* directors. The giant Taylor-Woodrow Organisation subsidises its own design company. The Max Factor Account in London was "brand-managed" for twenty-six years by one man, W. W. Whitby, who became a director in turn of each agency which agreed to handle Factor products, going from Crane's to Smee's to Alexander Butterfield's, and the "internationalisation" of Max Factor (*see* Chapter II) took place only on Whitby's retirement.

Sometimes a complete turnabout occurs, as when the Assistant Account Executive in the agency which handled Carmen Curlers suddenly left the agency to reappear as Brand Manager for the client. A similar instance happened with the World Record Club account some years ago. It is much to the credit of the clients, agencies and all executives concerned that the relationships didn't founder under this Looking-Glass situation, and, in the Carmen case, that the dénouement of the famous opera was not re-enacted!

GIVING "PUSH" TO A PRODUCT

In following the progress of an advertising campaign it is tempting—indeed, it's the usual practice—to invent a product, such as an imaginary cosmetic or kitchen-tool, toy or book. I have rejected this approach as far too limiting, since all observations would be restricted, sometimes severely, by the nature of the chosen invention. Comments on a girdle would always have to be qualified by comments on fertilisers or after-dinner mints or other bracing topics. No, let us play the game of devil's disciple and assume that the Brand Manager of a company has been put in charge of promoting "Brand-X." This is the product most discussed and least used, the most universally unknown product in the world. I think it is high time Brand-X got a break. So let's sell it.

Before approaching an advertising agency the Brand Manager for X will have had his company's own promotional resources to explore. The firm's market research department will feed him information on the "user-pattern" across the country for similar goods under rival labels, the Advertising Manager will tell him how much money is available for the campaign and what the sales-targets are. The Production Manager will fill him in on the factory capability on call to back up anticipated consumer demand, and the Sales Director will brief him on distribution arrangements, how the sales force is organised, where the wholesalers are located and in which areas of the country Brand-X will be put on sale, in what shops, at what price—and when.

All this data will be duly passed on to the advertising agency, of course (with the Brand Manager pretending he has prepared all this ground-work personally). If an agency is now to be selected from among several applicants the above data will be part of the initial brief given, from which competitive creative presentations may be desired.

Sources of all this information may include MEAL statistics (to assess how much rivals are spending on the same targets), the Nielson Retail Index, the Attwood Consumer Panel, figures published by the Department of Trade and such government publications as the *Economic Survey* and the *National Income and Expenditure White Paper*. The Brand Manager may or may not have already consulted one or more of the consumer survey tables which his agency will certainly soon be quoting to him (*see* Chapter IV), depending on how large a company he works for and how sophisticated his senior management.

The senior management may not be as sophisticated as he is paid to think. Sir Paul Chambers was Chairman of the Advertising Association for two years before discovering that his own Royal Insurance Company was not a member. "I am hopeful other financial institutions will follow suit," said Sir Paul virtuously, having hastily enrolled. But, one hopes, rather more speedily.

THE "MARKET MODEL"

If he is trying to be more "with it" than Sir Paul, the Brand Manager may well have made use of a "market model" in determining his plans for Brand-X, and for up-staging the Account Executive. This new fad is not, as the name suggests, either a toy or a plaything (or is it?)—it's the latest "in" method of marketing. All it really means, however, is that it provides an exhaustive in-depth analysis of a given problem, with a subsequent supporting layout of buttressing facts. The aims of a marketing model have been explained fully in his book on the subject by Clive Mann, a senior marketing consultant, and these aims include the discovery of:

1. the market potential;
2. the company's present and projected share of that market;
3. how to exploit this market;

and so on and so forth. It seems to this writer a bit like old wine in new bottles (almost identical objectives were specified by John Hobson, Chairman of Hobson Bates, in the second of his Cantor lectures delivered in 1964 to the Royal Society of Arts), and its use will, I think, be determined more by the quality of the vintage than the pop-design of the bottle.

After the contents are decanted from the market model, everything will still come back to the age-old street-vendor's cry, "Who will buy?"—which is why Advertising and you and I exist. We are not in the Frankenstein business (though I say it as shouldn't, since it was my great-great-great-great-aunt, Mary Shelley, who invented him), nor will the Brand Manager need a model to reveal to him, in Mr. Mann's words, that "the bigger the risk, the greater the re-ward—and the higher the cost of failure."

CHOOSING AN AGENCY

The decision revolves around the question: Which is the best agency for selling Brand-X? This is the Brand Manager's most funda-mental decision, possibly indeed the hardest he'll ever be called on to make. Many agencies will be willing to make it for him, in double-quick time. First, however, something else needs deciding: *does he really need an agency at all?*

Heresy? Re-read Chapters II and IV and think again. The possible choices bearing on his decision are these:

1. If his company is very large the chances are that it employs more than one agency already, using different agencies for different brands or different types of product. Convention decrees, for example, that an agency can't handle products which directly compete with each other, so while it may undertake advertising campaigns for a manu-facturing group's jam account, it can't handle the group's coffee pro-duct if it already services the coffee brand of another producer.

2. If he requires only a certain limited type of promotion, for example, television and poster media, then he will look for agencies specialising in these fields (though "presenting" agencies may try to change his mind on this).

3. He may prefer to use a creative consultancy instead of an agency in those cases where his company is big enough to have its own market-ing and research facilities. Or he may request the agency to confine its services to non-creative areas like space-buying and production, so that copy and design can be carried out by freelance outfits of one, two or more people. His company may even boast its own design de-partment, like the vast Scaffolding (Great Britain) Group or Gala Perfumes or Paul Hamlyn, or the big ethical pharmaceutical groups like Bayer, Glaxo and S.K.F., and occasionally require no more than an outside copywriter.

These considerations are reflected, for example, in the attitude taken by the Spillers people, who spread their flour, bread and pet food accounts (totalling several million pounds and including such nationally-known brands as Wonderloaf, Choosy, Homepride, and regional brands such as Tyne Brand Canned Meats) among at least half a dozen top-rank agencies, plus small consultancies. In a rationale of this diversified spread their Group Advertising Controller wrote: "Agencies gain reputations for certain strengths ... but these can reflect weaknesses in other directions, as end results sometimes show: an excellent colour concept calling for good reproduction placed in a poor-colour-reproduction publication; a first-class TV Commercial placed against the wrong audience ... an otherwise good campaign badly timed, due to inadequate marketing data."

The amount of money client has to spend need bear no relation at all to the number and size of agencies and/or consultancies the respective Brand Managers may choose. The practice of C. & A. Modes is cited elsewhere. The largest passenger shipping line in the world, P. & O. Lines, uses Davidson Pearce Berry and Spottiswoode agency for its press advertising and turns to consultancies, design groups and frequently freelance talent to produce its brochures and mailings. Birds Eye Foods Ltd., commanding two-thirds of the nation's frozen food business, has used agencies as large as Lintas and as small as the two-man Klein–Peters Consultancy.

Lines Bros., the deceased giant toy combine which made Triang Toys, Dinky Cars and Meccano (besides owning Hamleys, the famous Regent Street toy-shop), divided their £400,000 billing between three agencies, two in London, one in Liverpool, all chosen for various creative and marketing reasons.

Understanding all these considerations, we shall, for our purposes, now assume that Brand-X does require a general all-round agency service from a good not-too-large outfit. To help him choose, the Brand Manager may ask an agency representative to call round or he may float rumours that he is "looking" and sit back awaiting applications. Or he may ask for presentations.

The "presentation" waltz

It is ironic (hence the heading) but unfortunately a fact, that the "moment of truth" for many an advertising agency—even the most hallowed in repute and respectability—is also their greatest moment of falsity. This is when Advertising, in thinking it is putting its best foot forward, is really flaunting its Achilles' heel. This moment comes on the day when the agency makes a "presentation" to the client (personified by the Brand Manager and others) in the hope of winning his account.

Before the Brand-X delegation arrives agency personnel dash round tarting up the premises, applying "make-up" liberally to their own corporate face as well as to the offices; the loos are declared off-limits to anyone below Board level, cases of booze are ordered in, a catering firm is alerted for the caviare, and generally the agency upholds the worst of the lay public's dire suspicions that Advertising is the prostitute-parasite of commerce. No Regency madame ever paraded her "girls" before the moneyed, half-cut dandies with more calculated abandonment and shamelessness than an Account Director showing off the talent he can offer his callers ("all tastes catered for").

The variety in presentations is enormous, but we can refine them (if that's the word) down to three basic forms: (1) an inspection by client of agencies' offices and facilities (and secretaries), followed by a showing of current agency work for other clients; (2) a "speculative" creative presentation, which involves the agency in preparing for "gallery" viewing by its distinguished guests a complete campaign for the client's product, in competition with other agencies, whose identities may or may not be known; or (3) a combination of these two, to greater or less degree.

Whichever the form of presentation, the ingenuity and sheer originality expended on landing an account frequently far exceeds subsequent effort and time expended on the actual advertising. Presentations are an absurd, affected and pathetic game, a marionette waltz, and often as disgracing to the client who demands them as to the agency which provides them, with a humiliating exhibition of pandering (sometimes literally), bowing and scraping to the potential patron. They disgrace and they degrade, they embody all that is worst in the profession.

Yet the client almost *wills* the deceits which are practised on him by the autocratic way he descends on the ad-house to assert his *droit de seigneur*. Client will have first "invited" a number of agencies to "pitch" for his account, perhaps as few as three, or as many as twelve (Hathaway Shirts may have established a record by making eyes at nearly a hundred agencies and inviting a "pitch" from twenty-five).

After then paying a state visit to each agency in turn the client keeps them all in an agony of suspense while he makes up his mind ... and sometimes selects one he hasn't seen at all! His decision can be based on the most trivial and irrelevant reasoning, for all his blather about his "marketing" theories: I've known one client reject an agency because of the colour of its carpets, another because the agency chairman wore a striped shirt which was considered damning evidence of undue "levity."

The prize and the price

When the Mattel toy account moved from Crawfords they invited
five agencies—Lintas; Leo Burnett-L.P.E.; Foote, Cone & Belding;
K.M.P. and Horniblow Cox-Freeman—to make a presentation. Mid-
way through the selection rounds the last-named agency was commissioned by Mattel to prepare a £20,000 campaign for their "Barbie"
dolls and Horniblow Cox-Freeman was delighted to oblige, feeling
naturally the victory was theirs—only to discover that, after all this
excitement and effort, Mattel had awarded the account to Leo Bur-
nett-L.P.E.

To say accounts are "awarded" is rather to devalue the verb. Many
people's livelihoods are utterly dependent on the comings and goings
of accounts in this arbitrary fashion. Last year, over 300 clients
switched agencies, and were wooed by their suitors to the collective
tune of £2 million. To their everlasting credit a few agencies firmly
refuse to make "speculative" presentations, following the line used
by David Ogilvy to K.L.M. Royal Dutch Airlines when he told them
bluntly "We have prepared nothing. Instead, we would like you to
tell *us* about your problems . . . we will then embark on the research
which always precedes the preparation of advertisements at our
agency." No doubt he still felt the wounds of a speculative presentation which had cost him £10,000 *but failed* (it was to Bromo Seltzer
and set out to prove that most headaches were of psychosomatic
origin—whether or not his own headache that followed bore out
this conclusion, he does not say). K.L.M. very sensibly took him
on.

The celebrated Bill Bernbach follows Ogilvy in this. In London
today, neither Doyle Dane Bernbach nor Young and Rubicam will
make such presentations.

These are still in a minority, however, in the teeth of the evidence
and of self-respect. Every day speculative presentations are rashly
agreed to, especially when the client offers a small derisory fee for
the purpose (I have known one "big-hearted" big-name client, with
an appropriation of about £500,000, offer a gratuity of £200, even
when the least expensive can scarcely cost the agency less than
£2,000!), and indeed some agencies have new-business sections,
whose sole aim is to solicit and prepare the displays. These departments get so carried away, fired by crisis enthusiasms, that they tend
to live entirely in an unreal universe of advertisements for clients they
don't really possess, where campaigns whirl like galaxies through their
star-filled heads. Finally, they wish-fulfil themselves right into Carey
Street with cost-ineffective presentations priced anywhere up to
£50,000.

Playing the game

Lewis Carroll (not to mention Pirandello) must be the patron saint of presentations; Carroll and Pirandello were both exponents of the "what is truth"—the reality–fantasy–reality puzzle—aspect of life and perception, and very apt, in my view.

I have often stood in solemn conclave with fellow agency staff while the Managing Director lectured us on the "roles" we were to play in some forthcoming presentation and on what titles we were to assume to imply departments which in fact were non-existent. At the time I was a Copy Group Head, but most of us were asked to take on roles above our station, so there was more than a hint of method acting involved and enjoyed. I have seen our staff-numbers swelled by the equivalent of "spear-carrying" extras at the Old Vic to impress an obsessive head-counting prospective client accustomed to believing that only a "cast of thousands" rushing about in all directions could adequately do his bidding—he was probably right, at that.

Outside freelance marketing and P.R. men are brought in to impersonate full-time staff (which can produce later embarrassments when clients drop in unexpectedly). On the whole, clients have failed to heed the advice given by John Orr Young, co-founder of Young and Rubicam, in his book *Adventures in Advertising*, in which he warns them: "It is easy to be beguiled by acres of desks, departments, and other big agency appurtenances. What counts is the real *motive* power of the agency, the *creative potency*." On one unforgettable occasion, in order to give a gullible Brand Manager an impression of non-existent acreage of office space, an agency Chairman urged the lad to "rest his feet" and to see the vast spectacular unroll before him on closed-circuit television. His offer was gratefully accepted and, scotch and cigar in hand, the client watched upon the screen (which had been hired the day before and set up overnight) an incredible procession of charades from imaginary "departments" in full frenetic activity which would have done credit to a Feydeau farce. The Brand Manager swallowed it whole.

Was the subterfuge, conducted on such a scale, ever discovered? No, because after that, most conferences were held at the client's own offices (many Chairmen consider it beneath them to visit their company's agents "on site") and whenever the Brand Manager came trekking along there was an ample supply of drinks and cigars.

Mrs. Sam Rothenstein, former Creative Group Head at Bensons, made, in a *Campaign* article of October 1970, this devastatingly candid revelation: "It would be interesting to find out how many clients know that the *creative* presentations [author's italics] produced for them have been done not by the agency but by outside consultancies."

She goes on, "the extent to which freelance talent is used (on these occasions) can be gauged by the fact that Cramer Saatchi was sometimes approached by more than one agency *to pitch for the same account*." Again, author's italics. "Who cares for you?" said Alice. "You're nothing but a pack of cards!"

Making the choice

Is there always a joker in the pack? Not always; in fact, the majority of presentations, of all sorts, are perfectly honest (within reason) and I would not suggest otherwise. They remain, however, extremely wasteful of time and money (client's money too, as the successful candidate will certainly contrive to incorporate the presentation costs into a future client invoice).

Whatever size the audience, too, there is simply no sure way of telling which presentation will win. In 1970, when three agencies went after a flirty Lyons Maid (whose dowry was worth £650,000 in billings), only one of them indulged in a creative presentation ... realising too late that the wayward ways of a Maid never change; they lost! The head of Young and Rubicam has estimated that as many as 99 per cent of presentations are unsatisfactory, and he's probably under-estimating. When the *Evening Standard* (worth £100,000) had *ten* agencies on the hook for their account, one of the prestigious danglers, McCann–Erickson, figured they had it made when they dreamed up the admittedly impressive and extravagant (but so irrelevant) wheeze of secretly photographing the paper's Managing Editor, Jocelyn Stevens (late of *Queen*) as he entered their front door. In just two hours the photograph was printed and reproduced as part of a brilliant *Standard* front-page facsimile, the headline reading "MCCANN'S STANDARD BID—NEW MOVES."

Stevens was appreciative. He chuckled and made all the conventional and polite noises. He said he found it "Very funny ... the paper was very slick, too." And then he gave his valuable patronage elsewhere.

This, then, is the ritual framework within which the Brand Manager of X (the unmentionable product we are about to advertise) will start choosing an agency for handling his account. Let's hope he chooses *you*. For the purposes of this book we shall presume he does, though neither you, nor I, nor himself, nor anyone else in this narrow world can be sure what makes him do it.

Whether you simply receive him in a plain office—having perhaps taken the two-day course in client presentation offered by Business Intelligence Services Limited—or proffer a lavish welcome in a lush suite whose walls are plastered with award-winning campaigns (some of them yours) and the carpets thick with bunny girls ... whatever

your angle or wherever your curve, every "pitch" amounts essentially to a variation on the old rhyme:

> The Codfish lays ten thousand eggs,
> The Hen lays only one
> But the Codfish never cackles
> To tell you what she's done.
> And so we scorn the Codfish
> While the lowly Hen we prize,
> Which only goes to show you
> It Pays To Advertise!

As for the Brand Manager, it would be inhuman to begrudge him
his petty kingdom for a day (or as long as he can drag his decision
out)—it's not his fault that the present farcical system decrees that
every agency shall be eternally in the position of Scheherazade, spinning the tale to stave off execution on the morrow.

Every client sees himself as just such a sultan, imagining himself
in the imperial position of Trans-World Airlines on that mind-blow-
ing day in New York in 1967, when they let word seep out, let rumours
fly hinting daintily that they might, just *might*, be about to leave their
present agency, Foote, Cone & Belding. Almost every major and
minor agency on Madison Avenue pitched for the $22 million
account, and made presentations (including shooting pilot TV commercials) costing up to $50,000 each—over $1 million in total.

In the end, Foote, Cone & Belding slipped quietly over to the West
Coast and brought back sole rights to Jim Webb's song "Up, Up and
Away"—and were permitted by T.W.A. to keep the account. Thus
Ulcer Gulch dropped $1 million—but a far from cool one—down the
drain, and a thousand psychiatrists from the Lower East Side up to
Spanish Harlem began dusting off their couches and shrinking heads.
The crunch that shaped the P.S. (meaning Post-Seizure) to the whole
sorry business came along only six months later, when a blonde Scheherazade named Mary Wells (*see* Chapter XIV), who had won
deserved fame for persuading Braniff Airlines to paint their aircraft
in shades of fuchsia and then persuading Braniff's President to become
her husband, calmly walked off with the T.W.A. account *without making any presentation at all*. The original Scheherazade was clearly a mere
Coronation Street wind-bag compared to our Mary! The wretched epi-
sode is hilariously described by Jerry Della Famina in his book *From
Those Wonderful Folks Who Gave You Pearl Harbour*, and he finishes
sadly, by saying: "It's not that all of the advertising business is crazy,
but there are times. . . ."

Are there no shoes or open-toed sandals on the other foot, ever?
There are indeed. Whenever the Brand Manager with whom you are

dealing and wheeling in ever-diminishing circles of frustration gets that "Up, Up and Away" look in his eyes, you can casually remind him of the seismographic moment in August 1969, when Papert Koenig Lois of London let the word fall soft as a whisper in Sloane Street that they were calmly resigning £1 million worth of business, including Hotpoint, Hilton Hotels, Jensen cars, I.C.I. and Potterton central heating.

The Sonesta rocked on its foundations, a *frisson* convulsed the David Hicks decor. Potterton said "a pity," I.C.I. allowed that it was "very upset," one agency said "strange" and frowned, another murmured "very interesting;" and so it was.

Chapter VI

PLANNING A CAMPAIGN—2

When your agency acquires a new account like Brand-X it acquires a new *corporate* personality. Corporeal, too, for many personal adjustments and accommodations follow in the wake of the acquisition (plus new offices and new furnishings, if the account can stand the weight). Mainly, however, and most significantly, the change is corporate.

Sometimes, of course, the reason is straightforward enough: the client *has* bought in and literally taken the place over. More often, however, it's because he only thinks he has, but there are times when this second variation results in more direct client interference than the first. The important factor here, especially in initial stages of confrontation, is the strength of character and purpose of the Brand Manager *vis-à-vis* the strength of character and purpose of the Account Executive. It is upon this trial of strength that much depends.

The new personality can therefore mean simply the invading presence of a new person, i.e. the client, as personified by the Brand Manager, thrustful and lustful of power, a nagging sense of "not belonging" in the agency environment prompting spurts of aggression. Or it can mean the all-pervasive presence of a suddenly new agency *self*. This does not stem from the nature of the product to be advertised; Brand-X can be anything from a car to a potato-crisp, a light ale to a laxative, a dog food to a deodorant; this is a very small element in the change.

What does bring about immense change is *the development of the client–agency relationship*, the mutation of the engaged pair into the marriage partners—a puzzling, painful, only intermittently delicious process. Alas, a more precise definition is impossible, in the same way that one cannot define a marriage properly, or even improperly. "All marriages are different," and Shaw's remark can be strongly applied here, though technically there is more resemblance to Moslem than Christian ceremony, with polygamy rampant ánd such ludicrous ease of divorce at hand (which, however, can be legally insured against by your agency).

"ADVERTISER" INTO "CLIENT"

The first full getting-acquainted sessions will probably take place in plenary grandeur around the boardroom or conference-room table at the agency. I refer now to the practical down-to-earth session, of course, because this confrontation is not the first by any means—during the honeymoon period it will have been prefaced, even after the presentation and "winning the account" by a number of state visits between "heads of government" on either side, at which many courses are charted and consumed, many healths simultaneously drunk to and impaired.

In addition, whatever the surface chat of mutual trust and respect, the client will have thoroughly canvassed your agency's reputation and methods from discreet phone-calls to those other clients already on your firm's books. Likewise, your agency will have sought out the client's previous agencies (or present ones, on other brands than X) to get a similar rundown, collating rumour, scandal and fact, sifting reports from sources as disparate as MEAL, stock-brokers and what any little receptionist can tell you—which is more than most.

So you both have now learned at second-hand how the opposite numbers look with hair down or toupee glued on, and where the skeletons are kept. The big-money talk is over and, eyeball to eyeball, discussion starts on what the advertising budget will actually be, how it will be spent and also, how quickly.

It's essential that these house-keeping details be settled very early on, for the foundations of either a happy, hippy or snappy marriage can be laid or mined as soon as this, unless frank undertakings are exchanged, and before witnesses. The advertiser who is now your client must no longer be misled over the services actually available at your agency. On the other hand, the advertiser who has brazenly woven seductive spells compounded from a brew of huge billings must not now propose spending "as a feeler" only one or two thousand. With agency profits on a permanent knife-edge, and not likely to improve dramatically in the foreseeable furture (*see* Chapter XIV), this is a point which must be ruthlessly established.

Forewarned is forearmed. The agency may have to plan rapid hiring of extra staff, on permanent or temporary basis, or contract for special services from outside consultancies (*see* Chapter IV), or lay off others. Extra premises, facilities and equipment may need quick lining up. Another client who takes up too much unprofitable time, energy and creative output, may have to be "resigned" (*see* Chapter V). Most importantly, before all else, fees must be negotiated—the more of a billing which arrives in agency coffers from fees, rather than the 15 per cent crumbs that filter back grudgingly from media commission, the better for all.

Table-talk: the spending

Ranged along one side of the conference table (there need not actually be one, of course—everyone may lounge round on transparent plastic foam or huddle in a broom-cupboard office—but the principles are there) will sit the client delegates, your new in-laws. These are the Brand Manager, his assistant, secretary and Production Manager (who oversees the physical production of X) and maybe his supervisor and superior, the Advertising Manager.

On the agency side will be the Account Director (who will soon take his leave after making his presence felt), the Account Executive, his assistant and secretary, *his* Production Manager (who oversees the physical production of the advertising), the Media Manager and Traffic Manager. The Creative Director may appear for a time, but he will duly appoint a Copy Group Head, or similar, to be on hand from the start, if possible and allowed. Both sides may, of course, have higher brass and lower brass, but the executives I have specified are the crucial ones who must take part.

It's not unusual, as Tom Jones would say, for some executives to table-hop over to the opposite side. The Advertising Manager of B.O.A.C. became Chairman of the airline's agency, Foote, Cone & Belding. In the other direction the Advertising Manager of Cadbury–Schweppes moved across from a post at Cadbury's agency, Leo Burnett-L.P.E. The Chairman of Doyle Dane Bernbach in London was originally his agency's client.

Having agreed, or at least settled, *how much*, the conference next determines the *how* of spending. This will primarily depend on the type of campaign required by client, suggested or modified by the agency for business or other selfish reasons. This in turn, apart from money available, depends on the nature of the product. Brand-X may be:

1. *A consumer product:* anything directly consumed by the buyer; that is, anything that when *used*, no longer exists, or exists as it did before; anything from food to clothing and perfumes.

2. *A consumer-durable product:* anything *indirectly* consumed by the buyer; that is, anything which, used once, can still be used again in its original form; anything from cars to refrigerators, from lawn-mowers to TV sets.

3. *A mass product or luxury product:* clearly depending on whether it is relatively cheap, frequently used and easily replaced, e.g. detergents, paperbacks and razor-blades, or expensive, of limited appeal

and, in most cases, of only "occasional" use, e.g. Havana cigars, leather desk-sets, mink stoles and jewellery. Items in these classifications may switch places, of course, as society prospers (*see* the socioeconomic class-list later in this chapter), and much clothing and food once considered luxury is now (in selling terms) a mass product. On the contrary, salmon was once the "poor man's" food. Then again, the mass product of Britain may be the luxury product of a developing country—and vice versa.

4. *Industrial or technical product:* the type is self-defined, the selling difference being that your target won't be the general public, but men and women whose interest in the product is technical or professional, the vital distinction here being that the money which buys X is far less likely to derive from a private purse.

5. *Ethical pharmaceutical product:* anthying which relates to the field of medicine or surgery, sold sometimes to the public, but more often only to doctors or chemists direct.

6. *A service product:* anything which is not a three-dimensional *object*, but a desirable *objective*, e.g. the relief of the poor or the provision of amenities; this category could include a package tour, a charity, British Rail, hotels, etc.

7. *A public service product:* anything to do with public welfare or concern that will directly or indirectly benefit the whole community, e.g. health campaigns, anti-crime, anti-smoking appeals. We might include, as a sub-section, the "group" or "generic" promotions, such as those which publicise the virtues of more Pintas, or of eating more E. for B.—such campaigns can legitimately claim a public benefit, even though they achieve a commercial goal.

Over countless cups of coffee both sides eventually reach agreement as to exactly what sort of product our Brand-X is purporting to be, in selling terms of presentation to the market. This definition, allied to the price, should make precisely clear just what kind of people are to be sought as targets. The client's Sales Manager will weigh in here, perhaps, and both sides may call in market research experts to support their preconceived dogmas and diagnoses, or to put in train new research and market-testing (*see* Fig. 2). When either side retreats in the arguments which ensue you can be certain it is to a "previously prepared position."

Table-talk: where to spend

The confrontation proceeds, spawning the odd, sometimes excessively odd, sub-committees. Conference succeeds conference, coffee-cup follows coffee-cup into the waste-bin and the eyes of delegates follow the passing limbs of chattering "temps" (short for temporaries

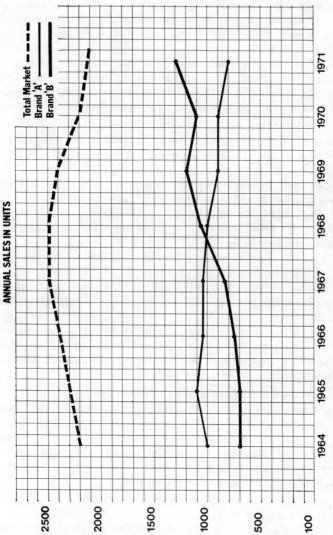

ANNUAL SALES IN UNITS

Total Market ━ ━ ━
Brand 'A' ━━━
Brand 'B' ━━━

2500

2000

1500

1000

500

100

1964   1965   1966   1967   1968   1969   1970   1971

Fig. 2.—Graph of market research statistics prepared for client by Account Executives to back up the agency campaign plan. Over a seven-year period, comparative brand sales are shown for competing products.

or temptresses, take your pick), while the talk wanders around search-ing for a point, or rather, selecting one point after another. Although establishing the *type of product* can produce a fairly rapid consensus, establishing the *type of advertising* can turn into a wide-open battlefield.

On this score the Brand Manager asserts that he knows best because he knows his product best; the Account Executive claims he knows better because he knows Advertising best. Both these assertions are, in general, true.

Choice has now to be made between advertising in the Press, tele-vision, direct mail, radio or posters, cinema, exhibitions or below-the-line. Within these media further decisions have to be taken and con-firmed as to which aspects of the chosen media best fit the product. These are as follows:

Press. National, local or regional newspapers, or magazines? General or technical and trade journals? Daily, weekly or monthly?

Television. Regional or London (i.e. national) networks?

Direct mail. To which addresses, general or specific? Should there be one mailing for all, or a "split-run" (*see* Chapter XI)?

Radio. Local or Luxembourg?

Posters. Nationwide or selected local sites? Tube-cards on the Underground or on buses?

Cinema. National or regional? An identical film to that used for TV, or different?

Exhibition. Travelling exhibits, in-store displays, or stands at Olympia (or similar)? Should exhibitions be designed for public or trade viewing or both?

Below-the-line. Shall there be cut-price offers? New launch reduc-tions? Premiums, giveaways, badges, competitions, etc. (*see* Chapter X)? Should there be combined promotion with another manufacturer?

Which of these media are used in the campaign for our Brand-X, and when, singly or in combination, results in what is called the "mar-keting" or "media mix" for a product. The "mix" depends not simply on the available cash for spending on advertisements, but on the client knowing *precisely* what he wishes the advertising campaign to achieve. This is where the Brand Manager's prime responsibility lies: he must be absolutely decided as to whether he wishes:

1. An "image-building" campaign, to familiarise Brand-X on the consumer consciousness.

2. An "up-market" or "down-market" image campaign, to alter the public's idea of the company or product, to change the appeal of X from, say, middle-class to working-class, or from dolly girls to duchesses, from the High Street into Harrods.

3. A "direct sales" campaign, to rope in a lot of buyers in the shortest possible time, to get the product moving off the shelves before any dust can settle.

4. A "prestige" campaign, to build up public goodwill for the product and its makers.

5. A "trade" campaign, aimed at "selling-in" the product, getting stores to stock X and put it on display. Of course, this is often done in conjunction with one of the above.

Having become very clear and self-convinced about the target and the desired sales-result, the Brand Manager should then leave it to the agency to determine methods of achieving them. He must also stick to his conclusions—and, when the creative work is half-completed (see Chapter VII), he must not suddenly decide to alter the target and expectations and then expect new work to be undertaken for the same fee.

It is by far the best for the aims and principles of the campaign to be thoroughly thrashed out, put in writing and signed by both partners. Marriage settlements always used to be conducted and finalised in this way, and marriages used to last a great deal longer.

Table-talk: how to spend

When media decisions have been settled in principle, the Media Manager then goes away to draw up his recommended "media schedule" (see Fig. 3) which will enshrine the "mix" in most practical terms, his purpose being to reach the maximum number of likely buyers while keeping within the decreed budget. Within this brief he will naturally also have a thought as to which medium will show the agency's work to greatest advantage (though this aspect is not mentioned, out of delicacy, to the client)—some agencies are strong in some media and not others. He and his Space Buyer and Time Buyer, plus a giggle of secretaries, will reach for statistics with one hand and telephone with the other.

The publication British Rate and Data, to which I have referred before, comes out in quarterly editions and will provide the media man with information for every medium, telling him prices for size or time, the audited circulation of most periodicals, data from TV companies, poster organisations or radio-stations—even the price of space under taxi-cab seats. In addition all these media will supply their own rate cards on request to individuals and automatically to agencies; these cards give details of straightforward rates, special-position rates and "volume-discount" rates, i.e. the cheaper-by-the-dozen deal.

Bloxhams Partnership Ltd. Wellington House, 6 Upper Saint Martins Lane, London, WC2H 9DR. Tel: 01-836 1237

Bloxhams
Media estimate and schedule

DATE: 21st March 1972
REF. NO.: Booked 1 JR/C
COMPANY: John Redford Ltd.
PRODUCT: Furniture
CAMPAIGN: Consumer Press
PERIOD: April/June 1972

PUBLICATION	CIRCULATION	NO OF SPOTS	SPACE SIZE	POSITION	SPACE COST	COMM.	COST PLUS SERVICE	TOTAL COST	3	10	17	24	1	8	15	22	29	5	12	19	26
									April				May					June			
Daily Express	3,390,049	1	13½"x6 cols	Early News	2,916.00	15%	2,916.00	2,916.00		10											
		3	7"x3 cols	"	693.00	15%	693.00	2,079.00				x		x			x				
Daily Mirror	4,388,446	1	Page	"	3,998.00	15%	3,998.00	3,998.00			20										
		2	6½"x3 cols	"	864.00	15%	864.00	1,728.00						x		x					
Sun	2,501,916	1	Page	"	2,173.50	15%	2,173.50	2,173.50	5												
		3	6½"x3 cols	"	425.25	15%	425.25	1,275.75				x			x			x			
Sunday People	4,761,017	2	6½"x3 cols	"	901.13	15%	901.13	1,802.26			16					28					
Sunday Mirror	4,677,999	2	6½"x3 cols	"	864.00	15%	864.00	1,728.00					7					11			
Daily Record (Scotland)	527,731	1	Page	"	472.50	15%	472.50	472.50				21									
		2	7"x3 cols	"	94.50	15%	94.50	189.00						x		x					
								£18,362.01													
						Production Reserve		1,637.99													
								£20,000.00													

Fig. 3.—Detail of media recommendations submitted by agency to client, involving weekly and Sunday press, of both national and regional coverage, over a three-month period.

Many media go beyond mere rate cards in promoting themselves and the advantages of advertising in their pages to their particular readers. They buy advertising space themselves in Advertising trade journals, comparing their circulations and readerships to the disadvantage of other publications. When *Titbits* printed a table which showed they led the field in the number of adults reached per £1 spent on advertising, the *Reader's Digest* promptly took space to show another table which proved (with "regret") that they led *Titbits* by about a thousand adults on the same "advertising £1" basis. "When *The Times* speaks, the world listens" states you-know-who, while another ad informs us that "Most influential people in Sweden begin their day with Dagens Nyheter," whoever she may be. The *Grocers' Gazette* tells you, without fuss, simply that "We make media sense," the *Daily Sketch* once threw aside inhibitions and said that they were "the only national tabloid flaunting itself in colour," showing a bikini-clad nymph to prove it ... in black and white. Whereas, if Brand-X is on the outlook for "The direct route to the Arab Markets" then it heads at once for *Huna London*, which is not the name of a new popstar, but the Arabic edition of the B.B.C.'s *Radio Times*.

Once you *heard* the *Melody Maker*'s rate card which puts all the data on a paper disc (assuming a handy record-player in the media department). Most newly launched papers and magazines make up complete "dummy" issues, well in advance of first publication date, which they send round to all agencies so that Media-Buyers can get a good idea of appearance and editorial content and perhaps recommend it to their clients. Thomson Newspapers supplied detailed region-by-region breakdowns of income, hobbies and jobs of its various journals' readers (these are called readership "profiles") as well as circulations and readership statistics, and offer prospective Media-Buyers complete merchandising and marketing facilities. The Northcliffe Newspapers had a book for media men which was called *Scanning the Provinces* which was over 200 pages long!

The huge Chadwick–Latz direct mail organisation, largest in Europe, supplied very sophisticated analysis of population groupings (including a free 103-page book), and elaborately cross-checked mailing lists for various trades and professions, dove-tailed with TV regions, plus their *Consumer Quality Index*. Each of the fifteen independent television companies themselves lay on marketing and research services which, provided you are buying sufficient time, include local retail and consumer research, test-marketing, audit-panels to sample Brand-X, distribution checks ... even a sales force!

As for posters, one can instance the Adshel Group, which would send you not only an elaborate brochure, but a free scale-model. Apart from the regular media ads media men will find in *Campaign*, that journal's detailed and frequent *Special Supplements* are extraordinarily helpful and comprehensive, whether dealing with a medium, a region, a selling method or a foreign country, with greeen covers for the Irish Republic, of course.

The I.P.A. itself provides agencies with their indispensable National Readership Survey (continually up-dated), their Poster Audience Survey and Television Audience Research, which convey such facts as that (1973) 52·4 per cent of the population are women, 47·6 per cent are men, that 17·8 per cent are aged 16–24 and 16·3 per cent are 25–34, and so on. Whereas, however, information supplied by the media is largely *free* (exceptions being wide-ranging surveys like the *1970 Young Spending Survey* published by I.P.C. Magazines), your I.P.A. survey will cost you £120 if you're not a member—and only £30 less if you are. And it is worth every penny, old or new, even though that only buys you Volume One!

Amidst all this welter of data you must take great care—and it's a mistake that can catch the most experienced professional off his guard—that you keep in mind the vital distinction between readership and circulation, for they are *not* synonymous. *Circulation* is the audited number of copies sold and/or read (since some may be given away); while *readership* is the estimated number of people who may look at those copies, i.e. one copy may be read by all five in a family, which means a circulation of one and a readership of five! The readership this gives old copies of *Punch* in dentists' waiting-rooms must be astronomical.

Table-talk: when to end

When the Media Manager has drawn up his schedule he presents it to the Account Executive for Brand-X, who then presents it to X's Brand Manager for approval. Once approved, the creative brief can be formally drawn up and copy and design got under way.

As with public relations and market research, a great deal of gratuitous jargon and mystique has grown up round the technicalities of media selection, which is, after all, simply the hunting of value for money in the media supermarket. But there *is* genuine expertise involved, whose cost-effectiveness can be reasonably measured, and the lack of it can ruin a good campaign. Media men have their own monthly journal *Admap*, with its very own rate card!

Rows over the advisability of media mixes have broken up many a promising client–agency marriage which seemed to have everything going for it. Such rows have in recent times tended to centre on the issue of "above-the-line" promotions versus "below-the-line" promotions, which suddenly become extremely fashionable and, just as abruptly, the focal point of much arduous back-pedalling, by pundits and punters alike. It is on the vexed but rather faddish pros and cons of this issue that Firestone Tyres, G.E.C., Ingersoll watches, Morphy Richards, Avon Rubber, Servotomic Heating and Uniroyal clothing have all been changing agencies within the last few years.

While taking an intelligent (and, where possible, informed) interest in which media are chosen for Brand-X, the Brand Manager should accede ultimate agency responsibility in this field (else why hire an agency at all?) and try to forget unworthy—if very occasionally well-founded—suspicions that the agency is obtaining an unethical "kick-back" from the media-owner. As the Director of Marketing and Planning at the J. Walter Thompson agency has put it: "Media buying is a creative thing, and buyers need freedom." But the ideal compromise has been expressed by the Advertising Manager of Pan American: "It is very difficult to find ... men with a knowledge of media ... but this is no excuse for leaving media up to the agency ... by taking an interest and involving the agency, it works better for us."

Some client interest is closer than others. Beechams and Cadbury–Schweppes make a bi-monthly report to their agencies on how the media-mix is working out in terms of actual sales—which may seem hard, but sales *are* what Advertising is all about, after all. Stevenson's remark on marriage is apt here, for he said "to marry is to domesticate the Recording Angel," and no doubt there are some agencies entitled to this sentiment in regard to their partners on the client side. Though Beechams certainly can, at least, lay fair claim to authority, since their founder, the first Thomas B., was no slouch at discovering new media for his message, from Christmas cards ("Hark the herald angels sing, Beecham's Pills are just the thing!") to the stranded hull of one of Nelson's surviving warships ("England expects Every Man to do His Duty and Take Beecham's Pills"). This was when the Cadbury ads were showing not only Queen Victoria, but the future Edward VII and his wife, Princess Alexandra, sloshing back their cocoa cuppas!

DISSECTING THE MARKET

Actual sales to whom? We've seen how the weapons of media are chosen and now we'll see how the targets are picked. By and large, all advertising campaigns—in theory, anyway—are aimed at a given segment drawn from the following six divisions or "classes," as set out in the I.P.A. *Readership Survey* (1970), with percentages of population, and these are accepted as definitive by most agencies:

A—Upper Management, top administrators and professional people. (3%)

B—Intermediate Management, administrative and professional people. (9%)

C$_1$—Supervisors, clerical workers and junior "white collar" staff. (24%)

C$_2$—Skilled manual workers. (30·6%)

D—Semi-skilled and unskilled manual workers. (24·4%)

E—Pensioners, widows of no independent income, casual and lowest grade workers. (8·7%)

I have included this listing since you will find frequent reference to it in Advertising, and they represent classifications to which all pay at least lip-service. Yet I have amended the I.P.A. wording slightly, leaving out the "social" class definitions (these are what are termed *socio-economic* groups, heaven help us!) since they seem to me increasingly unreal in an age of rampant wage-claims, when a casual labourer, coming in theory under Group E, can, even if illiterate, earn £100 per week ... which, though none is declared for tax, is certainly spent.

When dustmen earn more than museum curators, both earn more than nurses, and temporary typists more than any of them; when students on grant receive an allowance for taking a holiday; when a man's earnings can rise readily by "productivity" agreements, even though he has been idle for eighteen months (all these are actual examples), then I must regard socio-economic theory as yet another dialogue out of our Hire-Purchase Wonderland ... a land where, at time of writing, girls in the age-group 12–18—in other words, the teenage market—have in this country £666 million to spend on advertised products each year. Between the ages of sixteen and eighteen, this desirable target rapidly escalates, via the market-researchers' graphs and educated guesses, to a disposable income of £919·4 million per annum. The scrumptious, sometimes scruffy, young ladies splash out nearly £14 million on stockings, tights and socks, just £2 million more than they spend on jeans. As befits their luscious age-bracket, natural confidence keeps their spending on bras down to £5 million— but still worth any dedicated adman's heavy breathing. Eye-makeup nudges close to jeans, although, contrary to popular belief, the tobacco men are on to a loser here; nearly 70 per cent of teenage girls don't smoke. Not tobacco anyway!

GETTING THE TRAFFIC MOVING

Once the Brand Manager has given his okay to the mix and the schedule the whole package is placed in the hands of the Traffic Manager, who then draws up progress-sheets (you'll remember the

Progress-Chaser is in his department) to show how soon, in days and dates, the creative department, finished artists and production department people must in turn complete their work on the advertisements, posters, TV commercials or brochures (see Fig. 4) in time to make media insertion dates, or dates of TV transmission.

The actual date of publication is not our concern here, whether as the actual day it appears on the news-stands or the date on the cover. No, what matters to the agency is the "copy-date," i.e. the last date at which journals will accept prepared advertisements for incorporation into any given issue. This varies greatly from journal to journal and depends very much on the type of ad involved—clearly a classified ad can be inserted more quickly than a full-page illustrated advertisement, and an ad in full colour takes longer still (you can phone in your classified to the London *Evening Standard* for insertion next day, while a colour ad for the *Observer Magazine* will have to be submitted *thirty-four days in advance*). Sometimes, negotiation is possible on this date—especially for big-spending advertisers—but media-owners prefer that it be met. It is, of course, included on their rate card, as well as in *BRAD* and the illustrious and heavily-laden *Advertiser's Annual*. But the required-in-advance booking complicates the media man's job and he must insist that it matches up with the capability of the manufacturers of Brand-X to distribute their goods to the point of sale ... failure in this area is a sad lack of much current British merchandising.

Those, by the way, who think of "next-day" insertion as a daring innovation may be surprised to learn that *The Times* promised this very service to customers from its first issue under that name in 1788 (the Bastille fell only a few months later, obviously recognising that there wasn't room on the planet for both of them). And this remarkable service was guaranteed "no matter how inconvenient" in the days when advertisements cost around one shilling per inch—in modern *Times* that inch (now, of course, measured in millimetres) has zoomed in value; one page of today's Top People's paper will cost the advertiser £5,824! But he will not be too carried away by the "Top People" tag, since two-thirds of AB-class adults are swallowed up by *The Daily Telegraph*, *Daily Express* and *Daily Mail* (until those papers swallow each other at least). And he will remember, thinking of *The Sun*, that it's the *Topless* People who might better afford his product, as well as being readers of the paper with the country's largest circulation, its page 3 "flashing" ahead even of the *Daily Mirror*.

The copywriter and designer are now officially "briefed" on the advertising they must produce (if they're wise, they will have eavesdropped long before this) and how soon they must produce it. The

ACTION REQUISITION - NON-PRESS

The appropriate section will be *completed* by the Account Executive, with the exception of the tinted area.
Incomplete forms will be refused by the Progress Controller.

SECTION	INDIVIDUAL	ACT.	ADV.	SECTION	INDIVIDUAL	ACT.	ADV.
Accounts	P. Cavill		*	Print			
Creative-Manager	C. Radley	*		Progress Controller			
Creative-Copy	P. Kelleway	*		Services Director			
Creative-Art	C. Barnes	*		Service Executive	B.Cullen	*	
Creative-Display				T.V. Admin,			
Executive Group	N. Ross	*		Typography	D.Hart	*	

CLIENT ...... RELIANT ....

PRODUCT.... Rebel ....

PUBLICATION Brochure ....

DATE .... 18/.7/.72 ....

CLIENT PRESENTATION ...... July 1972 ....

For Progress Control use only	
DATE ISSUED	
COPY DUE	21/7
SCAMP DUE	
VISUAL DUE	26/7
REQ. NO.	RL 273

REQUIREMENT

Prepare a simple and very cheap leaflet
showing the Rebel Saloon, Estate and Van
in a good modern and acceptable setting.
Copy points and economy - 700 c.c. Reliant
engine, glass fibre body, strong chassis.
Long lasting vehicle. Car is small, could
be good second car; Estate is most likely
area for increased car sales. Priority
is Estate, then Van, then Saloon but you
must start story with Saloon. 4 colours
allowed, but one side only, and
sparingly used. Previous material
available.

NON-PRESS	
No. of Pages	
No. of Colours	
Size	
Quantity	
Leaflets Size Flat	
Leaflets Size Folded	
Max. Finish Art Cost ?	£
Max. Finish Print Cost ?	£
Are Proofs Required ?	YES/NO
Despatch Date	

Signature.... *Nigel Ross* ....

Fig. 4.—Requisition form by which Bloxhams set in motion, *to a strictly
adhered to time-schedule*, the creative and production services for providing a
selling leaflet on "Rebel" cars for Reliant Motor Co., Ltd.

Account Executive tells them all he has gleaned from client and agency research. And so, the client–agency marriage is consummated. In the next chapter we shall draw aside the modest veil from the facts of agency creative life and see how the offspring are born, the union blessed.

Chapter VII

PLANNING A CAMPAIGN—3

It was once reported in the Press that a number of London advertising agencies were visited by two young girls from New York. Their names were Carole Anne Fine and Rita Conner, and they were brazenly offering their services for only £100 a day—"I'm a little rough," sighed Carole Anne, "Rita's a little romantic," and both, we may assume, were highly mercenary.

Strong stuff for a middle-aged Creative Director or Art Buyer to find on his welcome mat on a cold December morning. But before the girls who advertise on the cards in Soho shop-windows start calling out pickets for wildcat action, let me quickly add that these enterprising damsels are freelance copywriters ... wild cats, perhaps, but of a much more rough and romantic game—trade, that is.

They are the future of their profession, of yours and mine. They form the basic unit of creative consultancy (*see* Chapters II and X) and they might just possibly be called upon to write for Brand-X. If they do you may be sure that X's Brand Manager will never be told about it, and the charge per girl will be £200 per day by the time it turns up on his agency invoice. However, let us keep our heads out of the clouds—the chances are against this happening, and we shall dolefully have to consider that your agency has an adequately-staffed full-time creative department, ready and raring to go, capable of meeting all the demands which the new-born Brand-X is likely to put upon it.

ART IS LONG BUT BRIEF IS LONGER

The brief given the copywriter and designer will principally be detailed to them by the Account Executive. He must therefore be expertly and tactfully insistent at extracting pertinent information from X's Brand Manager; and the copywriter must be equally expert—he need not bother about tact—at extracting this data, as unalloyed as possible, from *him*, "untouched by human hands" or by feet-in-mouths. The required information will fall into these six parts:

1. Exactly what is Brand-X? What does it do, or claim to do, and what benefits does it confer?

2. What sort of company makes Brand-X, and is this information of value as a selling-plus? Should the company be puffed, or hidden (if indeed those options exist)?

3. What price is X (for the public and the trade) and how does that price measure up to comparable competitors?

4. Who is being asked to buy Brand-X? What is their age, type, sex and income (*see* Chapter VI)?

5. What size of ads are required, and in what medium will they appear?

6. When is the campaign required (*a*) in "rough" form, and (*b*) in "finished art and copy" form, ready for printing?

Some simplification is here, obviously. The creative people will need to know if the claims are as solid as the Brand Manager insists; if colour is to be used; will associative editorial matter be placed next to the ad, etc. ... but everything falls within those six points.

Since the essential "gospel" news is conveyed in words, the copywriter carries prime responsibility in most agencies for initiating the ideas. And, where agreeable to all, he and the designer will talk *directly to the client*, as well as communicating through the Account Executive, while gently reminding the client always that he needs no help in his task; telling the client, as Ogilvy puts it: "Why keep a dog and bark yourself? Back-seat driving knocks the stuffing out of good creative men." Incidentally, it knocks the stuffing out of the success of X's campaign, too, which Ogilvy, being perhaps the finest copywriter this country has ever produced, no doubt wished to imply.

But, alas, the client is only one source of the lavish "help" which will now come flowing in, sometimes threatening to drown the creative people, as part and parcel of the brief—questionable aid which makes the process of absorbing the brief one of the longest stages admen learn to endure.

Facts versus dreams

"Facts are better than dreams"—thus wrote Sir Winston, and quite right, but only up to a point, and that point is vital in Advertising because every fact was once somebody's dream, and Brand-X itself will have started life as someone's dream-child, a gleam in the eye. Moreover, facts should be sifted and rationed. Churchill also was noted for requiring strictly that *his* briefs be just exactly that—brief! Once he went so far as to demand of the First Lord of the Admiralty that he "state this day, on one side of a sheet of paper, how the Royal Navy is being adapted to meet the conditions of modern warfare." Emphasis on that one side of a sheet of paper. Fortunately for the First Lord the size of the sheet wasn't specified.

Bitter experiences impel me to admit that, more times than not, the brief you receive is liable to be bolstered (or smothered, depending on the viewpoint) by a torrent of information in which technical statistics concerning production and formulae are combined with dubious data from X's own marketing and research departments, the whole mess topped up with Brand Manager's intuition.

None of this should be spurned by the creative men and women. They welcome all the background material they can get (and free samples!) and they appreciate sound professional guidelines laid down in regard to the six points already mentioned. Beyond that, however, creative people should be let off the leash.

In common with all artists working in any medium, they must be free to select and highlight from this flooding congestion of "assistance" what seems to them to be the most selling and saleable points about the product, with close reference to the various targets at which their advertisements will be aimed (when I speak of ads, let it be clear that I am speaking of all types of promotion and—apart from instances where otherwise stated—that under this umbrella-flag of convenience I am including television, posters and so on).

Suggestions, technical advice, informed hunches, all are welcome within reason—i.e. there must be an agreed moment when the dam-gates are closed—but the creative specialist must be considered to know his job, which is *advocacy*. This does not consist, as lay critics believe or pretend to believe, of the telling of half-truths or non-truths (politely called non-facts). Advertising is the art of how to improve on the truth without actually lying. The copywriter's and designer's advocacy is employed in representing the most attractive and persuasive aspects of the product in their judgment.

If they don't honestly feel that they have been given sufficient information of the kind they need, they must press for it from the client, and their Account Executive must give them every support in this. Inevitably there will be frustrations, even with "helpful" Brand Managers. One of my clients, when pressed for more varied illustrations of the product in use, gave me free-run of his company's carefully filed photographic library, taking up half one floor of the office-block. From several thousand negatives and prints, I finally, after a morning's rummage, chose twelve as a "short list" to discuss with my designer—only to have the client resolutely refuse to give me permission to use any one of them!

Brain-storming or washing?

You will find a plethora of "aids" being offered to creative groups as they struggle in labour. This help tends to resemble the treatment accorded to royal mothers during palace confinements in previous eras, when all fresh air was rigorously excluded from the bedroom, a constant roaring fire maintained to make sure that nothing less stifling than the necessary stuffiness prevailed, and princes, ambassadors, the court and any passing commoners were permitted to crowd the room almost to suffocation, to maul and gape at the poor endeavouring princess. The wonder is, under these conditions, not that the mortality of good advertising campaigns is high, but that any survive at all. Among the "lying-in" hazards to be sustained by the creative group are the following.

Brain-storming sessions. Sired by Madison Avenue but now rife in Mayfair, these are open-end discussions held in the agency during which the problems of promoting Brand-X are set out and comments invited from all and sundry—the "let's kick it around" syndrome which proves, if it needed proving, that in creativity wherever two heads are better than one twenty heads are worse than none. The sundry can include anyone from the Chairman's brother-in-law to the tea-lady, whose ladylike behaviour has ample room for scope in the shouting-match which eventually ensues. Suggestions from the floor (often literally so), ranging from the pathetic to the bizarre, are chalked up on a blackboard by the head kibitzer, and the consensus, or otherwise, assessed and summarised—usually by everyone *except* the creative people who actually have to produce the campaign. These sessions are frequently conducted as a word-association game, in which everyone is asked to call out their instinctive automatic response to a statement or word concerning Brand-X (one such session in which I took part concerned a world pre-eminent shipping line, and the general reactions to the word "cruising" were so uniformly libidinous that one was led to assume that the line must have been founded by the Emperor Nero). Amidst much loud and confused hilarity the sessions are climaxed by a sententious summing-up from the Creative Director. They are utterly useless. Since, by the large numbers who participate, camouflage gives blanket coverage to mediocrity, brain-storming sessions remain popular (naturally, the valuable time thus wasted is charged to the client), and they have recently been given an even greater mantle of "in" respectability by being called "synectics." Not, however, by me!

Consumer panels. These are gatherings of ostensible cross-sections of the presumed potential Brand-X public. They are assembled—sometimes off the street or by invitation card—in the agency's presentation room, given samples of the product X and asked for their opinions about it. Later on they will be asked to judge the proposed pack-design and advertising too, or to give "marks" for acceptability to a range of current rival products. (In one such test of a TV commercial for Gulf Tyres in the States the promotion passed with flying colours—

till, when double-checking the marking-cards next day, it was discovered that 20 per cent of the panel thought the manufacturers were
Goodyear!) If the products are items like sanitary towels or powdered
and perfumed toilet-rolls (both of which have now received clearance
for advertising on TV), one can see that consumer panels for these
would require an exceedingly permissive society; on the other hand,
many of my readers may be surprised what many housewives will
do for a day out and a free trial sample.

Copy-testing. This is an attempt to insure scientifically against failure
of the advertising campaign, about as precise an experiment as guessing next Thursday's temperature at noon. The procedure requires
the creative team, mainly the copywriter, to compose a series of ad-
approaches—perhaps up to a dozen—which are then put up on a
metaphorical pillory for any passers-by to throw rotten vegetables at,
or take chamber-pot shots. The agency sometimes deploys *agents provo-
cateurs* to get things thrumming. The "jury" may be demographically
selected from the socio-economic categories (*see* Chapter VI), they
may be badgered through the mail or collared on the corner; they
may simply be agency personnel, or the client Chairman's family and
friends. Retail and wholesale distributors may be canvassed for
comment (often causing great annoyance, for they are busy men).
Whatever the method it can at best give cold comfort because, of
necessity, these are copy and design "roughs," incomplete advertisements, which are shown for opinion, and their creators already know
perfectly well which one is the best. If they don't then they should
not be in the profession. Your true creative adman doesn't need a
committee to reassure him he's right. The effect may indeed have
an opposite effect, for the genuine original thinker will accord with
Wilde that "When people agree with me, I always feel that I must
be wrong."

Think-tanks and stuff and all other nonsense on these lines. America
has popularised the "think-tank" idea in politics and industry (the
true think-tank is, of course, the computer) and a number of British
agencies have now adopted the principle—as indeed did Mr. Heath—
which is at its most futile and absurd when applied to creativity and
art; it may take any form from a creative supervisory board to an
actual think-room—at one period I was accustomed to being isolated
in one of these with the doors bolted firmly against creative escape.
If the imprisoned group was a mixed bag creative happenings did
indeed sometimes occur, though they had nothing to do with the campaign in hand. In practice, of course, the only dependable think-tank
exists within the creative man's skull—his brilliant ideas come to him
while shaving, on the Tube, sardined on station-platform, or thumb-
ing through *Penthouse.*

Research versus creativity

After all this assistance, provided the putative creators haven't been brainwashed down the drain, they can attempt to proceed with their job. As a consultant psychologist, and ex-Copy Group Head, wrote in a *Campaign* article of May 1969, entitled "Does the Copy Man Lose the Argument Too Often?" the copywriter's case "tends to lose out, unless he himself is a very persuasive and argumentative man, because it is in most cases an intuitive one" which he has found imaginatively "because to do so is part of his craft and training ... He has got as close as he can to the mind of his public ... and he has 'imagined' how the minds of such people could possibly be changed," and yet this precious imaginative commonsense may in fact be "less violently misleading than rigidly held models based on quantifiable, but partial evidence" of various tests and researches, such as we have discussed in these pages. To which we might add, in regard to the evidence of such "models" (*see* Chapter V), that for all its quantity, which will be awesome and intimidating to the novice, there are seldom any two executives you can find who can whole-heartedly agree *what* it is all evidence of!

Here I will again quote David Ogilvy, whose marvellous eye-patch idea for Hathaway Shirts—which was to bring him his Byronic awakening to find himself famous—came to him in a taxi during rush-hour holdups (in exactly the same locale and circumstances that Sir Noël Coward composed the complete words and music of "I'll See You Again"). He correctly indicts many market researchers for spurning judgment and for using research "as a drunkard uses a lamp-post, for support rather than illumination."

THE COMING OF AD BUDGE

A very contemporary recruit (it is too much to hope he is just temporary) to the ranks of the foes of the creative man in Advertising is the ever-looming presence of the computer, which many firms in the States—and several, like Wilkinson Sword, in this country—are already confidently using to predict success or otherwise of promotions. Certainly, one of the more influential personalities on the marketing scene today is an executive (I refuse to call him a gentleman) named Ad Budge, who is employed by P.A. Management Consultants on behalf of quite a few clients—but who happens to be a data processing machine.

My personal prayer is that in twenty years or sooner we shall be asking: "Whatever became of Ad Budge?" and asking in vain. In their book *The Computerised Society*, James Martin and Adrian Norman cite the true incident of the researcher who, upon instructions from his computer, knocked at the door of a woman aged 107, and asked to speak to her mother! They also mention the grocer who employed a computer to take down customers' orders, with the result that one housewife who ordered cereal was sent enough packets to fill her living-room. A personal acquaintance of mine once received, via computer, a summons for over-parking in Tite Street, Chelsea, the previous weekend, even though it was at least two years since she'd even passed through the neighbourhood and was, in fact, at a party (with her car) in the wilds of Essex at the time. The incident would have amused a former resident of Tite Street, who once remarked, and it could well have been about computers: "Science can never grapple with the irrational. That is why it has no future before it in this world." One trusts the future will prove him right, but meanwhile one can add to Wilde that though Science can never grapple with the irrational, it can, alas, certainly surpass it ... my Essex friend was just one out of more than two thousand car-owners erroneously accused by this terrible new P.C., Presumptuous Computer.

Some firms also hire computers to mull over proposed brand-names. This has become a very delicate aspect of new product development. Brand-names must be distinctive and memorable, but they carry their own built-in liabilities for success. Thus nylon, thermos, hoover, gramophone, aspirin, sellotape, biro, margarine and linoleum are all, in fact, brand-names, though now fated to be used in a much more general sense (the name can be patented, but for a very limited time) and by inference their qualities can be implied as dwelling in other brands. You will have to overcome this dilemma when you think up a name for Brand-X.

You must learn to scan the whole consumer market, so as to avoid coincidences and confusions, the sort of situation where today "Global" can mean a package tour or a Russian wristwatch. You can try to make the name convey its benefits, the gospel in capsule, the prayer on the point of a pin—Ogilvy and Mather gave Helena Rubinstein's face-cream the name Deep Cleaner, since this exactly described what it claimed to perform. When, however, the consumer public was constantly being told "Don't say Brown, say Hovis," the ever-present danger was the reverse, that instead of saying Hovis they'd say Brown—this is one reason why we are no longer being urged to say it (the name derives, by the way, from the truncated Latin of *Hominia Vis*).

Once decided upon, a brand-name is rarely changed, and then at great risk, as happened two years ago when R.H.M. Branded Foods altered their "Extrafine" Flour (the built-in promise approach) to

"McDougall's McD," with the help of TV recipes from Jimmy Young—though not with the hoped-for upswing in sales.

CAMPAIGNING IN THE ROUGH

At long last, then, with as little aid as he can persuade others not to give him (he would much rather, like a Red Indian mother, self-deliver his baby inside the nearest bush and pass on to the next household chore), the copywriter evolves an agreed *copy-platform*, i.e. the basic appeal and approach upon which the Brand-X advertisements will all be constructed, whether the product removes understains, gives a good night's rest, has man appeal, drives women wild, builds strong pets, makes teeth that dazzle or decorates your perm with halos, makes cars or women go faster, longer, or both at once.

Dr. Johnson's "promise, large promise" remains as ever the soul of the copy-platform, and with it the copywriter must still incorporate what Addison had said in *The Tatler* even half a century before that, that "The great art in writing Advertisements, is the finding out a proper method to catch the Reader's Eye."

No computer can ever supply *that* ingredient, a magic touch that is much harder to find today when Gallup reckons that no more than 26 per cent of national newspaper readers ever trouble to *look* at a full-page ad, let alone react to it! One extra set of hurdles of which Addison could scarcely dream in 1710 was that a "proper method" now has also to be found to catch the *client's* eye before the ad can ever smell print, plus a whole "blind" of executive eyes before that, for the copywriter and designer have first to "sell" their work to the Creative Director, then to the Account Executive and Account Director, then to the agency's Managing Director and its Chairman (if the money's big enough), then to the client's Brand Manager, then to his Advertising Manager, then to the client's Managing Director, his Chairman, and possibly his entire Board. Only after all these gentlemen (and perhaps our friend Ad Budge) have passed the work as okay, will the campaign be ventured before the eyes of the consumer—who, though he remains the "point" of the whole operation, is nevertheless only at the apex of a gigantic meringue pyramid of puffery.

During these stages, within agency and client walls, the work is in "rough" form: that is to say, the copywriter has written headlines and subheads but probably not much of the body-copy (the paragraphs in detail), while the designer has executed only fairly sketchy illustrations, using the superb magic markers (which have revolutionised design and studio techniques) or similar implements, which perhaps he has amplified by pasting in cut-out pictures from magazines. Some clients will foolishly insist (though it's time-wasting and expensive) on a more polished "rough" presentation of work than others and there are independent studios that specialise in this service to agencies, thus leaving top creative people free to concentrate on original ideas. As a rule, the more sophisticated the client, the more "rough" he is prepared to accept the work.

Once client approval has been received, body-copy will be written in detail and cut-outs will be properly photographed from life, of course, or a specialist in figure-drawing or technical-drawing commissioned (*see* Chapter XIII), and so on. For the "rough" stages fairly wide licence is permissible to the designer, however; though he is wise to steer well clear of the brick-dropping accomplished by the Collett, Dickenson, Pearce agency, when they once submitted roughs for a Ford Escort advertisement, pasted up with photographs of a Vauxhall Viva!

GETTING ADS "THROUGH"

Working one's creative work up through the puffery pyramid is an exhausting and exacting task, which can use up far too much of the creative man's time and effort. He has sufficient battles within the agency, long before the client appears in the lists, to justify him saying, with the Sicilian bandit: "I can look after my enemies, but God protect me from my friends."

Showing creative work through agency channels involves questions of office politics and executive jealousies common to any business organisation. Rival copywriters will sabotage each other's ideas, or steal them. A new Creative Director may deliberately turn down (and use as his own later) the best ideas of a designer whose ambition he fears. The manipulations of office "empire builders" may cause to be cancelled out equally brilliant, though opposing, plans of campaign. Trojan horses clog the corridors of power. The raw enthusiast will concentrate on the fire in his belly and neglect, till too late, the pain between his shoulder-blades. Beware the blood-brother—you may be his brother but it will be *your* blood. Agency intrigues can be of Kremlin complexity, and just as implacable.

Once through the agency labyrinth and past the executive gauntlet-thrashings, getting the campaign for X okayed by client is something else again. The creative people should have the Account Executive in their corner for this bout, but one cannot rely too heavily on such support; the executive may have his own short-term "political" reasons for toadying to the Brand Manager (though, long-term, this is likely to serve him ill) with whom he may even contemplate swapping positions! Aided or not, any creative man will count himself extraordinarily lucky to be told by a client: "We are about to start advertising ... If you take it on, I will make you a promise: I will never change a word of your copy." Yet this is no potted fantasy; these were the words used by Hathaway Shirts when they approached David Ogilvy who, on this hint, proceeded to forge a maximum reputation from a minimum budget.

I'm delighted to report that one of my own major clients expressed the same flattering outlook in regard to my own output on his behalf, but such lovely sane creatures are a regrettable rarity in Wonderland.

OBJECTIVES VERSUS OBJECTIONS

The process of finalising a campaign which both agency and client will approve is like running an obstacle-race through a minefield. To start with there are a number of straightforward, fair objections your client is entitled to raise. You may be insufficiently aware of a certain quality appertaining to Brand-X or its use which needs more weight in your promotion. Client may legitimately point out that your campaign duplicates a competitor's much too closely. This can happen dramatically, and still quite unintentionally—can it really be true that "When *The Times* Speaks the World Listens" if at precisely the same time "People Listen When *The Listener* Speaks"? On a partyline, perhaps? If B.O.A.C. "takes good care of you," can Japan Air Lines really take "good care of you, too" (J.A.L.'s agency agreed to alter this line, even though they had beaten B.O.A.C. to "Love at First Flight" by a dozen years)?

Is it wise for Oxo Cubes and Martell Brandy both to show an almost identical big wedding-party in a lush garden? Could the Quaker Oats Company launch "Fruitipops" breakfast cereal, when Cadbury–Schweppes already had a sweet in the shops called "Fruity Pops"? Can your illustration show smiling nuns riding along on Honda scooters in a mass of traffic, when the newspapers are already full of ads showing smiling priests riding along on Vespas? Can Berry Magicoal and Sunhouse Electric Fires both claim, almost in chorus, that their use "makes a home"?

Client resistance to your ideas may, on the other hand, stem from his unhappiness that your ads are too *unlike* those of his competitors. Me-too-ism is virulent in some Brand Managers. Or the objections may be utterly arbitrary; the Advertising Manager's wife—who has peeped into his briefcase after dinner—may complain that your ads are too sexy (the model used too pretty and "unrepresentative"), or the client Chairman may even insist that *his* photograph be included, even if it upstages the product ... your attitude to this belligerence is indicated by the little rhyme you will find in Chapter X.

The Brand Manager may occasionally get stage-fright, and evince belated concern that you have taken his own fervent assertions about Brand-X too literally. He may ask you to dampen your enthusiasm and tone the copy down, looking perhaps nervously across the Atlantic where, in 1970, the U.S. Federal Trade Commission—an extremely powerful body—accused Lever Brothers, Colgate–Palmolive and Proctor and Gamble of making totally unwarranted advertising claims for enzymes in their respective detergents. He may be worried that the copy or "visual" (another term for the illustration) in your ads is "knocking," i.e. that it too directly denigrates a competitor. Your answer should be that *all* advertising does this, if only by implication (why else are we in business?), but he may have in mind occasions such as when the Advertising Standards Authority banned an ad for Rootes cars whose visual pictured clearly a *Ford Cortina* being towed to the junk-yard. But care must be genuinely taken, since the A.S.A. continually receives, and acts on, complaints by the public. Recently, an irate traveller complained about "Sealink's" offer of a 48-hour excursion to France, pointing out that the excursion had given him only 25 hours and 20 minutes in Cherbourg. "Sealink" was duly abashed and British Rail reimbursed the complainant.

TELEVISION AND TESTING

If your promotional campaign for Brand-X includes television, your own agency is less liable to be over-involved in wrangling with client since an outside consultancy will probably be involved.

This is not to say, however, that your TV commercial will be made right away, with no interference of client at all nor his blushing opinion. I can, however, cite one exception, which was the commercial for *The Sunday Times Magazine* "Churchill Issue," a special edition which had been prepared, printed and stacked ready and waiting in a number of warehouses round London prior to the great man's death. When his passing was eventually announced on a Friday morning, a TV commercial was made in just two hours on Friday evening and shown on Saturday, enabling those warehouses at last to be emptied for Sunday distribution. It was a good commercial, too, even though its impact was almost guaranteed. *The Sunday Times* has always enjoyed an outstanding performance record in this medium—it produced one of the only two British winners of Gold Lion Awards at the 1970 International Advertising Film Festival at Venice—but then, as noted previously in connection with Thomson Newspapers, the client and the "agency" were one and the same, which always helps (*see* Chapter II). When the *Daily Sketch* tried to get this sort of "instant" brilliant creativity, Horniblow Cox-Freeman resigned the account!

In the ordinary run of events your client will be shown the script of a Brand-X commercial before it is shot. Or he will be shown a story-board, i.e. a large "strip-cartoon" styled presentation of the action, with either photographs or drawings set out in panels on big display-mounts, with captions explaining action and dialogue beneath each picture. Or a film may be made, showing a series of still photographs, which gives an admirably vivid impression of how the proper version will look—indeed, some commercials actually use this technique, and very effectively. Sometimes the whole commercial will be shot in rudimentary form (perhaps with agency personnel instead of actors) on video-tape, a type of film which can be wiped clean and re-used time and time again. This is just for private "house" viewing, of course, or actors' Equity would have strong things to say.

Even after the client has given approval the commercial must be passed by the I.T.C.A., the Independent Television Companies Association, whose copy clearance staff must okay the script—this it will usually do within three days unless special problems seem evident, in which case the script will go before the full Copy Committee, which meets every ten days. When the film is duly made it must then once more receive the I.T.C.A.'s blessing. This censor-body sees about 8,000 scripts a year and turns down no more than 13 per cent on average, though the percentage does not help endear them to advertising people, who find them far too straight-laced (they are also astoundingly impervious to Freudian innuendo, as any regular TV viewer will at once perceive). Besides "sex" improprieties, offences which can veto your commercial include (1) knocking copy, (2) action which shows badly-behaved children, (3) even mild profanity, (4) naming of rival brands, and (5) unsubstantiated claims—to check on the latter, the I.T.C.A. retains experts in medicine, nutrition, finance, dentistry and so on. Only recently have TV commercials been permitted to show false teeth (always referred to as dentures, of course) and lavatory-pans for our delight and instruction.

After your various media promotions for Brand-X have finally "got through" agency and client obstacles, all or part of the campaign may still be wrung through the same gamut of consumer testing and sampling as already described in regard to the product itself. With advantages and disadvantages, this is a tight-rope stage when the distinction between the product and its advertising does, in fact, begin to blur.

There are many ways of conducting these tests and new ingenuities are constantly being concocted. I will list only a few. Advertisements may be run in selected regional newspapers, contrasting the message of one "gospel truth" with another, till the ad of apparently widest

appeal is then launched nationally. Similarly, differently angled TV
commercials can be tried out at special preview showings to housewives who are asked to write their comments on appropriate forms;
these commercials can then be tried out on different regional
channels. Consumer panels will be asked for their views on pack-de-
signs and their colours, as was the case with our new decimal stamps,
when panels of women (why only women?) were asked to select a
choice of colours from twenty-five, their preference being stated as
levels of "confusability," a typically revolting specimen of market-
research tags.

NEW PRODUCT LAUNCHES

When all this effort is directed towards launching Brand-X as a
new product, poor results from these tests can result in X never reaching the national market at all! For example, a great deal of money
was once spent testing commercials for powdered and perfumed toilet-
rolls on restricted regional programmes, but results happily did not
justify their being gaily unrolled during intervals of any nationally-
networked show. It is of course possible that the paper we did eventually see unrolling over stately lawns pursued by a stately tabby was
impregnated with catnip, but that is a different approach entirely.
The terraces of football clubs seem a far more promising medium for
this product, and we may yet see them sold in various Club colours.

Articles in *The Financial Times* have estimated the failure-rate of
launching new products at up to 90 per cent—even big names like
Gallahers have failed with Conquest and Mayfair cigarettes, Proctor
and Gamble have gambled dismally with Dawn Soap, Gleem and
Crest toothpastes, while Gibbs have flopped with their Daylight
Shampoo (only South Wales ever saw *that* Daylight). Yet these
gambles, when they pay off, pay handsomely—P. and G.'s enzyme
detergent Ariel led its field within three months of launching. Name-
changes of established products need careful testing, too ... when
"Extrafine" became simply "McD," it lost its position as a brand-
leader (though, of course, the magnificent Homepride TV commercials played a great part in this as well).

I don't propose, however, to take Brand-X into a campaign as a
new product launch, though I may still make side-reflections on that
aspect from time to time. We'll now assume that, after much over-
acted heart-searching bluster and wrangle, our client has at length
accepted in full the advertising our agency has produced. So we have,
we hope, a lusty infant, an offspring fit to let loose upon the blithely
unsuspecting world. We have chosen the baby's names. The long, long
confinement is over, and the first few days in swaddling clothes. The

christening is to come, or, in agency parlance, the campaign is ready
"to break." For its first public appearance, in whichever media, we
must see to it that this child, Brand-X, has the finest, best-tailored
christening-robes possible, with a minimal amount of mewling and
puking in the nurse's arms. True, 50 per cent of new products dis-
appear within five years, but by then most of you will be with a different agency, anyway. But first, let us examine some of the major
theorising that may have impregnated your campaign, which thank-
fully the paying public is at last about to receive.

Chapter VIII

THE THEORY PRACTITIONERS

To me, it seems a significant paradox of the Advertising milieu that although it breeds a group of professionals who are probably less malleable to "system" than any other group in commerce and industry, there is also no other professional body more in love with the seductive *idea* of a system. These men and women who fill the daily media with workable come-ons, and who must therefore be pragmatic above all else, possess a deep atavistic yearning for proof positive that what they do is in truth governed by some set of eternally valid laws. If only those laws could be found.

There is certainly no lack of law-givers, either in Mayfair or Madison Avenue. But our dreams melt in their clammy grasp, the law turns into lore, the "rum seer into the bum steer," as I once heard a colleague picturesquely describe the up-and-down saga of one of the more noted ad-philosophers ... or Theory Practitioners, as I have chosen to label them (though I shall reserve my reason till the end of this chapter, after the evidence is in).

The yearning is very natural. It's the longing of a gypsy for a home ... in which, of course, he will roam at will and pay no rent. It springs from the everlasting and mutual antagonism of client and agency in their "marriage of convenience," of Adam and Eve, who can never forgive, nor live without each other. Who can never make a living out of life without each other, and whose interdependence is begrudged but total, as vividly expressed in the already quoted remark of that son of a grocer who said (remember my advice to be Copy now to Men of Grocer Blood?) that "half the money I spend on advertising is wasted, and the trouble is I don't know which half."

Meanwhile, the partners circle round, turning each other warily and charily, with here and there some scattered surges of ecstasy— and which is truly the "better half," nobody dares discover. They both know that the Garden is closed to them for ever. This is what keeps them young, in spite of the Cain they raise which slays the Abel offspring and always ends in Nod. But if this couple ever had to admit to themselves there was no Garden! ...

THE LEGEND OF INNOCENCE

Yet, *were* they ever there? I doubt it. At any rate, there was no innocence there. The first Point-of-Sale may have been that fig-leaf, but the very first Advertising in Creation was earlier still, and we are told of it in the second chapter of Genesis (you'll find Jehovah's "campaign" is well-called by that title), in verses 16 and 17: "... Of every tree in the garden thou mayest freely eat: but of the tree of the knowledge of good and evil, thou shalt not eat of it ..." than which no more potent "teaser" approach was never devised. For that section of the market which is deemed thicker and needing the message more spelled out, a comic-strip serpent is invented to whisper, thirteen verses later: "... in the day ye eat thereof, then your eyes shall be opened, and ye shall be as gods, know good and evil ..." The promises don't come any larger than that, and all we need do here to round off the perspective is to understand the percipience of the dialogue in Wilde's *A Woman of No Importance* (who naturally turns out to be of outstanding importance) ... it is at the end of Act One:

> *Lord Illingworth:* The Book of Life begins with a man and a woman in a garden.
> *Mrs. Allonby:* It ends with Revelations.

And no one, but No One, is really in the business of growing forbidden fruit. Eve was cleverly selling the veto, not the apple. She was giving the apple a "brand-image," which we'll come to in a moment.

To achieve revelations when chips are down, you must start the bidding with a cover-up. Eve also had far too much sense than to name the fruit in question (and what a question!) ... at least, in the Bible no fruit is named. Recent research suggests that she more likely offered Adam a nibble at an apricot (of which we in Britain today import more than any other nation—how does that grab you, symbolism-lovers?). It remains ominous, all the same, that if it *was* an apple, the Fall of Man was accomplished by what botanists call a "false fruit."

The concept and image of the Tree of Life has figured for thousands of years in many religions, but it took our Eve to attach a Hands-Off sign to the bark. You'll have spotted for yourselves, I'm sure, that the very notion of Forbidden Knowledge is self-contradictory. "Here I am ... Don't Touch" is okay-talk for the Playboy Club (and explains amply its attraction for ageing Adams) but simply won't do for the genuine Eden—nor for the prototype bird of paradise, for that matter.

Yet the anti-advertising lobby (and some vestige of corrosive guilt in the soul of most advertisers) clings to the notion that there *was* a time of commercial innocence which the Coming of the Admen sullied irretrievably. This feeling haunts the dark nights of many agency men, too, though it is manifestly untrue, as we saw in Chapter I. But it does explain why the coming of a new "Bible" is always welcomed, on however flimsy grounds, new Prophets hailed and stoned, and a look-out always kept for the Tablets to be brought down from Sinai.

PROPHETS=PROFITS?

The tillers in the field of our "It's an Ad, Ad, Ad World" can't really be blamed for their naïve hankering after the respectability of a governed passion, to prove that a successful client–agency partnership which begat profits was never "just one of those things, one of those cash-register bells that now and then rings," but a solidly-based marriage, legitimate and solemnised. Unfortunately, sometimes when they have achieved an excess of solemnity, they have mistaken the gravity for law, seriousness being, in Wilde's words, "the only refuge of the shallow."

So there have been rich (and I do mean rich!) opportunities for bearers of Sinai Tablets. Most of their theories have been developed in the States, though the thinking has not mainly been American in origin (theory being an un-American activity, in Advertising as in much else, though few U.S. citizens are aware that it was not they, but us, who invented radar, the jet, hovercraft, the hot-dog and the neon-sign!). This superiority in Theory Development, which parallels the way their TV technology has exploded beyond us, along with radar and neon-signs, led to one of our periodic fits of inviting other nations to come and teach us how to suck eggs last year, when an American business consultant, Dr. Donald Schon, came over to give the Reith lectures for the B.B.C., on "Change and Industrial Society"—upon arrival, he told the Press "it is the task of Advertising to make human responses uniform so that they fit corporate operations." Which sounds about right from the head of an institution which calls itself the Organisation for Social and Technical Innovation—since this body boasts of being non-profit making, one wonders if it isn't time for Dr. Schon and colleagues to rethink first principles.

All these prophetic theories are, of course, useful in some degree—but as you accumulate Advertising experience, you will learn to keep such dicta in their place—not vice versa—polishing them up and honing them as the useful tools of your trade, not the manacles of your slavery.

LAWS AND THE PROPHETS

Before I deal with three outstanding Prophets, the most notable Theory Practitioners of today—and I confess at once my choice is arbitrarily personal—I will list three unquestionable ideas, seminal in their influence, the knowledge of which is indispensable before you can truly begin to comprehend the nature, resources and bias of modern Advertising practice ...

1. *Brand-image:* This is the main theoretical contribution articulated by David Ogilvy (Madison Avenue's favourite Briton), who defines it as the "sharply defined *personality*" you give Brand-X. At greater length, to the American Association of Advertising Agencies, he affirmed in an address, "it is almost always the total *personality* of a brand, rather than any *trivial product difference* which decides its ultimate position in the market." Brand-image is the "feel" you have about a product, it is *the way you think about it*, the instinctive connotations that arise in your mind at sight of a Rolls-Royce or on hearing the word "Chanel." Hippy, Red-brick, Capitalist Lackey, Swinger, Dolly, Square, Tory—these are brand-names, too ... all identify a brand of thing or person, all are indelibly branded with your preconceptions. It is one of the hardest tasks in life to change an established brand-name and is wisely seldom attempted. In modern politics, the new term *charisma* is brand-image spelled backwards.

2. *U.S.P.:* These initials belong to the phrase Unique Selling Proposition, which is the law propagated and promulgated by Ogilvy's great rival, friend and one-time brother-in-law, Rosser Reeves, Chairman of Ted Bates and Company in New York. Reeves has laid down three essential qualifications for establishing the U.S.P. of Brand-X: (*a*) it must state a *specific benefit* for the purchaser, (*b*) this must be a benefit which is offered by no other product and (*c*) it must be a benefit that produces *sales*! Reeves takes care to emphasise that where technical or medical claims are involved, these *must* be verifiable (not to be confused with certifiable, which would apply to quite a few claims we see on today's TV). He also qualifies (*b*) on a professional basis, saying that the special benefit need not be one that is actually *not possessed* by another product, simply that it is not being mentioned in the rival product's advertising ... a very different thing.

3. *Subliminal Advertising:* Also called "sub-threshold," this theory embodies the idea that you can infiltrate a person's subconscious, and persuade him to buy Brand-X, without him knowing that he didn't do it all on his own. You manage to motivate his initiative by flashing the X-name on a TV or cinema screen at irregular intervals during the running of a film, *but for only a small fraction of a second each time.* The viewer is not conscious of seeing these flashes at all, or even of having heard of the product involved, but he will at once be filled with a seemingly unaccountable urge to go out and buy Brand-X. You can do the equivalent in sound on the radio or on records and

tape. In practice, the value of subliminal advertising is extremely doubtful (as with hypnotism, you cannot be compelled to do anything which, in an uninfluenced state, you would not be inclined to do anyway), but the theory can always be relied upon to raise the hackles of opponents of Advertising, and of course in its extreme manifestations is now forbidden by law in this country (though, if it was successful, how would one know?). Its chief proponent is James Vicary, also a fan of the British-originated theory of *Mass Observation*. Vicary's devilish subliminal experiments were "revealed" (though not Vicary's name for "the authorities in question are unwilling to come any further into the open") in a *Sunday Times* front-page article in 1956—the journalists being apparently themselves unaware that the device had been pioneered in this country twenty-two years earlier! But in 1934, Watson-Watt first demonstrated radar, too, and who remembers? Vicary's Mount Sinai Tablets bear extra weight, of course, from his membership of the American Psychological Association, not to mention the Society for Applied Anthropology!

THE DICTA OF DICHTER

All such Tablets will, naturally enough, be Tablets with a Difference—a crucial Difference. Thou Shalt Nots must give way to Thou Shalts. For every adman worth his salt believes desperately in the "power of positive thinking" which, though also the title of a wildly best-selling book by Norman Vincent Peale, has informed from the start the in-depth research theories of Dr. Ernest Dichter—who actually anticipated Peale with a very similar book called *Successful Living*, in the days before he became one of the Adworld's Great Prophets, the first of our Highlighted Three.

Dichter is the prophet of *Motivational Research* (M.R. as distinct in the dictionary from M.O., which is Mass Observation), the man who galvanised the Advertising scene twenty years ago by advising every agency to throw aside modesty and guilt and win proud acceptance as "one of the most advanced laboratories in psychology."

He soon advanced into the global spotlight by telling us all about our sordid sexual relationship with cars, how the convertible was a "mistress," the saloon-car a "sober wife," and so on. What women (or men, for that matter) were actually performing when they changed gears, was mercifully left univestigated—though the K.M.P. Agency of London, in their poster-campaign for Regent petrol a few years ago (*see* Chapter XI), had no such inhibitions, with their phallic flourishing of hose-nozzles while the "cowgirl" forecourt attendant invited us to "Ride Regent—the Lively One." But Dichter started the jag, and with qualifications even more awesome in his line than Vicary's: he holds a Doctorate in Psychology and is President of the Institute for Motivational Research near New York.

GETTING DOWN TO (MOTHER) EARTH

Dr. Dichter is very preoccupied, in a rather predictably heavy Teutonic manner (he was born in Vienna, though not so light-heartedly as Richard Tauber, leaving it in 1938, the same year as Freud) with analysing behaviour in consumers, telling one grass company that "the lawn is an upholstered way of getting a direct feeling, direct contact with Mother Earth." He conducts research at his Institute in the most modish Group Therapy style (in Viennese days, he practised as a lay analyst), with in-depth interviews, psycho-dramas, the lot, all filmed and tape-recorded.

After all this deep probing of panels of family volunteers (doorprizes are given on the way out), the doctor then submits recommendations to agency or client, pointing out to his amazed recipients the erotic qualities of their product—telling the Ronson people, for example, all about the connection with Eros of the Goddess of Light, the symbolism (how could we miss it?) of the flame, the "erotic implications... of primitive fire-making devices, discovered" (where else?) "at a small German university." If his clients became as overwhelmed by the Importance of Being Ernest as the good Herr Doktor, they would soon believe that modern commerce was one big Sex Supermarket, an Emporium of Universal Porn ...

While it is easy to mock the worship of such grave images as Dr. Dichter, he influences many admen still, on both sides of the Atlantic. But while deference is not what it was, he has done, in my view, a great disservice on balance to the advertising profession, both by oversolemnising it and by making the profession an easy object of public scepticism and despite—Vance Packard's *The Hidden Persuaders*, which the ever-panicking *Sunday Times* described as "alarming, but entertaining" (thus hitting Advertising with the usual old one-two) was largely oriented about the Dichter-torial decrees of Motivational Research, including the Doctor's unmentionable theories on why some people are so fond of ice-cream, plus his now-classic observation, "The Prune is a Joyless Puritan"—or, I would hazard, contrariwise.

Perhaps we can garner reassurance in the fact that all this may not, after all, be so "scientific" ... When Dichter was asked how the image of ground-coffee could be improved, in the face of instant competition, he suggested the coffee should be illustrated as being served in glamorous settings such as back in Old Vienna!

A MAD, MAD, MADISON AVENUE WORLD

Since Mayfair Advertising is largely the delayed echo-chamber of Madison Avenue practice, Dichter's influence has been strong over here. His emphasis on *gestalt* thinking, or thoughts "by association," has become what today we call "lateral thinking," thinking sideways, which are just new words for old. His main acknowledged British disciple is Harry Henry, who has written *Motivational Research* to prove it. Motivational Research, however, has never helped an adman's left hand to know what his right is doing, or helped in the why and wherefore of his hiring and firing. This is a fundamental weakness of all Advertising theory ... its remoteness from everyday mundane human irrationality—which, alas, admen persist in calling "rationalisation." Humpty Dumpty, thou shouldst be living at this hour!

There may, however, be a wind of change, which makes coincidental but significant the fact that Dr. Dichter's last official visit to Britain—for a Creative Workshop sponsored by *Campaign*—was *not* a triumphal procession. Yet one could not fault the Doctor's pronouncement at the Workshop that his job is "to find out what goes on in the mind of the consumer. We don't give a damn what goes on in the mind of the copywriter." Except to amend that these two processes should be one and the same, perhaps.

The influence, then, remains, but diluted. "The English," said Oscar Wilde, "have a miraculous power of turning wine into water." But this can be much to the good at times, and it was refreshing to hear the admission from one of Dichter's detractors at the Workshop, the Creative Director of Collett Dickinson Pearce, that in creating campaigns "We often have to guess"—we do indeed, and the comment was in clear contrast with Dichter's chat about such things as "ego involvement, identification and psychological distance." Professional guesses are, of course, never hit-or-miss affairs; they take intuitive account of much faddish or factual data, some of which is Dichter's.

It's the garnish that distresses. At bottom, the good Doctor is often bang on target. After all, it remains undeniable that detergents have superfluous suds foamed on to their formulae, which have admittedly nothing whatever to do with the cleansing process—simply because most housewives happen to *feel* that suds are an integral part of becoming clean.

A.D.=AFTER DICHTER

The German bandwagon was closely followed by another. One would be sufficiently content with admen dethroning their prophets in turn, if they didn't always try to hurl out baby with bathwater (despite Dichter's emphasis on tailoring research to client, he ends up flying by the seat of his pants, like everyone else), and promptly proceed to enthrone another in the tyrant's place.

One of the Top Prophets is a Canadian don named Marshall McLuhan. He originally came into his own with *Understanding Media*, published in 1964, which must be one of the most frequently quoted unread volumes of the past decade (a splendid qualification for a Bible). The Director of the Centre for Culture and Technology at Toronto University, McLuhan accumulated such accolades as *Life*'s "Oracle of the Electronic Age" (that is an accolade?), *Fortune*'s "one of the major intellectual influences of our time", *The Times Literary Supplement* has placed him "at the frontier" (of what, I'm not sure), while *The New Yorker* has gaily ranked him with Oswald Spengler, D. H. Lawrence, F. R. Leavis, Hannah Arendt, old Uncle Tom (T. S.) Eliot and all. Climbing rapidly to the summit over a dozen of speaking engagements (at £400 per luncheon, plus 50 per cent of the profits) all over North America, he came to Britain in 1969 to receive the President's Medal from the Institute of Public Relations, where he told his audience that all jokes were grievances and soon proved that *his* certainly were. But then, the fact is known to any Shakespearian Fool.

Prophets being by tradition bereft of honour in their own country, Toronto Advertising men take a less bedazzled view of their home-grown sage than ourselves and Madison Avenue. Or the West Coast, for that matter, where TV's *Laugh-In* purportedly based all its techniques on McLuhanisms. Indeed, one of its most reiterated catchphrases was at one time ...

> "Marshall McLuhan,
> What're yew doin'?"

A very fair question, to which he eventually cabled a reply ...

> "I'm just clue-in."

Whether or not McLuhan really ever possessed the Philosopher's Stone, I feel certain he will eventually sink like one, taking the gall with him. What we must be careful of is that we are not dragged down, too.

THE MEDIUM IS ... THE TEDIUM

Read McLuhan for yourself, though, and make your personal assessment. His most celebrated concepts are (*a*) the "global village" and (*b*) "the medium is the message." By (*a*) he means that the swift-ness and totality of modern communications have made the whole world one in tastes and attitudes. By (*b*) he means that *how* you say a thing is very much more important than *what* you say, that context is what matters, not content, that means are the end in themselves.

My opinion is that half a truth is worse than none, and that almost every one of McLuhan's paragraphs are inimical, where not utterly irrelevant, to Advertising. No two sets of people could be more dis-parate than those living on opposite sides of a fence, much less at oppo-site ends of the street, much less still of a village (a village with any character to it)—and to conceive of the earth as a single "global vil-lage" is to succumb to the prevailing hallucination in that skyscraper on Manhattan's East River that nationalism is a thing of the past, whereas its resurgent manifestations in some continents make the European boundary-squabbles of the Middle Ages seem positively matey. Even behind the Iron Curtain, tragic events of recent years have proved there is no economic global village there, and never will be.

As for modern communications, it only takes a wildcat walkout to paralyse the hottest lines in the world. Moreover, as Advertising grows more sophisticated in its less-gimmicky research methods, it is evident that since what will do for an ad in one country, or even one *county*, will not do in another (*see* Chapter XII), how much less is the same campaign for Brand-X going to be as applicable in Kenya as in Kiev or Karachi, Kuwait or Kyogle or Kyoto, not to mention Kansas!

As for the medium being the message (or the "massage" as a sub-sequent McLuhan book has sadly taken it), no one would take excep-tion to the dictum, in so far as it meant the same idea as Oscar Wilde's view that we would never again go to war with France "because her prose is perfect" (the national trait embodied in syntax), nor indeed in the sense of *le style est l'homme même*, forgetting Wilde's counter-dic-tum that "only the great masters of style ever succeed in being obscure" ... forgetting, for McLuhan's sake. But the Toronto don would suggest it means much more, going so far as to imply that the impact of a medium was a constant factor, no matter what message it contained, or whatever personality informed that messsage—which is patently absurd. If the medium was the message, today's genera-tions would never have heard of Shakespeare, much less seen him—having no Globe to burn, no Blackfriars, and Somerset Maugham would be correct in his claim that all you had to do to compose a Wildean epigram was "to loop the loop on a commonplace and come down between the lines." As Shaw sardonically remarked, "As far as I can ascertain, I am the only person in London who cannot sit down and write an Oscar Wilde play at will. The fact that his plays, though apparently lucrative, remain unique under these circumstances, says much for the self-denial of our scribes."

McLuhan writes of "instant total awareness," and believes he scores decisively when he reminds us that no one ever thought "to ask what a melody was about, nor what a house or dress was about." This, however, was only true where *no communication was looked for or intended*—Louis XIV certainly intended his nobles and people should know what Versailles was all about, Chopin that they should know what his *Polonaise* was all about, Beau Brummell that they should understand what clean linen was all about. If the medium is to be the sole message, then there is in fact *no message*. To be "totally aware" of Scotch will not sell Johnnie Walker instead of Haig. To be totally aware of everything is to be *aware* of nothing.

THE "LOCK" OF THE PAST

McLuhan at one point in his argument quotes Socrates approvingly as saying that "the discovery of the alphabet will create forgetfulness in the learners' souls, because they will not use their memories." Thus, suggests McLuhan, did the Greek philosopher regard the medium of the written word as anathema. Yet Socrates himself left us not one written syllable; he is remembered, and has always been so, only through the written words of Plato, and to a lesser extent the writings of Aristophanes, Xenophon and Aristotle ... we must take *Plato's word* for Socrates, as must even McLuhan. Small wonder then that the leader of the anti-McLuhan revolt in his own backyard, the dynamic Toronto adman Jerry Goodis, has asserted unequivocally, "I consider McLuhan a menace to the communications industry, an incompetent communicator deliberately bent on misleading everyone." (Note if the medium was the message here, that term "deliberately bent" would have unfortunate connotations this side of the water.) What McLuhan has to say, in sum, has nothing, but *nothing*, to do with *communication*, and thus nothing to do with Advertising.

The sage who has written "the goose quill put an end to talk" still contrives to chatter merrily to *Playboy* magazine for a cool fee of £7,500, so presumably the goose did nothing, at any rate, to put a gag on money. And still lays golden eggs. Meanwhile, McLuhan lays eggs of other variety in abundance ... why, one wonders, is he judged so devastatingly original? When he censures mankind "because we look at the present through a rear-view mirror. And march backwards into the future," one's mind instantly jumps via a nifty piece of

"lateral thought" to the final harrowing lines of F. Scott Fitzgerald's
The Great Gatsby:

"Gatsby believed in the green light, the orgiastic future that year by
year recedes before us ... tomorrow we will run faster, stretch out our arms
farther ... So we beat on, boats against the current, borne back ceaselessly
into the past."

If the medium was the message, then McLuhan's words should be
in effect as superbly evocative and disturbing as those of Fitzgerald.
But they are not. In fact, any reader of Fitzgerald's splendid novel
knows that it was precisely Gatsby's naïve belief that context and content were one and the same thing, which drove him to his doom.

"Words," McLuhan said in an interview quoted in *AdWeekly*
magazine, "involve all the senses—as the rock singers know." Every
sense, I would add, except sense. Shakespeare would have agreed with
him, but then Shakespeare wouldn't have meant the same thing as
McLuhan.

THE "SHOCK" OF THE FUTURE

My third and final highlighted example is the latest and the
youngest of the Prophets of Advertising. His name is Alvin Toffler,
and *his* book *Future Shock* (but *Present Laughter* all the way to the bank!)
has caused as great a stir as McLuhan's *Understanding Media* fourteen
years ago (perhaps admen have a seven-year itch for these things).
One large New York agency has bought 200 copies for distribution
and study by key executives, and no less a chronicler of prophets than
the author of *The Hidden Persuaders* has called Toffler's theory "a tremendously important warning about the threat of too-rapid change
to our rationality."

Pause for double-take. To our *what?* Right away, here then comes
the first shock, for our previous prophet-theorists have predicated the
results of our *irrational* psyches, and assumed the irrational dominance.
But Toffler storms on producing further waves of shock, each more
traumatic than the last (at least, to fellow pundits), strutting with
ease in the robes of the Prophet of Doom, always a sure ear-bender
and attention-grabber: "We are creating and using up ideas and
images at a faster and faster pace," cries the new Prophet. "Knowledge is becoming disposable."

With the sole exception, one presumes, of the knowledge contained
in *Future Shock*. To me, the biggest shock is that any of this should
be deemed shocking. There is no posture of shock within this passage
... "the modern world, with its new conceptions of philosophy and
religion, its reawakened arts and sciences, its firmer grasp on the reali-

ties of human nature and the world, its manifold inventions and discoveries, its altered political systems, its expansive and progressive forces . . . a fresh stage of vital energy in general, implying a fuller consciousness and a freer exercise of faculties" . . . but then, John Addington Symonds was writing about the Renaissance, which regarded such swift movement in thought and material invention with pride, not shock.

We all surely know already that Man since the Middle Ages has progressed at a more rapid rate than for thousands of years previously. We know that medical science has advanced more in the past fifty years than in the previous fifty million. As for being the "throw-away" society which Toffler deplores with a Wages of Sin fervour, how much better to throw away plastic toys, non-returnable bottles and TV dinners on disposable trays, than chamber-pots out of windows, the lives of little children by stuffing them up chimneys, shoving them down mines or dropping them from the gallows for stealing sixpence . . . or throwing away the leavings of death in dens "of infamous resort . . . where iron, old rags, bottles, bones and greasy offal, were bought . . . hidden in mountains of unseemly rags, masses of corrupted fat, and sepulchres of bones," places so familiar to Charles Dickens when he compelled poor Scrooge to stare upon them!

CHANGES FOR THE BITTER?

Advertising is indicated by Alvin Toffler, of course, as one of the key villains in his drama, a prime disseminator of this Disposable Madness, as he views it. Which, by the justice of the gods, rebounds on admen in the increasing disposability of their jobs, for, he adds, boots going in with malice aforethought . . . .

"High turnover characterises the mass communications industry, especially advertising. A recent survey of 450 American advertising men found that 70 per cent had changed their jobs within the last two years . . . (and) the same musical chairs game is played in England."

So what else is new? So we travel more, change cars more often, alter our acquaintances and careers, romp round from one residence and community to another, changing patterns and behaviour (what price the "global village" now?). We see more of the world, become familiar with new national types, maybe losing our own in the process . . . we have even, he suggests, accepted the notion of "serial marriage," having wives is succession, as a mealy-mouthed Western substitute for polygamy.

But has Toffler read no history or literature of the past? Let him be as ready to investigate the media of yesterday with the relish for castigation he bestows on media of today. All that has happened is that possibly more people are "doing it" and making it their thing—certainly, more are openly talking about it, from over cocktails to the casual TV interview on the street—than ever before. I'm sure that if Toffler took a good look at the Scott Fitzgerald twenties ("they were careless people ... they smashed up things and creatures and then retreated back into their money or their vast carelessness") he would discover quite a prevailing rage for serial marriages.

Now, had Toffler expressed concern about the general switchover to "cereal marriage," reflected in the breakfast-food image of family life expressed in current ads of impossibly antiseptic homemaking, then we might all get together, pooling our collective wailing heads, on a prophet-able Worry-In!

WINDFALL OR SNOWFALL?

But no. This new Sage of Anxiety is getting freaked-out and turned-on by the perennial situation of humankind, summed up by Sean O'Casey's immortal cry of anguish emitted by the Paycock in 1924 as the world being "in a state of chassis." It always has been in a state of chassis—this is, I fear, one of the "thousand natural shocks that flesh is heir to"—and while it might be a consummation devoutly to be wished by the Prophet that this were not so, the changes were, in their context, no less traumatic in Europe from before and after the watershed impact of Attila the Hun, the Armada, Waterloo or Passchendaele, or the change in the way of life of the American Indian after the galvanic dozen years between the Sand Creek massacre of the Cheyenne in 1865 and the final flight of the Sioux towards Canada following Custer's last stand and the white revenge. There are more *things* and trivia, wherein these changes are made manifest, that is all. The change is of degree, not kind.

Toffler quails before the spectre of choice. But it is rather a choice spectacular! Choice is what Advertising is all about. Of course, there are inherent dangers, as in all delightful things—the same perils of Future Shock, you might say, as were threatened by those Cassandras who opposed the Reform Bill of 1832.

Lord Snow, praising Toffler highly in *The Financial Times* for his "remarkable book," feels himself almost entirely on the side of the young Jeremiah, even implying some approval that "the weight of official Soviet society is deliberately and consciously negating a whole spectrum of those changes." A charming way of alluding to the official abuse of Solzhenitsyn and persecution of all writers and others who have attempted to drag Soviet Russia into the modern world, not by decrying the Tovarich Top-shop, G.U.M., or Venus probes but by campaigning for the end of "cancer wards." Euphemism, it seems to me, can go no farther... East Germany, Poland, Hungary, Czechoslovakia and now Poland once more, in the holocausts of the old Stettin, know all about the "weight" to which Snow playfully alludes. *Their* Future Shock is now!

Still, C. P. Snow warns me that "if this book is neglected, we shall all be very foolish." Well, I have not neglected it, let the record show! However, I confidently expect to go on feeling foolish as ever, since our Advertising Prophets are as transient a phenomenon as any other ingredient of the Throw-Away Society—and no doubt new prophets and theorists will arise long after we have forgotten both our shocks of the future and our snows of yesteryear. I think the winds of change blow hard, but no harder than they ever did (though possibly with more hot and rising air), and will bring in their wake as many windfalls as snowfalls.

FOLLOW YOUR DON'T-KNOWS

You will soon discover for yourself many more theories than those I have singled out for some attention in this chapter ... and I shall, from time to time, refer to others myself in coming chapters. But these will suffice to demonstrate the conflicting or complementary witness of the body of theory, criticism and law-making that surrounds Advertising today ... and remember, every law that is made breaks to some degree a law that is already in being—that is, literally, on the books.

We have seen the range. From Dichter who believes you can analyse the apparent irrationalities of choice, through McLuhan who believes that no real choice any longer exists, to Toffler who contends that we have too much choice and that it will drive us mad ... and whose sentiments are essentially those of the frightened Alyosha in Solzhenitsyn's *One Day in the Life of Ivan Denisovich* who is scared silly at the very idea of escape from the Siberian labour camp, and wails, "Things that man puts a high price on are vile ... Why do you want freedom? In freedom your last grain of faith will be choked with weeds."

I have called these prophets the Theory Practitioners, because, though a few of them, a very few, actually practise and earn their living in Advertising—neither Toffler, McLuhan nor Dichter do so, though they advise those who do—most of them practise rather the *profession* of theorising, of "kibbitzing." More and more are taking up this profession, this practice of unsought comment, which is anything *but* "freely" given ... kibbitzing is a "growth industry," like carcinoma, and sometimes, the more ill-informed, the better. I should not wish to knock theorising *per se*—but Advertising is one field of endeavour where talk is *not* cheap and in fact can come very expensive to both client and agency. True Advertising, like politics, is the art of the possible, it is practice not preaching.

So by all means make yourself familiar with such erudite eructations as *lateral thinking, cognitive dissonance, critical path analysis*, the *complementary benefit principle* and the rest, because, from time to time, advertising executives (both on the administrative and the creative side) are hooked on such things. If they are not, their clients may be, and you must be prepared to defend your "weasel words" as defined by Dr. Mario Pei in his theory-book *Words in Sheep's Clothing* (*see* Chapter XI).

Apart from this, pay them no heed, and get on with your job, *our* job, which is Advertising, *selling the goods*, getting Brand-X off the shelves and producing that Sold Out notice. Don't, as Wilde counselled, "be led astray into the paths of virtue," remembering that "morality is simply the attitude we adopt towards people whom we personally dislike" and that "wickedness is a myth invented by good people to account for the curious attractiveness of others." Treat my own theorising in the same manner.

GUIDE TO "MARRIAGE"-GUIDANCE

Those client–agency partnerships which quail before the prophets and their tablets from Mount Sinai are usually motivated by fright, by lack of confidence in themselves. But "Getting Married" booklets hinder more young couples than they help, taking care of the bed part all right, but not the bored. I believe there is a better road to public respect and security, and I'll discuss this in Chapter XIV. The Dichter proclamation of 1951 that successful Advertising "manipulates human motivations and desires and develops a need for goods with which the public has at one time been unfamiliar—perhaps even *undesirous of purchasing*" (my italics) has caused lasting damage to the public image of Advertising, and is quite untrue. Even the "subliminal" experiments, as I have said, have shown that one cannot persuade anyone to buy or to do anything which he has no predilection for already. We are not hypnotists—if any of us have aspirations to become Svengalis, we wear our own trilbys into the labour exchange.

The client–agency "marriage" need be no less permanent because of the mutual admission (after bliss) that the partners were "sold" on each other by presentations (*see* Chapter V), as beyond the suitor's income as those of any other eager beau. Selling is communication, and communication is life. Let us investigate what our Brand-X campaign can learn from the experiences of others in the market-place, but only to the extent of Wilde's further precept "whenever I think of my bad qualities at night, I go to sleep at once."

We can leave insomnia to the Theory Practitioners. The only sacred cows in Advertising are those 8,500 which Thomas Lipton threatened to place on Queen Victoria's doorstep. To them, I bow ... but to none other.

Chapter IX

SOME CASE HISTORIES

You are not about to be subjected to narrative about various brand campaigns in detail (with one exception), though I urge you to consult them where you can ... there are some excellent books, such as *The History of Bovril Advertising* by Peter Hadley and *The Lipton Story* by Alec Waugh, not to mention a string of memoir-anthologies (some in, some out of print) which you may find in public libraries or secondhand bookshops. But, apart from that sole exception, which I'll come to presently, they belong to a different type of study than this.

No body of work for one particular brand is typical of *all* Advertising of its type or period; and the course which campaigns for one product have taken across the years, while they may indeed tell us much about the product, and about its maker as client, and by reflection something of the era in which both flourished or otherwise, they don't usually convey a great deal that is helpful about our profession's overall outlook and techniques.

The very year Lord Peter took up employment at "Pym's Publicity" (*see* Chapter III), was the year that Cadbury's agency started advertising their Dairy Milk chocolate by showing two glasses of milk being poured into the bar ... the wrapped bar. No, you are not inhabiting some time-machine ... forty-two years later, the same agency was still using the same visual gimmick with the same product on television, as you will have seen for yourself. With excellent reasons, of course—principal one being that no one has yet come up with a better idea: it tells the fact, sells the benefit, using a metaphor that is true and real. Short of saying that Dairy Milk has some of this, some of that, and a bit of the udder, it's hard to see how the creative people can be more specific and stay polite.

Until the day when some white-coated test-tube technician discovers that milk gives you cancer, rabies and gonorrhoea, plus serious psychotic disorders, Cadbury's and Leo Burnett-L.P.E. are fixed on a winner. Yet a history of this one product would tell us little of the ups and downs and doublings-back-on-their-own-tracks of Advertising and admen.

SEX MAKES US ALL COPY-CATS

Everything changes, nothing changes. You will come across the remark in French several times in this book ... my aim being to impress the truth of it on students more and more, as they grow to appreciate my theme, which is to underline the eternal purpose of all good, sound Advertising—highlighting the benefit, impelling the sale.

We may think, at first contact, that Badedas, the "bath additive," is straying a bit too near the mark when the copyline of its ad says "Things happen after a Badedas bath ... quite simply, *lebenslust.* Which the British, masters of understatement, call joie de vivre" (thus making sure it becomes, of course, a massive over-statement); but 200 years ago, another "bath restorative" product was sold on the copyline "Admirable for those who have been almost worn out by women and wine ... it will render their intercourse prolific," which is really an identical claim, without recourse to Teutonic or Gallic pussyfooting.

On somewhat squarer topics, students may note that the 1969 Press Ad "Give him (her or them) a Guinness" duplicated word for word, apart from the product-name, a Bovril ad of fifty-six years before. And compare these two examples of the method of "selling" the classics of literature:

"Be fascinated by sensuous Cleopatra! Shudder at murderous MacBeth! Chuckle with Falstaff! Thrill with lovesick Romeo! ..."

"Understand the fascinating contradictions of the Russian soul ... the madly voluptuous Dmitri Karamazov ... the tragic Anna Karenina ..."

who would readily guess these ads were nearly half a century apart? One may be a trifle more polysyllabic than the other, but sensuous Cleo and tragic Anna are sisters under the skin—and equally adept, make no mistake, at selling their favours. In the twenties, as E. S. Turner shows in *The Shocking History of Advertising*, the Dialogues of Plato were represented "as topical, challenging and smart" ... and in 1958, a Press Ad was still hailing the indisputable fact that they "hit so many nails squarely on the head today."

FADS IN FAGS

But this is no worse, and quite as justifiable, as the Bard himself lifting passages wholesale out of Montaigne. For we can find plenty of change, too. Where cigarettes are concerned, we have gone through a complete reversal of appeals. In 1898, an advertisement was urging "Don't you wish you could smoke all the time? Why not!", and it has taken only seventy years for the tune to change to things like "You can't scrub your lungs clean." Also, it's amusing to view the current efforts to promote new "slim line" cigarettes to appeal to women, and recall that in Victoria's day cigarettes were considered effeminate and the image of the Players bearded sailor (*see* Chapter XIII) was a successful attempt to promote masculinity into smoking.

Mind you, it was much easier to become a constant smoker, and stay that way, when smokes were five for a penny ... on the other hand, much harder to clamp down on cigarette advertising when it is worth nearly £24 million to agencies and the media and when a new taxing system (based on the value of cigarette and packet instead of weight of tobacco) came into force in January, 1978, which will enrich the national Exchequer with an ever-larger annual percentage of the £2,000 million now being spent by the nation's smokers.

One constant feature in cigarette promotion, however, no matter how medical opinion veered (and in the 1880s, a cigarette in the United States was sold in chemists' shops as a *cure* for catarrh, colds, asthma, hay fever and all throat diseases!) has been the insistent belief in the magic colour of gold. In November 1901, *The Star* carried four pages of ads—including the entire front page—for Guinea Gold cigarettes, and that gold standard is more alive today than ever, with Gold Leaf, Embassy Gold, Sovereign, Gold Bond, the "Pure Gold" of Special Filter, and all the other brands which disport themselves in golden packets, in luxurious settings of shimmering, elegant drapes (their ads are not only alone in being the only product-type which supplies no product information, but they are virtually interchangeable) ... closely followed, of course, by cigars such as Gold Foil and Cambridge Gold. The erstwhile long "naval" dominance is losing out before that devilish glitter, except for Players and Senior Service, though Three Castles has it both ways, showing a galleon sailing on a sea of gold.

Cigarette advertising has another constant feature ... the gift-stamp. Manufacturers in recent years have seized upon Green Shield as a buckler against doctors and do-gooders; but, back in 1933—again, and very aptly, the year of *Murder Must Advertise*—the Kensitas Company announced that they would henceforth be enclosing five gift certificates inside each pack of twenty, certificates which were "exchangeable for articles of finest craftsmanship." But whether murder must advertise or not, I'm afraid the modern claim that we cannot scrub our lungs clean would have washed even less in the last century than it does today, for an indefatigable marketer named Dr. Scott advertised an electric "Flesh Brush" which could scrub away everything from toothache to malaria, and all ailments situated in stomach, liver and kidney ... true, nothing was mentioned about lungs, but he had an "Electric Cigarette" especially designed to take good care of *them*!

I think we may permit ourselves a wry smile of astonishment at the continuing conflict, moral, therapeutic and economic, over a habit which Dr. Johnson rashly asserted had "completely gone out" in 1773. But the conflict was always there, right from the start, when Sir Walter Raleigh introduced tobacco from America into the English Court, and his king, James I, who detested smoking (and had hoped for gold) promptly beheaded him. As for cigars, it was Wellington through his Peninsular campaigns who gave us those, as he gave us the boot and the stiff upper-lip, while his aide-de-camp gave us the Raglan sleeve. Thus are product-names born.

THE CUPPA CAMPAIGNS

Drinks of varying potency were the subject of some of the first Press Ads in this country—the first ad for tea appeared in 1658 (approved "by all physicians") though potential customers were directed, of all places, to a "Cophee" House. But this promotion had been beaten to the Press six years before by Jamaican Coffee, which was not content to boast of its nice taste but also claimed to chase away consumption, gout, scurvy and "hypochondriac winds" ... which, as we all know, blow no one any good except perhaps the odd psychiatrist.

So you will see that some degree of medical benefit from drinks has been part of the adman's arsenal from the very beginning (as Turner points out, it's a very brisk step over the centuries from "rectifying the stomach and blood, cleansing them from all impurities" to waking up your liverbile or, more pertinently we might say, to "soothes your stomach; corrects digestive upsets; tones up the liver and checks biliousness," for ad-wise, there is little to choose between Famous Drops for Hypocondriack Melancholy and Andrews Liver Salts). The modern claims of Bio-Strath have nothing on Riga Balsam, which invited this test a hundred years ago ... "Take a hew or ram, drive a nail through its skull, brains and tongue, then pour some of it into the wound, it will directly stop the blood and cure the wound in eight or nine minutes"—far safer, one feels, to confine one's efforts to keeping Henry Cooper's right arm with a purpose in life or the standard of leisurely weekend cricket up—or down, depending on the viewpoint—though Bio-Strath may heartily endorse Riga Balsam's biblical text: "The Lord hath created medicines out of the earth, and he that is wise will not abhor them."

Testimonials (*see* Chapter X) have always figured largely in drinks promotion, though endorsements tend to be less extravagant than in the past ... tea may take Lulu through her TV rehearsals and Jackie Stewart round the world's top car-racing circuits, Sch ... You Know Who may enable actor William Franklyn to whip Rod Laver at tennis, while a certain brand of beer may even take Sir Francis Chichester round the globe—but Lord Roberts and his troops, we are led to believe, not only won the Boer War on Bovril but thoughtfully chose a route of attack which spelled out the brand's name on the map (thanks to an agency cartographer at "Pym's Publicity"). The only remotely comparable geographic feat in our own staider times is Typhoo putting the "T" in Britain, one of the most endearing of television commercials (but "join the T-set" several years ago meant buying a Scimitar GTE car!). Ogilvy tells us that Maxwell House Coffee's famous slogan "good to the last drop" originated with Theodore Roosevelt, though he does not make clear whether the President-cum-Rough Rider took San Juan Hill on a cuppa. What is true is that a friend of mine in Canada threw Maxwell House into a tizzy by persistently writing to ask them what was wrong with the last drop.

Putting "T"'s into the United States has naturally been much more of a challenge (or tease?) to admen, since the days of the thirteen colonies, and American distributors duly called on Dr. Dichter to come to the aid of the Boston tea party (he also gave coffee a lift— *see* Chapter VIII). The high priest of motivational research urged a more virile approach, so the ads started to show hearty sweating he-men dashing down their cuppas instead of a circle of imbibing genteel hostesses (ironically, with opposite ends in view, beer ads of this period showed a famous concert pianist, in tails and white tie, swilling his pints back after rolling over a few Beethoven sonatas). However, since the song "Tea for Two" was such an outstanding hit of the hard-boozing twenties on Broadway, I personally feel the doctor could have been a mite subtler. He could have researched in time rather than in depth and discovered that the archetypal American rebel, Paul Revere (who rode so hard to warn folks at Concord that the redcoats were coming) probably refreshed himself afterwards with his celebrated silver tea-service, and that the American clippers which won a fortune for the Astors were mainly carrying tea!

For the amusing historical truth is that it is *we* who were a nation of coffee-drinkers, who later switched to tea (when we speak of a cup of "cha," we are speaking Chinese), while our "colonial cousins" are the reverse. Lack of historical perspective also cost tea-makers and their sluggish admen a famous slogan, for the original coiner of the phrase "that sinking feeling" was a Duchess of Bedford two centuries ago—and she cured it, not by drinking Bovril in her pyjamas but by serving at Woburn the world's first "afternoon tea."

THE HARD STUFF

In any product-area, it is vital for admen to distinguish between fact and fiction, before they start to select a prime benefit appeal. Scotch whisky, for example, is regarded by many as almost a British symbol (abroad, Johnnie Walker is often muddled with John Bull)— yet the truth is that consumption of Scotch is increasing in almost every western country *except* Britain . . . as Alan Whicker's interview on TV with the charming "king of champagne" demonstrated, when that delightful aristocrat's own favourite drink was shown to be Scotch! Price is not the reason either, for what *is* rising is our national consumption of vodka (which is frequently more expensive) . . . a rise directly attributable, in the first instance, to that seminal moment in the original James Bond adventure *Casino Royale* when 007 ordered vodka to be added to his dry Martini "made with grain instead of potatoes" and served in a deep champagne goblet "large and very strong and very cold." And, heresy of heresies, Bond is, of course, a Scot.

The advertising of vodka has carefully followed up on this cue, particularly the Smirnoff and Cossack brands. The latter proceeding from the promise of "sweet-talking kissable Cossack drinkers" in 1967, through the startled, tousled honey-blonde who is advised to "keep it quiet" in 1969, to the weary damsel in 1970 whom we saw staggering out of bed to the window, to be reassured "next morning, you'll still feel the same about it" (though the damaged goods appears a bit uncertain, with lover-boy ruffling the sports-pages over his hairy chest under the sheets behind her, calmly awaiting his breakfast . . . with vodka?).

Black and White whisky has also trendified its image, with a rather different emphasis, from the 1965 ads which associated their product with Shakespeare and Milton, to their ads in the early seventies which related to Hattie Jaques and Muir (encompassing the whole range of current TV "humour"). Campari has produced a blend of extreme sophisticated fantasy and brilliantly sly social comment in commercials which show an elegant young man on a Venetian terrace trying to impress a beautiful creature he has just encountered at the bar with his continental *nous*. The vision of loveliness responds to his elegant drawl (clearly phoney) by uttering through perfectly carmined lips the most uninhibited monosyllabic platitudes in appallingly common accents. "Nice, innit?" she remarks over her drink and her unaffected appreciation conveys a genuine tribute to product and setting. That White Horse going everywhere has taken to strolling into milady's bathroom (perhaps under the impression that she is Catherine the Great), while Vat 69 has even been so reckless as to lose its number (which has almost the impact of a loss of virginity) ... there is some risk here, of course, since this brand-name is also the tag-line of one of the hoariest and whore-iest of school-cum-barrack room jokes. Still, no tight-rope of taste can be flinched from, it seems, when exports of Scotch are rising by the melodious pipe of nearly £43 million every six months (the first six months of 1977 saw exports reach earnings of £231,222,000)! How long, I wonder, will it be before the new penny drops and distillers remember that at least their product matures in 007?

During the liquid, party-mad twenties, advertising of alcohol ran at £2 million a year—and was condemned by a Royal Commission as "almost a public nuisance"—but by last year drink advertising in newspapers alone exceeded £4 million, with no righteous howls from any quarter. Possibly because so many righteous mouths were busy imbibing the record thirty million gallons of *spirits alone* that vanished down British throats in 1976.

BEER KEEPS AHEAD

Centre of the promotional stage, however, stays firmly in the hands of the brewers... despite all the plethora of glamourous "What do you want to drink" drinks, the dream-worlds of Cointreau-addicts, taking the "cock" out of Cockburn's and the "LLY" and "T" out of Noilly Prat, getting stoned or crabbie on ginger wine, discerningly drinking Campari, having it way up there with Dubonnet or some yo-ho-ho with Captain Morgan, being pale and interesting as a Croft Original on a warm romantic evening with Casal Garcia, being young and bold with Courvoisier like the good old days with Justina, meeting Martell's Mr. Brandyman, experiencing "it" soon with Booth's gin, with the big pay-off in Dry Sack, following the brave example of Nelson, who drank Pedro Domecq before Trafalgar (and got pickled in brandy after), putting a port in every girl or a hundred pipers in "a watery grave" ... and so on.

The scene is naturally dominated by Guinness, but the plot is best summarised in that marvellous Carlsberg lager ad "Swallow the Leader." That the media themselves know the cash-flow disparity in Advertising between Ale and Arty was perfectly shown one autumn when, in an issue of *Campaign*, both the *Birmingham Mail* and Ilford's Colour Display division, used foaming tankards in their visuals and, two issues later, the new trade journal *Food and Drink Weekly* launched its first appeal to agencies with a beer-can and bottle illustration ... letting spirits keep themselves up by association, or not.

Why the Guinness domination? Because the durability and continued effectiveness of its campaigns have been a constant spur to the profession for over forty years, while the techniques used by several generations of admen on its behalf have often set the highest standards in their own and other product-fields (Guinness was on the "drink that goes with everything" kick, twelve years before the Coke merchants tried the approach, praising their own daring in doing so).

GUINNESS IS GOOD FOR ADVERTISING

Actually, it all began way back with a 21-year-old artist named Hablôt Knight Browne, who in 1836 won over the strong competition of drawings by Thackeray to become illustrator of *The Pickwick Papers*. Signing his pictures "Phiz" (to match Dickens's "Boz"), he drew Mr. Pickwick on the hearth just beneath the clearly lettered name of the great stout ... perhaps a sly comment on Pickwick's girth! So Guinness has had a free "plug" for itself every time a copy of this masterpiece has been opened since. And that *is* P.R.

Though the product's Advertising proper did not begin till the late twenties (with Bensons—or "Pym's Publicity"—who also had the Bovril account booming for them), the Guinness family down the intervening years had plenty of the right Irish instinct for "below-the-line" activities—one of them became Dublin's first Lord Mayor and another restored St. Patrick's Cathedral. In 1928, however, came "Guinness is good for you" and the saga had really begun.

The "tonic" angle persisted through "Guinness gives you strength" in 1934, and was dropped only when the account, at that time worth £1 million in billings, moved suddenly to J.W.T. several years ago—though it remains "good for you" in the Equatorial countries, where the inhabitants imbibe more Guinness than we do. Meanwhile, the Guinness poster illustrations became famous, and their series of comic animals (like the runaway seal, balancing a stout bottle on its nose) on the "My Goodness, My Guinness" theme.

Pastiche has always been a strong point of the visuals, ranging from Alice in Wonderland adaptations of the Tenniel characters, like the Walrus and the Carpenter, back to nothing less hallowed than the Bayeux tapestry ("Battle of Hastings 1066—Bottle of Guinness 1966"). A high level of accomplishment was displayed in Coronation Year, when Guinness animal posters dispensed with the brand-name altogether (a feat achieved in recent years only by Heinz baked beans Advertising).

The contemporary posters and Press Ads are much tamer and pitched to a lower key, built round the slogan "Give him a Guinness," trying to broaden the appeal-base, showing all manner and classes of people in widely-differing situations, from choir-singing to a very kinky chap who spends his time surrounded by women's shoes. Even trendy "sophistication" is sometimes ostentatiously stretched for, with such ads as "Sunday morning . . . One tall jug, champagne, Guinness, the posh Sundays and you two," with the opposite extreme catered for by a photograph of those reluctant pandas, Chi-Chi and An-An, in the vain pursuit of love, and the suggestion "Give 'em a Guinness" (what about Cossack vodka?). It's hard to say which extreme is more absurd.

IS THE VINTAGE OVER?

The "now" Guinness advertising (we are told by pundits and creative directors that it's a campaign "for the seventies") does not impress me, but form your own judgment, taking each ad and poster on its merit and presumed intent. The agency admen themselves in solemn conclave have awarded some of it a Best Ads 1970 accolade in *Campaign*, to whose interviewers Stanley Darmon, marketing director for Guinness, confided with pride: "We have had a lot of letters about our supplement advertising" . . . and this book will have failed if any students finishes it without appreciating that this reason is, to me, one of the worst possible. Let customers, not correspondence, be your aim—unless they are one and the same (*see* Chapter XIII), with order or payment enclosed!

Huge, full-colour, copy-crammed double-page spreads like "How to make a Guinness" and the "Guintelligence test" are splendidly written, well laid out, a joy to read, even more joy to write . . . but are they busy selling agency or client, or one to the other? Is medium or message on sale? Enough to drive one to Harp lager's less intellectually demanding "Blonde in the Bar" . . . except perhaps this lighter touch is not so different as we thought—ever seen that harp on the label before? Mae West to the contrary, "My Goodness" had a great deal to do with it.

The Guinness TV-commercials have much more interest, in their simplicity and purity of selling stance—at least, the ones which show how you can take a pen-nib and write your initials on the "head" or explain disarmingly how the concept of Irish coffee originated from the natural look of a Guinness, etc. . . . all good tongue-in-cheek blarney, while we are held by the sight of the lusciously velvet and dark hard-stuff being poured. Certainly, the Guinness admen are so convinced of the efficacy of their TV-ads that in 1976, by spending £2,219,700, they made their product the biggest spenders on the box (with British Leyland £300,000 or so behind in second place). We can also note that Heineken have paid Guinness the supreme compliment of doing a friendly take-off of the famous "man with a girder on his head" poster.

My outstanding favourite among today's drink ads, however, is the one with the headline "After four pints of bitter, a double scotch, two gin and tonics, a lager and a curry, you need a drink." It is, of course, the promotion for Fernet Branca and how it sets about mending your "morning-after" feeling. These ads not only amuse but, as I have grateful cause to testify, they are literally true, both in facing the fact that its taste is "so evil, your taste-buds will run for cover" and in claiming "once you've endured the first few minutes, you'll soon learn to forgive."

Wit, intelligence, humanity, the benefit clearly stated with the "defect." The marvellous gospel truth. It's wonderful. Pity it needs a hangover to find it.

SOAP-BOXES AND SOAP

I regret very much there is no room to deal here with advertising in politics, though it is an inviting subject. But I will just draw your attention to the stated opinion some years back of three leading West German agencies that the then Chancellor Willy Brandt's opposition leader, Rainer Barzel was "unsellable" because he was burdened, they said, with the colourless image of "the schoolmaster of the nation ... tough, stubborn, uncomfortable ... he sought the best solution and not the greatest applause ... his uncompromising courage in being unpopular, in fighting for something better, was urgently needed in that time of iridescent bright colours."

Does this sound familiar? These are seriously supposed to be "unsellable" qualities that the electorate will not buy? How reminiscent these views are to those expressed by the pollsters about Nixon and then Heath! President Nixon's own TV-producer during the election (*see The Selling of the President* by Joe McGinniss) said bluntly of his own candidate, "Let's face it, a lot of people think Nixon is dull. Think he's a bore, a pain in the ass ... who was forty-two years old the day he was born ... like somebody hung him in a closet overnight and he jumps out in the morning with his suit all bunched up and starts running around saying 'I want to be President!'."

But this is the man who won in that election, and "handsomely." And Heath had his moment of victory. We in advertising have much to learn in this area, which will become of increasing importance, not on TV alone, but on the big, influential medium which commercial radio has certainly become (*see* Chapter XIV) ... now that Heath's shaking shoulders and Nixon's blue chin no longer lead the motivational researchers astray. Would Roosevelt's fireside-chats in the depressed thirties have gripped America as they did (and I heard many of them) had we had those dark suitcase-pouches under his eyes always before us, that enormous back-slapping grin, that cigarette-holder?

And though I did eschew noting whole brand-campaigns at the start of this chapter, with one exception, we must now come to that exception—which, of course, is Pears soap. Maybe a natural follow-on to political soft-soap-boxes. Pears appears often throughout this book, and I think can fairly be claimed as the most influential product-name in Advertising history, ever since the day in 1875 when Thomas Barratt took over, with the words every client should frame above his great slab of executive desk: "Any fool can make soap. It takes a clever man to sell it." He had no hesitation about the identity of that necessary clever man, and hastened to prove it. Within five years, his "puzzle" posters for Pears were tantalising crowds of people round the hoardings, using "subliminal" or "op art" techniques, and his first powerfully simple ads were shouting out the catchphrase of half the world: "How do you spell soap? Why, P-E-A-R-S, of course."

PEARS WITHOUT PEERS

Barratt's idea was to make the words soap and Pears synonymous, and he did not spare money to get what he wanted. For a time, he largely succeeded, with such slogans as "Good morning! Have you used Pears' Soap?" (plagiarised many years later by "Have you Macleaned your teeth today?"). Apart from the Millais Bubbles, other memorable posters were the reproduction of the *Punch* cartoon by Harry Furniss, showing a filthy, tattered tramp scribbling his testimonial: "Two years ago I used your soap—since then I have used no other;" the picture of the baby in the bath reaching for the soap, over the caption "He won't be happy till he gets it;" two monks washing with "Cleanliness is next to Godliness;" and reproductions of the marble statue of the reluctantly scrubbed urchin, sculpted from life in a Preston "Coronation Street" milieu, called "Dirty Boy," which Barratt bought for £500 from Focardi, an Italian artist.

Barratt also managed to place advertisements on the back of the penny and halfpenny postage stamps (they still seem to taste of his product) and had "Pears" stamped into 250,000 specially imported French ten-centime pieces. The Pears campaigns became the subject of a learned paper delivered at an eminent American University, and Thomas Barratt and all his works soon became the object of mounting jealousy from fuming and fierce competitors.

The eventual usurpation came from the future Lord Leverhulme, with his Sunlight soap, but while Barratt lived, Pears remained a dominant brand—it's still there but today, ironically, it forms a minor segment of the Unilever "Lintas" empire (itself undergoing change and upheavals, having exchanged as Creative Director one of McLuhan's most fervent disciples for the happy husband of the Yo-Ho-Ho girl of the Captain Morgan ads). The great days of Pears, however, made its advertising a household word—some households using different words to others—and as near as dammit to immortal. And certainly never, of its kind, bettered.

TRAVELLING HOPEFULLY

We have thus far touched on case histories from two of the three largest-billing categories, drinks and smokes; the third is food (whose national newspaper advertising expenditure last year was 57 per cent up on 1975) but that has so many ramifications and sub-divisions that it would require a book to itself. So let us complete our lightning packaged tour in the promotional world that gave birth to the phrase, with the Advertising scene for the fastest growing industry in Britain and the largest on earth ... the travel industry. In this country, total expenditure on ads by participants is the fastest-growing, too—last year, the total ad expenditure in the national press bounded by 33 per cent to over £12 million—it will be appreciated that if all TV commercials and brochures were included, the total appropriation for travel promotion has risen to staggering heights.

Spent on what? Well, by far the biggest cash-allotment of the promotion goes "below the line" in brochures, and the media Advertising—partly on television (although that blonde clasping her bosom as she skittishly rolls in the surf and dashes through foliage and sand-dune is, believe it or not, advertising cigars not holidays-with-play) but mainly in the press and mainly on Sundays—is aimed at getting potential customers to send for the brochure, either directly from the tour operator or from local travel agents.

The brochures vary tremendously in quality, as you would expect. Some are extremely expensive publications, employing top-class writers, photographers and designers. British Airways' various Sovereign Travel brochures probably produce the heaviest total output of standard platitude fantasy and Worldmark, with a more exclusive target, one of the most outstanding in quality—for the different markets they are sighted at, both set remarkable standards. One must admit, nevertheless, that, on the whole, levels of press advertising in travel do not measure up to the print.

Why this paradox? Partly, it is because of the relative newness of the industry, and its unwillingness to employ sufficient Advertising expertise in its service. In the eye-opening (one hopes) words of Walter H. Johnson, Jr., when he gave a lecture a few years ago to the Travel Industry Study Group ...

> "I know of no major business in the world that is less marketing oriented than the business of travel ... I know of no business in the world that buys 15 billion dollars' worth of equipment without knowing whether the market exists for it or not. I know of no business in the world which has devoted as much time and energy to working to sell the product of engineers, who have neither the willingness nor the time nor the interest to consult with the traveller ..."

to which prescient comment, the Rolls-Royce débâcle over the RB211 engine for Lockheed's TriStar airbus, ten months later, wrote an appalling endorsement. Barbara Griggs underlined it in her *Daily Express* column: "The average air-traveller wonders fleetingly why nobody ever bothered to ask him if he wanted to fly in a TriStar in any case. He doesn't, necessarily. What he wants is to get from point A to point B as fast as possible, as comfortably as possible, and as cheaply as possible. But not necessarily in that order."

TRAVELLING LIGHT, TRAVELLING RIGHT

Sometimes it is, I believe, the ignorance that the selling expertise exists, which results in low standards—often down to crudity—of press ads for travel. And sometimes, it is an inability to distinguish good selling advice from bad, which can take the form of wilful blindness brought on by ideas of false economy (the brochures having cost so much). While charlatans are seldom cheap in our profession, low fees are no guarantee of respectability of character, as Lady Bracknell might observe.

However that might be, of the three types of client in this "boom" field—the tour operator, the carrier (of tourists, not germs), and the holiday resort or country—only the carriers are achieving any recognisable degree of selling sophistication. The television commercials of British Airways, Pan Am and T.W.A. (*see* Chapter V) are often beautifully shot, the message of the airline concisely conveyed, assisted by some superbly orchestrated backing on the soundtrack.

But the principal liability of these ads (as with the Cunard and P. & O. commercials), and the TV-ads for resorts and tour operators is that *they all look alike*. We can only look and wonder ... is that shipload of laughing, dancing, eating, merry-making passengers just edging on to the screen through the calm waters of the heat-haze carried by P. & O. or by Cunard?

GOING PLACES ... FAST!

The bewilderingly rapid changes in the travel scene were graphic-
ally summed up by Brian MacCabe, chairman of Foote, Cone and
Belding, in his address to the Institute of Marketing (in the same series
as Walter Johnson's talk) on 20th January 1970, entitled "Travel
Marketing in the Seventies." As an ex-B.O.A.C. advertising executive
himself, he was able to portray the post-war growth with dramatic
exactitude:

> "My first long-haul flight with B.O.A.C. was in a Lancastrian—a con-
> verted Lancaster bomber—to Australia ... Nine passengers sat facing the
> fuselage for $2\frac{1}{2}$ days ...
>
> And now, here we are, bracing ourselves against the impact of the Jumbo
> Jets, arriving and departing with clockwork regularity ... containing
> nearly 400 people; the Concorde flying 140 people at 1,450 m.p.h. across
> the Atlantic in $2\frac{1}{2}$ hours ... Some change in 25 years!"

Some change, indeed. A dizzying, dazzling prospect. But are we keeping up with the change, where promotional opportunities are concerned? I fear not. We are held fast in another corner of Lewis Carroll
countryside where "it takes all the running you can do, to keep in
the same place." Our *impression* that we have moved is arguably a
delusion on a par—and sharing much affinity with—with McLuhan's
"global village" theory (*see* Chapter VIII), and it makes our Advertising in travel emphasise the apparent same-ness of the world, not its
variety.

MacCabe himself embraces this delusion, when he refers to the
Paul-at-Damascus style revelation he experienced, that convinced
him "the more that large numbers of people of every country tra-
velled; the more they knew each other, understood each other; and
built friendships with each other; the less likely they were to fight
each other."

The slightest glance at history should dispel this cloud-cuckoo
(however admirable) vision ... since Cain and Abel, the most fero-
cious wars of all have been civil ones, the most persistent hatreds inter-
necine—from the European reformation and counter-reformation to
the Indian–Pakistani partition, from Gettysburg to Biafra, from Drog-
heda to Hue, from Belfast to Amman—between, in fact, those who
knew and understood each other far too well.

TRAVELLING BRIGHT?

We know people, familiar or unfamiliar as they may superficially
seem, better for valuing our differences, not our same-nesses. Bernard

Shaw, who hated being dragged off on cruises by his wife (we will not mention the shipping-line), gave as his chief complaint the exactly opposite point of view to that which forms the basic premise of most modern travel Advertising: "I dislike feeling at home when I am abroad" and shattered another cornerstone of travel promotion philosophy by hating the journeys but revelling in the destinations he reached.

Alice on the Looking-Glass chessboard, felt the same way, to her credit, and made her opinion as usual known to the Red Queen with crystal clarity. As Elinor Goodman wrote in *The Daily Telegraph* in November 1972, "Simple sunshine, sea and sex are not enough ... with everywhere from Margate to Marbella offering golden beaches and bikini-clad nymphs." At the end of his world cruise, Shaw could only say "one place is very much like another," but it was the organisation of the cruise which had made him think so.

Yet still, in press or on television, the same strips of sand confront us, the same massed white blocks of balconied beach hotels, the same golf-courses, the same water-ski-ing ... is this Miami, Majorca or Mombasa? ... is this Spain, South Africa or Suva? ... are those tropic palms in Devon or Dalmatia or Damnation? Who knows ... and does anyone care, as long as the postcards of proof are plentifully supplied? Does it matter where we arrive, as long as we travel hopefully?

VIVE LA DIFFERENCE!

In all Advertising, from travel to tin-tacks, Ogilvy's words in relation to Advertising Great Britain to Americans hold good:

> "My English friends seem to know exactly what I ought to put into my advertisements for Britain ... fishing, horse-racing, sailing, golf, modern architecture and night-clubs. It does not occur to them that Americans can enjoy these same amenities every weekend ... Our surveys show that the American tourist wants to see what he can't see at home ... *We are not advertising to Englishmen* ... Research has demonstrated that it pays to advertise what is *unique* in a country."

From most travel advertising today, you would never guess it. In place of the old "wogs start at Calais" mentality, we have substituted the no more creditable or civilised "all the world's a Lido" outlook—which, if anything, is worse. At least, our forefathers, however offensively they may often have done so, accepted that wogs were different ... even if the difference was that they were Westernised Oriental Gentlemen! Travel seems to be in danger of ceasing to be "abroad" in any real sense at all ... many people feel more alien in the King's Road, Chelsea, than in its namesake on the other side of the world (in Fiji).

How much the travelling public is prepared to pay, how far it is
prepared to go, to find the difference it hungers for, is evidenced by
the ten thousand advance bookings Pan American Airways have
already received for their first moon flight.

Of course, the public want to be reassured about their standards
of comfort and safety; what MacCabe rightly pinpoints as "the fear
of foreign languages, people, food, hotels and habits . . . that they will
not be let in for more than they can afford; that everything has been
arranged for them and that (hopefully) nothing will go wrong to cause
them anxiety." The Hilton Hotel groups (with over 70 hotels in
operation across the globe) had the right idea precisely in their slogan
"Hilton International. Different as the country it's in." In a more
naïve way, so did the Victorian ad which showed H. M. Stanley opening up the continents on a steaming cup of Bovril.

SELLING THE STEAK, NOT THE SIZZLE

You will usually hear it quoted the other way round, but this is
the way to solve your problem when you genuinely *do* have something
different to offer. MacCabe gave the estimate that in 1975, there
would be 650 million tourists sailing and soaring, hiking and honking
their way round the world. By 1980, there would be 1,000 million!
And yet, as he says, "the most complex advertising problem there
is" produces ads that ". . . show an exciting angle photograph of a
ship or an aircraft or a train—or a golden sun, a blue sea and a blonde
girl . . ." which are anonymous and nothing. Like Lord Brothers send
a co-sponsored expedition to photograph models in Nelbarden swimwear or like Clarksons spent £10,000 in sending top photographers
swanning round the Mediterranean to snap hotels and cruise-vessels.

More research is definitely not the answer—at least, not the kind
of motivational research which has revealed, in a U.S. survey, that
tourists' preference for rooms with balconies has nothing to do with
fresh air or sun-tanning before breakfast, or hearing the dance-band
below while sharing an intimate *cuba libre*, but is caused by a need
to "expose themselves to the environment," . . . we do not need research, I trust, to remind us that you do not advertise a play with
a portrait of the proscenium, that you do not promote a circus with
a picture of the tent. *The difference lies in the destination*, the different
scenery, people and customs.

People today are prepared to take for granted that decent transport
and healthy, comfortable accommodation will be provided for their
money—yet the Advertising directed their way mostly emphasises
these factors alone, not the destination at all. And since hotels and
ships and trains and planes tend to look alike—even as all the airports

on earth are really one airport—so the advertisements merge into one another.

Travel Advertising should show us *where* we are going, not how we get there, should emphasise that the new and strange still exists in the world, but is more akin than we realise ... therefore, that we our-selves, and the lives we can lead, are more interesting than we realise or try to make them. Everyone's backyard is a far-away place with a strange-sounding name to someone (read Chesterton's *The Napoleon of Notting Hill* to see what I mean) ... so, conversely, travel ideally should show us that the most strange, most exotic, erotic or beautiful is always the backyard for someone. This is the excitement of travel that ads should convey ... the world is one world, but it's a world of difference.

Lions you can see in the wild at Longleat, but the Ngorongoro Crater, that's abroad ... elephants you can watch at Chessington, but the Khedda Roundup, that's abroad ... Canterbury Cathedral, next to miles of gorgeous surf-crested sands, that's abroad ... a girl in a bikini, that's a broad. Our product is the destination.

"ONLY CONNECT ..."

Advertising that confuses the pot of gold with the rainbow is always, in my view, bound to fail ... people know that gold is touch-able, they know that rainbows are not and how long they last. Which I think is the trap too much of the travel advertising we see all round us at this time of year (January–February are always the big-spending months in the media) falls into ... it confuses means of travel with ends of travel.

This hazard lies in ambush in all advertising. You must always make double-sure you are emphasising the proper benefit, the real difference. Make sure your visual relates both to the difference and to the benefit ... Napoleon has been used successfully to illustrate shaving-soap, hair-spray and tooth-brushes (quite apart from brandy). And do make quite sure you are presenting the benefit in a positive manner. In one issue of *The Observer* colour magazine three years ago, there were two ads for TV-sets, separated by only a couple of pages: one showed a husband slumped in his chair, gazing at the box above the headline "After a hard day at the office, Bush doesn't expect your eyes to work overtime" but no wife; the other showed a woman in négligé, gazing at a Murphy set and thinking "Mother didn't tell me there'd be tellies like this" but no husband. Both sets are manufactured by the Rank Organisation (which automatically means one ad is useless to the Group, anyway) and both, in effect, portray television as a home-breaker extraordinary. Was this the message? Two different agencies, but with a single absence of thought—and the same client, which sometimes means the same thing.

The key-words of our profession are the theme of *Howard's End* by E. M. Forster—"only connect." I do not mean simply connection in itself; but connection with the reality of the world as the customer knows it and the reality of the benefit as *you* know it.

The ads and campaigns cited in the case histories we have touched on in this chapter will indicate to you which ads made connection and which ads did not, either to the eye, heart or purse-strings. All of them were intended to stand out and be heard amid what Thomas Carlyle called the "all-deafening blast of puffery," by which he referred to the amusing, but devastatingly accurate, subdivisions laid down by Sheridan's Mr. Puff in *The Critic* ... "Puffing is of various sorts: the principals are, the puff direct, the puff preliminary, the puff collateral, the puff collusive and the puff oblique, or puff by implication ..." and the best campaigns have used them all, in due course and time, from that article in *The Times* which hailed tobacco as being "good for the Head, Eyes, Stomach, Lungs, Rheumatism, and Gout, Thickness of Hearing, Head-Ach, Tooth-Ach or Vapours" to the film *Doctor at Sea* which, apart from displaying Bridgit Bardot in her first English-speaking role, also displayed bottles of Guinness being used to cure sea-sickness.

It will pay you to study as many past campaigns as you can, and I think you will find the ads of fifteen years ago are little different from those of fifty years ago ... improvement in design standards especially have been startlingly recent. Now we shall consider how you may, in your turn, improve them still more, keeping in mind that the ideal of every advertisement is the ideal of the barber's pole ... whose red stripes are the red of blood and whose white stripes are the white of bandages. At one stroke, sharp and painless, the trade-mark of our calling is to wound and heal.

Chapter X

THE ADMAN'S ARSENAL—1

The various types of campaign you can institute for Brand-X were discussed in Chapter VI. With this vital point decided and the brief finally placed in their hands, the copywriter and designer must set about creating in words and pictures the ads which the customer will see and hear (the hearing will become increasingly important, as commercial radio spreads—*see* Chapter XII). It will be noted by this time, I hope, that I am happier with the word *customer* rather than *consumer* ... the rampant breed I like to call theory practitioners talk and write about the latter, and could be referring to anything from pigs to petrol tanks. Admen deal with customers, i.e. the reasoning, irrational human being who has the power to think and to choose and is able to choose between more and more products and services every day.

I think it wise to dispel the popular lay notion at once that creative people in agencies do this in a spirit of cheerful cynicism. While the adjective is completely correct, the noun is not. Realism, certainly—but this is a very different thing. We can accept entirely for the admen the Wilde definition of a cynic as one "who knows the price of everything and the value of nothing." Such a work-principle would be disastrous for good advertising, and the sooner a beginner understands this the better. Neither, however, should he stray into the counter-side of Wilde's saying (much less frequently quoted), that a sentimentalist is one "who sees an absurd value in everything, and doesn't know the market price of any single thing." Sentimentalism belongs to the client, not to the adman, who must hold the balance between both extremes.

Apart from any other argument I might advance, it needs only to be stressed here that the copywriter rarely knows the price until the last minute—sometimes he must ask that a price-alteration be "pasted over" on the artwork just before the block-maker receives the job! Where trade advertising is concerned the retail price is often only indirectly relevant. The creative people know that their prime consideration is not *how much* the product costs in the shop but *what benefit* accrues to the person buying it.

PRESS ADVERTISEMENTS

After receiving his briefing from the Account Executive the copy-writer gets together with his designer-partner to assess and evaluate the purely technical data, i.e. which medium the advertisement is going into, and what space-sizes have been booked. The writer must know first of all just who will be reading his words and how much room he has got to word-play in.

At this stage the creative people will also swap ideas on the type of visual most likely to produce results. They will be concerned not just with the ad's subject-matter, but the relative proportion of space which words and picture should occupy. Which brings us to the relative importance of the copy and design, and their respective functions. This relationship is always in flux; now design is fashionably on top, now copy. Some indicate the fact that our lives today are dominated by two key-words of pop culture, "The Word" which, as Genesis tells us, was there at the beginning of all things. Silent films are a cult, the howl replaces the lyric in the hit parade, the tape-recorder is replacing the exam-paper. On the other hand we live in the most verbose age in history; every day, in Britain alone, 26 million newspapers are read—which on average means one newspaper for every other person.

Through one medium or another we are all exposed to the message of words which are telling us over 1,500 gospel truths a day—one sales-pitch for every single minute of our lives! McLuhan, as usual, tries to have it all ways: he talks of "depth penetration" and "synethesia" as fast becoming the norm of communication in propaganda, but then censures Advertising for "the lengthiness, the prosiness, the redundancy of its verbal message." As one who writes "lengthiness" for "length," *he's* one to talk! It all depends on the message and the time and audience on hand—Dr. Goebbels' main verbal technique was redundancy of message brought to a fine art.

Perhaps the ideal copy-visual adjustment of all time was achieved by the picture-writings of the Pyramids, those first advertisements for runaway slaves which still can be read in their "sacred carving" medium (or, in Greek, "hieroglyphics") and which achieve the ideal synthesis of word and picture to which every press ad should aspire. Both ingredients are of equal status and their sum is greater than the parts ... a unisex of communication.

Words and pictures: which does which?

"Words, words, words—I'm so sick of words," sings Eliza Doolittle to her bashful suitor in *My Fair Lady*. She then goes on to proclaim what many designers in Advertising regard as a grievance they must immediately rectify. "Don't talk of stars, tell me no dreams—Show me," urges Eliza. "Don't talk of Spring, Don't talk of Love—Show me . . . Sing me no song, read me no rhyme, don't waste my time—Show me!" And one is really tempted to believe she has made out quite a case . . . until we reflect that, for all her protestations, her song expends all of 203 words (I've counted them) to prove her point.

As Alice remarked in scorn of the book her sister was reading: "What's the use of a book without pictures or conversations?" What she meant, of course, was that her sister's book was not *communicating*. For that, you need words *and* pictures. As to their relative importance and precedence, argument on this is as sterile as the conundrum of the chicken and the egg. Unless you happen to know beforehand, it's impossible to guess which came first on your morning newspaper's political cartoon—the drawing or the caption. Both words and pictures are doing *their own* thing, but combining to accomplish the *same* thing.

When Oscar Hammerstein II was writing *Showboat* he waited for Jerome Kern's melodies first, then added the lyrics; when, sixteen years later, he was writing *Oklahoma!* he wrote the words first, then Richard Rodgers added the music. Both shows were landmarks in the development of the stage musical, both packed with magnificent songs, yet who could tell in which case words followed music, or vice versa? Ask the next chanteuse who assays "Just My Bill" to guess whether Hammerstein or Kern started the wonderful song, and could she do it? Of course not. She'd be wrong either way, because it so happens that Hammerstein got stuck on that one, and P. G. Wodehouse came through with the jolly old rhymes. That's show-biz. That's Advertising, too. So is the fact that when "Ol' Man River" went bouncing round the world's bathrooms the tune hadn't really sprung full-grown from the mind of Kern, but had started in the brain of one Maury Madison (real name, Renwick Smith) with a song called "Long-Haired Mamma."

An ad generally acknowledged as one of the best in 1969 was a press advertisement for the Health Education Council, intended to shock readers into practising better food hygiene. Was it a "copy" ad or a "design" ad? The headline (*see* opposite) contains *seventy-three* words, and yet the design is just as important in the impact, as those explosive words. Though the visual occupies only a quarter of the space of the ad (because there's also a baseline!), the plate of food it shows makes the ad doubly effective. It was a product of the Cramer Saatchi "hot-shop" (*see* Chapter II). So who should get most credit for the food hygiene ad—Saatchi as writer or Cramer as designer? Neither—it was composed by one of *their* copywriters! That's Advertising. That's show-biz.

THIS IS WHAT HAPPENS
WHEN A FLY LANDS ON YOUR FOOD.
FLIES CAN'T EAT SOLID FOOD,
SO TO SOFTEN IT UP THEY VOMIT ON IT.
THEN THEY STAMP THE VOMIT IN
UNTIL IT'S A LIQUID, USUALLY STAMPING IN
A FEW GERMS FOR GOOD MEASURE.
THEN WHEN IT'S GOOD AND RUNNY
THEY SUCK IT ALL BACK AGAIN, PROBABLY
DROPPING SOME EXCREMENT AT THE
SAME TIME.
AND THEN, WHEN THEY'VE FINISHED
EATING, IT'S YOUR TURN.

Though I would emphasise that the initial impetus belongs almost always to the copywriter (*see* Chapter VII), I do not subscribe to Ogilvy's blunt assertion that "Advertising is a business of *words*," but prefer to go along with Cramer's comment in regard to the food hygiene ad referred to above. "We decided ... to get the message across as directly as possible ... It's much better to tell it straight than use all kinds of graphics."

Better to tell it straight. That legend should be written in fire on the foreheads of every designer and copywriter who ever courted their Muse-sense at the expense of their News-sense.

Believing and persuading

There are two main objectives in a press ad (which apply to most forms of Advertising, but since we are taking press ads first, we'll deal with those objectives here) and these involve the duties of *recognition* and *responsibility*—that is, making sure that the identity of the message is instantly *recognisable*, and then the *responsibility* of making sure that message has the right content. I regard recognition and responsibility as the two outstanding factors in the protocols of communication in Advertising, and that the first is primarily the job of the designer, the second the copywriter's job. The potential customer must accept the ad as credible and the message as persuasive; *seeing is believing but reading is persuading.*

The design visual establishes the immediate *rapport* with a reader which good advertising demands. To do this the designer presents his customer with a recognisable element upon which the attention can focus (like Cramer's plate of food in the food hygiene ad). The element of recognition may be a familiar situation—a kitchen crisis, a school sports-day, a restaurant *tête-à-tête*, gossip in a supermarket— or it may depend on the presentation of a familiar type of product in such a way as to provoke the sensation of unfamiliarity.

The copywriter is not, of course, excluded entirely from the recognition chore. His words may achieve it simply by announcing the brand-name and saying "X is Different!" or "You've Never Seen an X like this before." But his words are there to abet the work of the designer, where recognition is concerned, as was amply proved when *Harper's Bazaar* reprinted in 1969 a selection of ads from their issue of forty years previously. They looked decidedly odd. This was nothing to do with the words, however, whose phrases—"Does Your Skin Need Freshening?" ... "A Coat for Any Occasion" ... "I once suffered from Superfluous Hair"—are depressingly familiar still in the pages of women's journals. No, the startling incongruity lay in the pictures, the hair-styles, the figure-drawing, the make-up, the whole visual presentation and effect. Today these do not communicate because few women (except perhaps the very advanced) can identify with them. Since they have nothing to do with us in appearance of dress and other externals we feel they have nothing to say to us. The recognition element is utterly absent where it primarily must be—in the design.

It is more than a matter of such obvious period sense, of course, as the indefatigable Dr. Gallup discovered when he tested "recall" on a press advert which featured a baby-carriage. If people remembered that picture of the pram at all (and only one in three ads are even remembered to *that* extent!), their recalled reaction was not "How pretty" or "How expensive" or even "Thank God I'll never need one of those things again!"—a few, just a few, merely wondered what sort of brakes it had. Actually, the ad was not promoting the baby-carriage at all, it was plugging a breakfast food!

The message-makers

The hurdle of recognition cleared, the responsibility for the effect of the advertisement devolves without compromise on the bowed shoulders of the copywriter, who is ever conscious that, in the average daily newspaper, his headline is competing against 350 others for the reader's attention. The design has, we hope, made the reader stop a moment and see, and recognise what he sees; it is up to the copy to tell him *what to think about what he sees*. Pictures can create a mood; only words can create action.

When an Old Master changes hands it is not a triumph of aesthetic principles and few pretend that it is. It's another success for commercial art, a market speculation, brought off not by a connoisseur of style but by a collector of assets. The purchaser may admire the work, he may be fascinated by the subject, but what he pays for is the signature. It's not what's on the canvas, it's what's in a name.

What's in a name is the copywriter's job. He will have already conferred with the designer on the visual, not only on the best approach for the particular selling job involved but the relative proportion of space which words and picture should occupy. He will have read up on recent issues of the medium in which the press ad will appear, to familiarise himself with the competition as well as with the editorial matter. He is no more likely to fling about clever allusions to *Paradise Lost* in *Reveille* than the designer is likely to put a blonde in a shower for the *Church Times*.

These preliminaries over, the copywriter will settle at his desk, go for a walk in the park, browse in shop windows, ride on top of a bus— whatever little private "ritual" frees his instinctive thought-processes (Shaw wrote his early plays on park-benches, Hemingway had a fixation about pencil-sharpeners). The headline will be sought, the hook that will catch the most inattentive reader who runs, whither by the promise direct or the promise indirect, the "arouser of curiosity."

The ideal line which combined both approaches turned up, in my opinion, in a press ad that appeared in the *Morning Post* two years after it had been founded by a syndicate which included both Mr. Christie and Mr. Tattersall (the paper lasted till 1935), in 1774. The advertisement read:

> "A Lady wishes to borrow One Hundred Pounds. The Security, though personal, may probably be very agreeable to a single gentleman of spirit. Every particular will be communicated with Candour and Sincerity, where confidence is so far reposed as to give the real Name and Address of the party willing to oblige the Advertiser. Gentlemen of real Fortune and liberal Sentiments, and those only, are requested to address a line to Y.N. at Mr. Dyke's Cross Street, Long-Acre."

One trusts that this particular Dyke was sufficient to dam the flood of replies! That phrase about "security being probably very agreeable" has advertising genius, no less. Another ad in the same newspaper the following year contained a counter-proposition:

> "A young Gentleman of the most liberal education and a genteel Address, would be happy in having an opportunity of devoting his services to a Lady of real fashion and fortune, who may wish to have some particular deficiencies thoroughly supplied, without subjecting herself to any disagreeable restraint. Any lady to whom such an offer may be suitable, will receive the fullest Explanation, in answer to a letter addressed to A. X. Turk's Head Coffee House, Strand."

This most apt address being not many yards distant from the one given above, it may perhaps be hoped that the advertisers got together to confer their promised benefits upon each other.

Promise can be conveyed in two ways. You can elect to promise something Brand-X will perform of itself, or you can promise that, as a result of what X can perform, the product will do something *personally* for the reader. To some extent every ad—just like those quoted—is selling its favours.

Promises, promises

Under performance, for example, the copy can promise that Brand-X will last longer, shine brighter or repel burglars. Under personal benefit, you can guarantee it will make the reader look ten years younger and bring invitations pouring in for the Royal Enclosure. The two types of promise can be combined. You can imply that not only will Brand-X groom you better or make your home more chic, it will also make the reader an instant object of admiration and envy, totally irresistible to the *au pair*, and bring him several seats on the Stock Exchange.

The copywriter may choose to present his promise in the form of a thinly-veiled threat, a promise that if the product or service is not used promptly all manner of dreadful consequences may ensue; if the reader doesn't use Amplex, ignores her ring of confidence, forgets to lock his car or consult the *TV Times*, passes up the *Daily Express*, ignores the under-stains, doesn't puff a suggestive cigar in his bird's face, doesn't move his office out of London without the mileage ingredient, has no egg for breakfast, no chocolate drink at night, doesn't have any idea who succeeded Shih Huang Ti nor who put the T in Britain.

In Advertising whatever works is right, whatever *sells* is right. There are rules good, and rules bad, and all are made to be broken by better ones. You will find some agencies very keen on a rule-book for copy and design, others who believe that the future of Advertising lies in throwing all such books away. Ogilvy has formulated a set of rules which he constantly breaks himself (e.g. the opening paragraph of body-copy should be kept down to a "maximum of eleven words,"yet his famous Hathaway Shirt ad opened with a paragraph of forty words and his ad for Puerto Rico, which he has claimed is "the most effective advertisement I have ever written" began with a para of forty-six words!).

The designer will do well to make good friends with the copywriter's headlines, which will be defended with far more zeal than the body-copy. This is because five times more people read headlines of press ads than ever read body-copy and the copywriter has lavished appropriate care on it. Nor will he ask the writer to shorten his heading unless he judges he has the most pressing of reasons; tests conducted in New York a few years ago showed that headlines of ten words *or more* sold far more of a given range of goods than shorter headlines.

As with Toulouse-Lautrec, the headline and the body-copy should form as integral a part of the overall design as any pictorial, illustrative element (*see* Fig. 5). As the composer sets words to music, so the commercial artist sets words to design.

Fig. 5.—Press ads—at stage of "presentation rough" layout—created for Royal Air Force recruitment campaign by Bloxhams. Note how visual components of the same basic advertisment have been adapted to fit varied sizes of space booked.

One final point. Though the visual arrests the initial attention, and the headline hooks it in, it is the body-copy that ensures the swallowing of hook, line and sinker, by logical, attractive, persuasive layout of fact. Moreover, since tests have also proved that, nine times out of ten, long copy outsells short copy (in one of his celebrated Rolls-Royce press ads, Ogilvy used 961 words) it is a vital aspect of the designer's art that his overall ad-design makes the words both eye-pleasingly displayed and *easily read*, two aims which are often in apparent conflict, yet must be reconciled.

Certain qualities of character should ideally be shared by both designer and copywriter. Dr. Barron, in an article "The Psychology of Imagination," published in the *Scientific American* of September 1958, said that "Creative people are especially observant, and they value accurate observation (telling themselves the truth) more than other people do... they have more ability to hold many ideas at once, and to compare more ideas with one another—hence to make a richer synthesis." My own experience feels closer to the views expressed by James Webb Young, last of the "golden age" of American copy-writers, in his famous lecture "A Technique for Producing Ideas:"

> "Every good creative person in advertising, whom I have ever known, has always had two noticeable characteristics. First, there was no subject under the sun in which he could not easily get interested—from, say, Egyptian burial customs to Modern Art. Every facet of life had fascination for him. Second, he was an extensive browser in all sorts of fields of information. For it is with the advertising man as with the cow: no browsing, no milk."

To all of which I enthusiastically subscribe, even at the risk of being called a silly moo.

POSTERS AND PACKAGING

I've spent quite a time on press advertising because of its domi-nance in the advertising budgets of most clients, but many of my comments will apply to other media, where the creative aspects are involved. In the realm of poster advertising (under which I also group tube-cards and bus-back-and-sides), where expenditure is roughly 5 per cent of the amount lavished on press media, certain unique crea-tive problems manifest themselves, and the agency never forgets that posters are being increasingly used in harness with that second biggest mopper-up of client-money, television.

The effectiveness of TV commercials can often be doubled, even tripled, by a well-planned poster campaign tie-in. For example, when we see a great sixteen-sheeter proclaiming nothing but two words BEANZ MEANZ, we don't need any further nudging to recall those Heinz TV spots. In the dismal light of past cutbacks in TV advertising one would suppose the television production companies (*see* Chapter XII) would welcome aid from whatever quarter, but last year the producers of the Proctor and Gamble detergent ads on the American networks, in my view, unwisely began a defensive assault of sly denigrations in respect of poster advertising, which prompted the Metropolitan Outdoor Network Incorporated outfit (note their initials spell MONI) to erect the following poster on one of the main freeways into New York. It read:

GO HOME!
According to "research"
You should be home
Watching P & G Ads
on TV

. . . a very effective reply—which was, from its siting, of course, quite unanswerable. It may suffer, however, from Ogilvy's stated intention one day "to start a secret society of masked vigilantes who will travel about the world on silent motor bicycles, chopping down posters at the dark of the moon."

The Duke of Windsor, when Prince of Wales, once gave poster-hoardings the accolade of "art galleries of the great public" and, looking back to Millais and Lautrec, and more recently to Dame Laura Knight and Graham Sutherland, agency designers may feel in excellently esteemed company. On the other hand, the National Council of Public Morals stated in 1917 that censorship of posters was "even more necessary than of films" and a celebrated ex-copywriter, Ogden Nash, once lyricised:

"Beneath this slab
John Brown is stowed.
He watched the ads,
And not the road."

And in another poem, he added:

"I think that I shall never see
A billboard lovely as a tree.
Indeed, unless the billboards fall.
I'll never see a tree at all."

One wonders what his sentiments would have been (as an American, he retained the ancient British term of "bill" for poster, of course) had he seen the days when the centre aisle of St. Paul's Cathedral was the most popular poster-site in London, outrivalling even modern Piccadilly and Times Square, over which G. K. Chesterton rhapsodised: "Magnificent—if only one could not read!" and the modern federal highways of the United States, which *Reader's Digest* has characterised as "a billboard slum."

Packaging, like posters, spearheads the purely visual impression that the customer has of Brand-X. The public *does* tell a book by its cover, in fact, and throughout the nation potential buyers will come to know X, not by its content but by its container; its face is indeed its fortune, as it lines the supermarket shelves or beckons from the chemist's window. The pack-designer of genius is a very rare bird indeed and the wise agency pays him accordingly. I count it my very good fortune to have worked with a star of this specialised firmament, Bob Williamson, a Canadian who makes London his base but whose reputation is international.

Picking the pack

Packaging is a prime factor, clearly, in the establishment of a "brand image." It is not the content but the container which makes the product "with it" or "square," that keeps it mod or musty, that exudes an aura of "Englishness" or "Frenchness," that proclaims the market it hopes to attract. The container announces whether X is for the young or the middle-aged (no one is *old* in Advertising), for men or women or—increasingly—for both, for luxury or practical everyday use. Perhaps the most obvious example of ever-changing trends can be found in the evolution of record-sleeve designs during the past two decades . . . it mutated from shots of performers, through "mood" covers to serried ranks of psychedelic, surrealistic and abstract designs which shriek on to Oxford Street.

The package may change in little or in much, and no client can be lightly persuaded to accept new design. Much depends on the age of his presumed market—"pack recognition" is a basic condition for campaign success and, even sometimes where the product is genuinely "new" and "improved," your client may decide that the face should remain familiar. With the permissive society racing past on the inside track, however, the packaging of contraceptives has undergone radical alteration (a friend once absent-mindedly flipped a pack under my nose, in the belief he was offering a light for my cigar!).

New pack-design may have a functional, and not primarily an emotional, aim, like the "refill" instant coffee packs introduced by Tesco, or the pull-open tops which appeared on Coca-Cola cans. The latter, as Coca-Cola admitted, were incorporated because "we felt that the best way to give impetus to our sales was to introduce ring-pull cans similar to those used by breweries." To a product whose bottle-shape had been for years an international symbol, this was a major decision.

For today's pack designers special problems exist which never threatened before. Apart from price, the Trade Descriptions Act requires that weights and formulae be clearly displayed on the pack—on top of brand-names, slogans, "house"-colours and trade-marks, this inflicts new burdens on the designer's imagination. Every cigarette pack must now carry a Government health warning. In addition, as Irene Sinclair, creative head of J.W.T.'s packaging department, once pointed out: "You're not going to design a bottle that will fall off a shelf or a box that won't stack ... one also has to face the fact that a package may be on the market for thirty years."

The cream of designers' work is shown at the International Packaging Exhibition; there is also an Institute of Packaging, and a World Packaging Organisation which concerns itself with what to do when the designers leave off ... and leave behind a cancerous wasteland of polythene, plastic and P.V.C., a forest of pyramids, each topped by that single invention which has done more to revolutionise pack-design than any world war, midnight oil, or executive ukase—the aerosol. We mustn't, however, omit to refer here to the special problem plaguing all Advertising creativity: in the words of Oliver Waley, head of the Packaging Group at Lintas (who designed a more "mature" wrapper for Walls chocolate ice-cream), no matter how much sweat and genius the designer applies to the package, "it will eventually be designed by the chairman."

From which, God save us all. But no saviour will arise or descend for the designer who forgets another prime demand he must meet. His package must not only lure the customer, proclaim honestly the contents and mollify the client, it must also look good incorporated into press ads, TV commercials and posters. If a package cannot make, in photographer's jargon, a good "pack shot," then *ipso facto*, it's a lousy package. Television we come to in Chapter XII. For now, let's return to the poster.

Writing on the wall

Yes, essentially, this is what all poster-art is, or certainly should be where Advertising's concerned. It all began, you might say, with the Stone-Age poster art in the Caves of Altamira, where the woolly rhinos and bison of Palaeolithic designers anticipated by several million years the morose bull in the wonderful poster designed in 1896 by W. H. Caffyn, who gazed (the bull, that is) at a bottle of Bovril and sighed tearfully: "Alas! My poor brother!" The Rosetta Stone was a poster whose writing on the wall boded ill for Napoleon (could he have read it) as the message "Mene, Mene, Tekel, Upharsin" did for Belshazzar. As it proved on the plaster at Babylon the poster should be as transient as it is indelible on the reader's memory.

Posters will fail if they are too fretted with art and not with craft, too wrapped up in splended graphics rather than hard graft (McKnight Kauffer's *The Art of the Poster* should be a beacon not a bible). The aim is always effectiveness, not effect, and there are eight distinct ways in which posters can help achieve the sales-targets hopefully prognosticated for Brand-X:

1. They increase the effectiveness of televison advertising, so that the two media are rapidly turning into a double-act.

2. They allow you to pin-point your target area, by booking strategic sites that will corner customers, the locations being chosen either for geographic, social or economic reasons. And they allow you, in so doing, to hit your target bang-on, again and again and again.

3. They give you the effectiveness of a super-large press ad, without the short life of the average advertisement—posters can come nearest, in fact, to achieving the much-feared "subliminal" effect. Your poster cannot be discarded with the morning paper or the Sunday Supplement (or hung up in that little room in the backyard). Moreover, it remains there every day for commuters to see and note on their way to work *and back*.

4. *Posters cannot be ignored*. They don't have to run the risk of faulty reproduction in newspapers or magazines. They don't have to compete with or defeat fascinating editorial matter (or, much worse, boring editorial, which the reader will flip hastily by, throwing out your "baby" with the bathwater). The poster runs no risk of your potential customer leaving the TV set to brew tea or answer the door or a call of nature or of telephone, while the commercial break flatulently expends itself.

5. Instead of having to compete for attention, posters are the sole distraction offered on railway and Tube platforms (not to mention that sole forum for respectable kinkiness, the Tube escalator), or, in the case of buses and Tube-cards, on public transport itself. Often your poster needn't be all that good, so long as it's *there*. In the love-making of Advertising, propinquity is all. If your girl model for bikini, tights or girdle gets a moustache drawn on her—or worse—little harm is done. Sometimes the contrary; Marilyn Rickards, who queened it for Nelbarden swimwear on the moving stairs for several seasons, is flattered by graphic emendations, she says. London Transport itself is duly transported, since it made £1·6 million in 1975 from giving their 2,000 million annual patrons the chance to show their artistry on the lady.

6. Posters can succeed in that sense where films still maintain an advantage over television. Its pictures are often larger than life, and remember that with many customers still this *does* automatically mean twice as natural and hence, twice as persuasive. Like Greek drama, which relied on the principle of conviction which Wilde enunciated about Man: "Give him a mask, and he will tell you the truth."

7. Coverage by posters is even higher than TV's fantastic peak of 85 per cent. Posters can reach 94 per cent of the target!

8. This final point is of utmost importance, when selling a brilliantly creative poster idea to the Brand Manager—posters are one of the cheapest media there is, in terms of cost per thousand. An I.P.A. survey, for example, taken several years ago, showed that a budget of £46,800, spent over three months on coverage of England and Wales alone, would reach an audience of 24 million *every week*, at a cost of only 3d per thousand so-called "opportunities to see."

Provocativeness (and maybe a pinch of provocation) will do fine on a poster, but the best use of such design will, I repeat, be in harness with other media on your Brand-X campaign. No campaign of substance can be built on posters alone. Goods are not sold on the poster-site ... but the "come hither" look *is* sold there. To get the message the passers-by must get the picture, in no uncertain terms. I have mentioned the analogy that all ads are really "selling their favours." Well, you're in business on the poster-site, making a proposition. Like the lady under the lamp-post, your poster will raise its enticing skirt on corners all over the countryside. It's the designer's job to make the best possible use of the pitch, so his visual language must be unmistakable and direct to the point (whether or not he uses words as an ingredient).

There was a recent poster in the United States which stated the analogy with utmost candour. Advertising its own services, an agency placarded these very words, in huge lettering on the billboard:

THE OLDEST PROFESSION
IN THE WORLD.
CALL 223-3888.

In a press ad you have body-copy, and if visual and headline have done their work well, time to explain and amplify your selling points. On a poster the time just isn't there. You can't arrest life, alas—certainly not twentieth-century life—like a stop-frame frozen on a film-projector. The reel spins on, and succeeding scenes compete for attention with your poster, just passed, gone by, maybe forgotten. In poster advertising you must catch the world on the run and everyone is running at an ever faster pace. At the last timecheck your poster has, on average, a maximum of five seconds to work!

WHO'S YOUR WITNESS?

Posters and press ads have a wide option of tactics they can employ, and illustrative angles. Most admen on the creative side are familiar with the rhyme:

> When the client moans and sighs,
> Make his Logo twice the size.
> If he still should prove refractory,
> Show a picture of the factory.
> Only in the gravest cases
> Should you show the clients' faces.

. . . all of which good, sound advice is regularly ignored in the advertising of politics.

There is one very potent weapon from the adman's arsenal which we have not yet touched on—the testimonial. The lay public is perhaps most conscious of it through the box, where Fanny Craddock—with Johnny's monocle gleaming encouragement to the "A" and "B" customers—not unnaturally tells us her partwork on cooking is the greatest, John Gregson told us how he somehow sensed a super cigar each time he saw the name Embassy and Anita Harris's loving Mum fills the thrush with Bisto, though my favourite will always be Clement Freud's lugubrious "dialogues" with his bloodhound. Meanwhile, the delightful Mrs. Cooper stokes up our sometime British and European Heavyweight Champion at the range, and even the great ex-Wimbledon champion Rod Laver is smashed hilariously off the tennis-court by the fizz of You-Know-Who!

These are testimonials, for which big money is paid (they helped boost George Best's income to £20,000 per year and Dusty Springfield got the far-from-dusty sum of £10,000 for her series of TV spots—though the earnings palm must surely go for ever to retired racing-car ace Jackie Stewart, who garners over £500,000 per annum from product promotions, including one for Glenfiddich Whisky, though he himself is a teetotaller). They are used extensively in direct mail, as we shall see in the next chapter, and we find them in many press ads and on the hoardings. Testify means literally "bearing witness," and every gospel truth must have its witnesses—only today agencies insist they appear more reliable than those celebrated four in the *New Testament* ("New" had its great selling power even then!), who in fact never laid eyes on Christ, wrote their testimonials fifty years after the event and had probably never been near Palestine in their lives. But slip-ups will always occur where least expected. An American agency which used actor Patrick O'Neal for a TV beer commercial, and paid $10,000 for the privilege, discovered too late that he was a member of that other A.A., Alcoholics Anonymous. Unfortunately, not Anonymous enough for the agency, who sued him for the cost of making the commercial, $280,000!

As James Webb Young, to whose lecture "A Technique for Producing Ideas" we have already referred in this chapter, spelled it out: "Every type of advertiser has the same problem; namely, to be believed. The mail-order man knows nothing so potent for this purpose as the *testimonial* ..." (author's italics). Mail-order is often confused with direct mail and certainly much direct mail is also mail-order, but the expression refers exclusively to Advertising which aims to elicit a *direct response*, usually by means of a coupon, i.e. you expect the reader to be so swayed by the ad that he at once picks up his pen and orders some Brand-X. This immediate response is likely to be elicited much more surely when the ad includes a testimonial.

BELOW THE LINE = BELOW THE BELT?

There are some who think so, who think about it at all. We shall pause to think on it a moment, since client spending on "Below-the-Line" advertising is on the increase, though to what precise extent is shyly shrouded in mystery by many on both sides of the client—agency partnership. The term simply refers to any advertising which does not directly solicit sales of Brand-X—since this can mean anything from incentive-bonus schemes for retailers to giveaway-buttons, from cut-price offers to coupons, Green Shield stamps and customer competitions, the creative department is clearly going to be tender on the subject.

At the Advertising Association's 1970 Conference, held at Brighton in May of a worrying topsy-turvy year, both approval and disapproval was voiced. The Joint Managing Director of the Spar–Vivo supermarket chain warned the assembled admen that retailers were fed up with coupons and added: "You should make sure that you are getting value for money from below the line activity." The Conference learned, however, that both Brylcreem and the National Coal Board had benefited greatly from such activity, the N.C.B.'s holiday competition costing £100,000 and bringing in extra sales of £3 million.

Obviously, artists and writers are only incidentally employed on below-the-line work. They may have to think up button-slogans like "FORGET OXFAM, FEED TWIGGY," dream up a picture-quiz like the New English Library's jigsaw puzzle of famous Great Nudes to make one eternal *Penthouse* "Pet" (on a joint-promotion with the magazine), design display-cards for giveaway coins or produce a book like the extremely successful *Dairy Book of Home Management* which earned over £20,000 profit. Often, however, these special jobs are given over either to the client's "house" creative team, or to one of the many firms now established to produce specialised promotion gimmicks, of varying quality, and nothing else.

The defensive posture adopted by creative people towards an activity which was once fringe, but now threatens quite a massive invasion of client appropriation, is understandable. Being entirely non-media the activity scarcely recommends itself to agency executives, either, who see their 15 per cent commission being steadily emaciated. Its chief heinousness lies, however, in the fact that it deprives copywriter and designer of their prime incentive (or what *should* be their prime incentive)—the positive reaction of the customer in terms of sales, the immediately traceable cause and effect.

How they must long for the days when slogans could be printed on the backs of postage-stamps (after licking, the message blossomed on the tongue!), when a one-volume edition of *Pepys's Diary* could include fifty-six pages of advertisements, when advertising slides— now tamely confined to cinemas—could be projected on to Nelson's Column and the outside of the National Gallery, when the "Mad" Major Christopher Draper could fly a banner advertising cream crackers over the head of King George V while His Majesty tried to declare open the Mersey Tunnel, when carriages shaped like bottles or top-hats could trot round London smothered in posters (anticipating our minicabs), when opened umbrellas were bedecked with ads and posters and, above all, when *Lloyd's Weekly Newspaper* could stamp its advertisement on copper coins which remained valid and negotiable ... after which, Shell's "Man in Space" and "Vintage Cars" coinage seem pretty tame stuff!

Touching on this—to creative men—sore subject, does, however, bring us to an area of advertising which is seldom "mentioned in public" or even plain-wrapper-covered print, and that is trade advertising. It seems somehow indecent to discuss parts of it, what one might call the private parts. Such glamour-image as Brand-X may possess is considered soiled, rather as if we were being reminded that our favourite film-star or top model goes regularly to the lavatory like everyone else.

CREATIVITY IN TRADE

This is a strange reticence, as you will see at once on consulting the pages of *BRAD*. In my particular copy there are seventy-eight pages devoted to various consumer publications. To list the full number of trade and technical publications requires two hundred pages, about *three times as much*. I would suggest that our general air of decorum (most unusual in Advertising) in referring to such "facts of life" is a Victorian hangover from the time when people draped maxi-skirts over piano-legs and, if ever they could bring themselves to acknowledge the world of everyday commerce, preferred to speak only of those regrettable folk who were "in trade."

It was, of course, in the Victorian era that trade and technical journals made their first appearance, though they then multiplied rapidly. Even as recently, however, as 1962, when Blanche Elliott was writing *A History of English Advertising* she discovered that her inquiries regarding trade publications "merely evoked a mild surprise that they should be considered of any interest at all." She goes on: "The value of the work they perform is scarcely appreciated by the public, who are for the most part ignorant of their existence, since they only circulate amongst members of each trade." She could have added that those who do subscribe to a particular trade journal are usually utterly unconscious of, and uninterested in, the fact that journalists exist for trades in other fields than their own, yet the British Association of Industrial Editors numbers over 1,100 members! Including me.

Nor must we forget that many of these trade journals exert an influence outside their technical sphere. *Lloyd's Weekly Newspaper*, mentioned above, was a trade paper of course. The *Drapers' Record* carried on a running feud with the dictatorial William Whiteley, founder of the world's first big department store in 1863, whose boast that he could supply anything from "a pin to an elephant" was later transferred in the public mind to an establishment south of the Park. The journal attacked Whiteley's tyrannical methods with his staff (he was later murdered at the store, in a *cause célèbre*). The *Confectioners' Union* usurped Pears' slogan of "cleanliness is next to godliness," which could have implied either that soap tasted delicious or that most sweets tasted of soap! The *Funeral Trades Gazette* could boast Oscar Wilde as a contributor at the same time as he was writing for the *Pall Mall Gazette* (later to become the *Evening Standard*) and his comments on some burial practices are still apt:

> "... If a man needs an elaborate tombstone in order to remain in the memory of his country, it is clear that his living at all was an act of superfluity. Keats's grave is a hillock of green grass with a plain headstone, and is to me the holiest place in Rome. There is in Westminster Abbey a periwigged Admiral in a nightgown hurried off to heaven by two howling cherubs, which is one of the best examples I know of ostentatious obscurity."

Few trade journals have scintillated with prose such as this, alas, but their pages are valuable storehouses of historical and social comment on the past and more of them should be appropriately esteemed in the present. After all, *The Financial Times* is a trade paper, while the lists of best and worst-dressed men in the *Tailor and Cutter* make headline news round the world.

Making trade winds blow

Bearing these remarks in mind the reader may now be less surprised than he might otherwise have been to know that much of an advertising agency's time—indeed, some of the creative department's most valuable time—is taken up with filling the advertising spaces of the vast area of trade media (films, show-cards, etc., as well as Press) represented by those 200 pages of *BRAD*.

The advertising profession would, quite simply, wither and die without trade advertising. So would most of our industry today: without its essential "plumbing" the commercial physique of this country would be very sick indeed. Some of the work I am most proud of (like the half-page ad in *Design* which led directly to my client being awarded a contract at Kennedy Airport) has been in this field, but the public never hears of such work, admen themselves seldom discuss it and it never receives any prizes. If it *works*, that must be the creative man's satisfaction.

Behind almost every glamorous consumer campaign lies the crucial trade campaign, and it effects the buying public acutely. Before the customer is presented with his choice the shopkeeper chooses what he will display on the shelves; before the public is wooed the publican must be won—and the creative effort here is, quite literally, wholesale.

The biggest single work on advertising film I've ever undertaken was a documentary for Churchman's Cigars, which was never intended for the eyes of the public at all. Yet the operation was as bigtime as any feature film—the production employed well-known actors, an ex-Rank Organisation producer, a top animation company (*see* Chapter XII), expensive effects and setting (all in colour!) and, if immodesty permits, an experienced screenwriter (since I worked for two years in cinema and television before entering the advertising profession). The sole audience for this mini-spectacular was to be groups of small tobacconists.

When the Press treats itself as a product its main concern is to address itself, not to the reader but to the advertiser—it is Advertising which finances the Press, not readership—and the A.B.C. circulation figures are important for their influence in attracting new advertisers, not as an outward and visible sign of success with the public. Before you started this book you may never even have heard of *Campaign*, yet a large proportion of the Press ads you see in the consumer Press would never reach your eyes at all if the journals like *Woman's Realm*, *The Engineer* and *The Times* did not first promote themselves and their audited circulations in the main trade medium of the advertising world.

Copy and designs on trade

The creative techniques employed by copywriter and designer will be exactly the same as those already touched on in relation to consumer advertising. But since the target is very different, there are two essential changes in the field of fire: (1) the target is much more canny and ad-weary, and (2) the character of the promise alters—it will still be as ideally "large" as Dr. Johnson recommended in his *Idler* essay, but the benefit will not be to make the customer better (or, as some admen prefer to say "a better person"), or healthier, wiser, stronger, or more lovely. Only richer. Following, we may note, precisely the Doctor's own example, when he himself was advertising the sale of a brewery's contents to potential publicans:

> "We are not here to sell boilers and vats, but the potentiality of growing rich beyond the dreams of avarice."

Your modern copywriter will refrain from putting his case that steeply, but his aim will be the same and have similar expectations of reaction to the bait. The materialistic society is no modern phenomenon, nor was in any age.

The shopkeeper who scans his trade advertisements is not looking for sweeter breath but sweeter profits. He's not after "happiness" but that far more elusive state, solvency. If your press ad can keep a promise on that score, then depend on it, that shopkeeper will certainly *feel* better, healthier, wiser and the rest, and he'll also seem the loveliest thing on two knees who ever crawled to his bank-manager.

The creative team is, at this stage, directing its efforts exclusively towards the "selling-in" process; selling, that is, Brand-X into the shop. A trade campaign persuades the retailer to order sufficient supplies for a handsome display, as well as adequate stock to meet hoped-for demand, so the trade "launch" may well precede the consumer launch by anything up to six months or more. Nevertheless, the creative work must be undertaken in parallel with the trade promotion—if possible, by the same copywriter–designer team—so that you can parade proofs of the consumer press ads (and TV commercials or whatever) before the stockist. He naturally expects evidence that the public will first *want* Brand-X, and then will come in and *buy* X from him in large enough quantities to justify the preliminary order your trade ads solicit. He must be convinced of the demand.

More pieces of eight

Your consumer-oriented poster may possibly stand use as a display-card in the shop-window or on the counter (though space is begrudged in that quarter), but completely new approaches are generally needed. Methods of selling-in can be conveniently grouped into another eight main divisions of creativity:

1. You convince the stockist that he may confidently expect demand for Brand-X. The first part of your evidence for this—a most vital part—is to show him your projected and prepared consumer campaign, explaining how and why you think it will work, telling him the various media in which it will appear, with dates and times of publication and/or transmission. The second part of your evidence consists of listing the factors which you contend make Brand-X so desirable, either in price or quality, or—if you're lucky (or a liar)—in both. You may send the stockist some samples, for his own or his family's use.

2. You dangle the personal benefit before him, making crystal clear the profits that are in it for him, and the mouth-watering discounts he will receive for large orders.

3. An *extra* benefit is then temptingly described. This has nothing to do with profit, but is directly related to sales; it takes the form of prizes for achieving given sales-targets, for attractive shop and window displays, or perhaps a competition which, while unrelated to sales-volume, is only open to stockists who are willing to order *now* a stated minimum quantity.

4. You send to the retailers some prestige and goodwill gimmicks. These may involve calendars (the Pirelli Tyre Company spent about £32,000 on its celebrated calendar of "lovelies" which were frequently "re-sold" as collectors' items for £25-plus by lucky recipients and—now discontinued—have been published as an "Art" volume), inscribed ball-points, ashtrays, even theatre-tickets or holidays abroad. Again, there are now a number of firms who specialise in providing "instant" schemes of this sort, with the attendant fixtures and fittings!

5. You convey strongly the *spur to action*. As with the consumer campaign, this urges the reader to buy—but this time the prices are the wholesale tags and often embrace various discounts, while the distribution arrangements are fully described.

6. You transmit to retailers a set of *sales aids* bundled up in an eye-catching pack. With these you explain to the shopkeeper that not only will your consumer campaign bring the customers pounding on his door, not only will his profits be fast and enormous, but you will boost him up the ladder of success, to millionairedom and tycoonery, by supplying him with FREE sales-aids, such as dump-bins, window-stickers, show-cards—maybe even a visiting pop star (for £200 per cut ribbon). All this altruistic, "disinterested" aid is of course to appropriate for Brand-X as much of his selling space

as you can. Often, however, your free offer of such aid will depend, as usual, on the size of his initial order.

7. Your copywriter and designer will extend their efforts to trade exhibitions (unless, here again, a specialist firm handles the assignment, *see* Chapter XII). Trade fairs and trade exhibitions are held on a large scale in this country and Europe, ranging from affairs at Earls Court and Olympia to smaller-scale confrontations where solutions are one-part creative sales-technique and three parts booze, bosoms and general *bonhomie*. Your back-up service to the front-up service of girl-guides will include design of show-stands for Brand-X, posters, distribution-racks, leaflets and various product displays. In 1971 Gallaher's agents Hobson Bates (in conjunction with Russell Artists Merchandising) thought up a Manikin distribution pack which had sections of a bikini-dolly on each side. If the retailer wanted to see the whole pin-up he had to buy five boxes to line up in a row!

8. Film-strips may have to be produced—these are essentially up-to-date versions of the old Magic Lantern, and they can be shown in assembly-halls, in boardrooms or on the Chairman's own desk.

Ethical pharmaceuticals

It is arguably true that the "Rolls-Royce" of trade advertising is the work done for (or, more usually, by) the big Drug Houses—the most expensive, certainly, and often the most imaginative. Firms like Smith, Kline & French and the Bayer Company employ their own large creative departments of extremely well-paid artists and writers to produce a continuous stream of promotional material the public never sees. Some of it goes into medical journals, of course, and trade publications like the *Chemist and Druggist*, but most of it goes in the form of direct mail (*see* the next chapter) to government ministries, chemists, doctors, clinics, university medical departments, and hospital technicians such as radiographers and physiotherapists. Many doctors get ten mailings per day slipping through their letter-boxes, and much of the work is very effective in that often these doctors then ask their patients to try them out.

Whatever the nature of the product, however, the design and copy approach to trade advertising for X must centre on X itself. The glamour of the reader is no longer implied, but the glamour of the product. In consumer advertising the creative people are aiming to give the reader a vicarious personality through the use of Brand-X; their psychological tool is empathy, the projection of one's personality into, and identification with, a contemplated object. Trade advertising aims to give the object itself a personality—this is called *anthropomorphism*, which is still, in a way, a profitable form of self-interest.

There are times, of course, when, by careful selection, the creative team can hope to land their press ad in a medium which will reach both the trade and the customer in one fell swoop. They can do this by having their advertisement in the specific issue of a trade journal which may well be read by an audience outside its normal circulation. *Campaign* runs a feature directory which can aid them enormously to reach such a twin goal, since it gives agencies advance warning of special-interest articles coming up in various magazines and newspapers around the country.

COST OF COMMERCIAL ART

In exercising the skills described in this chapter the creative department have used a lot of client money; the Brand Manager will have been prepared for a large percentage to be eaten up by press ads, of course, for both the trade and the customer. The Account Executive will have to see that he is also prepared for the cost of the other creative elements of the campaign for Brand-X, whether "above" or "below" the line, and settle on fees that leave the agency a decent profit that will pay for a first-class creative service.

Many clients have still to be educated in how much money creative talent does, in fact, cost; that, as Vance Packard instances in *The Waste Makers*, the package can sometimes cost "ten times as much as the product inside" and that "the average United States family today spends five hundred dollars of its income each year just for the package!"; that for every £1 of profit, Cadbury's spend over £1 on advertising; that Lord Beaverbrook's various promotional gift schemes were once running at a cost of 41p (8s. 3d.) per new reader (and succeeding beyond his wildest dreams!); that Esso and Shell spent £500,000 each within three months on their respective "coin" promotions; that the Decimal Currency Board spent about £450,000 (which means *we* spent it!) on posters and giveaway booklets; that racehorses have been paid, and paid well, for "testimonials;" that the Labour Party (through K.M.P.) were happy to pay Alan Aldridge £600 for his Tory "puppets;" and that, as long ago as 1888, Thomas Barratt was happy to pay £20,000 for his Bubbles poster!

Now we shall take a look at how the copy and design men and women deal with direct mail—a subject to which a recent book about "campaign planning," over three hundred pages long, devoted exactly *twelve* pages—an item of advertising expenditure which is hardly ever mentioned in any learned survey of billings though it consumes over £120 million annually, a medium which deploys the third highest advertising expenditure in Britain.

Perhaps I am prejudiced. Together with Gordon Crossley, the designer for the Oxfam account at the time, I once wrote a letter and leaflet for the famous charity that brought in over £200,000 including two cheques for £5,000 each. So naturally I consider it a medium well worth our attention.

Chapter XI

THE ADMAN'S ARSENAL—2

Let us begin by recalling to mind one sultry evening in the deserts of Asia Minor, when the victorious general in that dreary Middle Eastern conflict which had dragged on and off for years, retired to his tent and wrote home to his theoretical (and chair-bound, back-seat-driving) superiors one of the most famous promotional letters in history. Three words only in it, *veni, vidi, vici,* have been enough to flame down the centuries between and illumine forever for us that extraordinary man and his times.

That was 47 B.C. Now, let us jump to 1769 and recall the deadly invective of an anonymous correspondent who helped destroy a Prime Minister with the words (which would have done for the much more recent incumbent):

> "You are so little accustomed to receive any marks of respect or esteem from the public, that if in the following lines a compliment or expression of applause should escape me, I fear you would consider it as a mockery of your established character ... You have nice feelings ... if we may judge from your resentments. Cautious, therefore, of giving offence where you have so little deserved it, I shall leave the illustration of your virtues to other hands ... You have done good by stealth. The rest is upon record ..."

and in another letter took King George III to task in an "open letter" for his attitude to the American colonists, cautioning His Majesty bluntly that he who "plumes himself upon the security of his title to the crown, should remember that, as it was acquired by one revolution, it may be lost by another." Unfortunately, the much-feared "Junius" brought down only one Cabinet to find it replaced by a worse one, that of Lord North. He ensured himself wide readership for his letters, however, by publishing them in the pages of the *Public Advertiser,* which also carried such notorious ads as those for "Harris's List of Covent Garden Ladies" which, needless to say, did not refer to dowager patrons of the Opera House!

Let's make another jump and land in 1943, when a certain heating equipment firm wrote a letter marking the culmination of an outstandingly successful sales campaign, which started: "We acknowledge receipt of your order for five triple furnaces"—and Auschwitz was in business.

THE GREATEST MESSAGE EVER SOLD

Three letters. One formed the legendary cornerstone of Triumphs which, though it spurred Caesar's assassins, also spawned that dynastic dictatorship of emperors which gave to Rome its greatest days before the fall. One terrified an entire ruling class and did much to encourage the insurrection of the United States. One put in train the implementation of a "final solution" in a concentration camp where three-quarters of a million victims were duly incinerated, including 400,000 Jews ... the most catastrophic of all the terrible events which impelled the re-creation of Israel.

This second founding of the Jewish nation came nearly two thousand years after its destruction by Roman butchers—with one million victims that time. And some twenty years before the fall of Jerusalem in A.D. 70 another sort of sales letter had been written ... composed by a Jew who called himself a Roman and wrote in Greek. Date-marked Antioch (in modern Turkey), the letter was addressed "unto the churches of Galatia." The greatest, longest-running direct mail promotion the world has ever seen had begun—one of the most recent "mailings" of all, signed by the most recent namesake of that first copywriter, set the Western nations in turmoil over the Pill.

No disrespect is, of course, intended, much less any blasphemy. The letters of Paul of Tarsus, as much as those today of Paul VI, were deliberately planned for promotion and persuasion, carefully designed, then as now, to be read aloud in churches. Though only the future will be able fairly to compare results from the promotional talents of Paul the Tentmaker, as against those whom some have called, provoked and provocative alike, Paul the Rentmaker (for the violent divisions of opinion among Roman Catholics caused by some of his pronouncements).

IN THE MAIL, ON THE MAKE

Nothing to do with promoting Brand-X? Perhaps you hold that epistolary days are past, and good riddance. In a limited sense you'd be right, of course. The telephone first, then the telegram, now telex and the computer, have combined in unholy alliance to bring a new age of illiteracy in communication ... S.T.D. has replaced P.S. But it still needed only one encyclical from Rome to shake the world; it required only one letter from Einstein to touch off the nuclear age.

The fact is that though we write fewer personal and public letters than ever—and those, worse than ever—we *receive* far more than we've ever done before. Even as the enchanting Millimant bewailed in *The Way of the World* as long ago as 1700, so may many a modern housewife say to the mounting tides of direct mail pouring through her letter-box: "I am persecuted with letters—I hate letters—nobody knows how to write letters; and yet one has 'em, one does not know why."

Not that the Post Office would echo her moans. With several thousand million items of direct mail being stamped each year, that's a tidy sum of revenue no government would willingly denounce or reject, let the anti-advertising lobby huff and puff as it may. Exchequer needs aside, however, I think this present chapter will do much to explain to that housewife (and to the student) a good deal of that anguished "why," and why direct mail clients deem it worth spending many millions of pounds per year on it. Mark Elwes, Executive Director of the Direct Mail Producers Association, while frankly admitting the difficulty of estimating total expenditure (many clients won't admit to using mail-shots) reckoned at least £20 million went on the medium last year, giving it third place behind TV and Press in the appropriation stakes.

The effect and repute of this form of promotion can be traced right back professionally to the "Father of Advertising" himself, one John Houghton, who in the August of 1683 (the same month that Pepys, recalled to high office from disgrace and near-execution, recommenced briefly the diary which failing eyesight had regrettably terminated fourteen years before) printed one of the first ads for hot chocolate in the twelfth issue of his publication entitled *A Collection of Letters*. You can trace it still in the recent best-seller from Eric Ambler who—knowledgeable of the power of direct mail as only an ex-copywriter could be—uses in *The Intercom Conspiracy* the plot-device of a series of embarrassing newsletters to the top spy-bosses of both East and West.

Not so astonishing then that when Garland Compton asked ten new recruits to the agency to make predictions for the state of Advertising in 1980, their Orwellian visions were dominated not by Big Brother, but by a sinister all-reaching Being called Direct Mailman!

THE INVOLVEMENT MEDIUM

I *don't* believe the medium is the message or ever was (I wonder, by the way, how long it is since Marshall McLuhan was called Horace?)—it is servant not master. The telegram can tell you you've lost a friend or won the pools, the hot lines of Cabinets and Kremlins can serve linkmanship just as much as brinkmanship, and direct mail was never as black as some have painted it—when, that is, they have not been too busy ignoring its very existence.

We will consider the term to include any written matter—illustrated or not—or any object or gimmick that drops through your letter-box with the aim of stimulating sales, mailings which make the recipient well disposed towards the product and determined to buy it as soon as opportunity occurs. Direct mail can be intended for the householder's breakfast-table, for the doctor's surgery (*see* Chapter X), for the office of a college principal, or for the desk of a Sales Manager or Managing Director—though some secretaries claim that mailing shots which arrive Friday afternoon or Monday morning are doomed.

However that may be, the creative team will often seek to turn goodwill into "opportunity to buy" at one stroke by including a coupon with their letter, leaflet, brochure or whatever, a coupon *which the recipient must fill in*. Take careful note of the emphasis, for it is very important to involve the recipient in actively *doing* something and doing something which can be made to appear vital and important. The coupon which just has to be mailed back in will almost never elicit the same response as one which compels the customer to "complete" it. It will certainly never elicit the same *selling* response. The coupon must require at least the ticking of a box, the affixing of a specially designed "gift stamp," the signing of a "certificate."

THE COUPON IS THE CRUX

Both copywriter and designer are aware, or should be, how crucial is the combined effort that goes into creating the humble coupon. For this, as they say, is where the action is, where it all happens or it doesn't and where all the imagination and originality they put collectively into letter and leaflet will, or will not, pay off. That small line in caps which says "Post Within Two Weeks To Obtain Free Offer" may be the most critical typographical problem facing the designer in the entire mailing shot!

The problem is by no means confined to the aesthetical, and designers must be thoroughly familiar with regulations as to cards and folders through the mail. These can be found in the latest *Post Office Guide* (make sure it is the latest, as it is constantly being updated) which contains such ignore-at-your-peril information as that the preferred thickness for business reply cards is 250 micrometres, that colours are permissible if they are pale and that all the lettering should be in one strong colour, preferably black. As to Direct Mail envelopes, U.K. authorities are more lenient than they were (almost anything goes in the States) and most colours are allowed except red, always assuming that the designer keeps in mind the sensitive retinas of Her Majesty's postmen. Such considerations may seem irritatingly trivial to a young adman, but carelessness on these points will leave the client most unimpressed with the brilliance of the creative department.

While not every mailing will include a coupon, the principles which operate behind those vital rows of dots are precisely those which make direct mail such an outstanding medium. And their key factor is literally just that ... a key. Every coupon is coded by an unobtrusive key-letter or number which lets the advertiser know at once from which region and town—even which street—the reply or order has come. (In press advertisements which are couponed, the same device shows at a glance which edition, of which page, in which journal, pulled most replies.)

There are many organisations which exist solely to process response to such mailings, and these firms are expert in tabulating keyed coupons for a wide variety of clients and agencies ... indeed, they may have supplied the mailing list, and if the list isn't kept up to date, some strange responses can result. One mailing not long ago went to the dean of a Yorkshire priory and came back marked "Gone Away"—further research revealed that this particular dean has been charged with sodomy and adultery and had been made rather forcibly redundant by Henry VIII in 1540 ... so indeed had the whole priory!

CREATIVITY IN DIRECT MAIL

The proper care and maintenance, however, of the mailing list are not the province of the creative people. What *is* their responsibility is the selling power of design and copy, and informing their instincts and inspiration in this regard will be another eight points:

1. Though admittedly direct mail is relatively expensive on a "cost per thousand" estimate, if their work brings results they know the promotion will prove far *less* expensive than other media on the basis of cost *per order*, which is the only reckoning that matters. In sum, direct mail can be an extremely profitable medium when correctly used—so neither copywriter nor designer should stint his imagination (certainly not on the first "roughs" they submit), always provided that originality never loses touch with the selling aim.

2. With direct mail, the creative men can aim to hit the target where he lives. In the home! And their sights can precisely zero in on *which* home, once the Account Executive has let them see the mailing list. Ideally, they will be familiar with the reader's probable income, sex and occupation, his age, his hobbies and his social and cultural interests. Direct mail has the inestimable advantage of being supremely *personal*, a point which can trip the amateur up but one which the real pro seizes on with avidity. It is in direct mail that creative men prove their true mettle, which is why so many shy away from it under such camouflage as that recently used

by a top copywriter when he confessed to John Winsley in *Campaign*: "I'm not awfully good at mail order, I find it so boring." The man who is tired of London, said Dr. Johnson, is tired of life ... and the same comment can be applied to direct mail moaners.

3. Everyone *likes* receiving mail. In this field the target comes halfway to meet you. Something in the morning post (no matter how temporarily) makes the recipient feel wanted and important; he knows that at least someone, somewhere, has *taken the trouble to look up his address*. Even the unwelcome reminder notice or income-tax form purveys the inestimable sense of power a handy waste-basket gives—fleeting though that power may prove! Even the importance of being a "consumer target" is better than no importance at all, and this is particularly true of the lonely, bored housewife, prime target of almost all mailings. Your recipient *wants* to believe, making a wonderful springboard for both copy and design to hold scepticism at bay (for what it's worth, one survey has suggested the Irish are the most naturally credulous of recipients, the least so being the Spanish).

4. Direct mail is a magnificent learn-by-trial-and-error tool of promotion. Because of the mailing list you can ring the changes of appeal more than in any other media, depending on whether the letter-box you're aiming for belongs to a Durham coalminer, a Surrey stockbroker or a belligerent Protestant from Falls Road. The copywriter can refine the test shots more than the designer, as you might suppose, since he can try out two different letters for opposite ends of the same street! When working on the Oxfam account (*see* Chapter X) I once, for the same appeal, wrote a dozen varied letters to categories such as regular-givers, occasional givers, emergency givers, annual givers, and so on—even presumed-dead givers, which (like that appeal to the Yorkshire dean) suggests a new extra-dimensional meaning to the phrase "advertising medium." For another client (who had better stay nameless) I once created a series of test-mailings spread over two years *for a product that didn't even exist* ... it was the tabulated and analysed results of those weird efforts that in fact brought the hypothetical product into existence. The product was, in the end, just what the customer had, albeit unwillingly, ordered. Such is the awesome power of the copywritten word!

5. Neither copywriter nor designer has any restrictions of space or length in direct mail, provided you keep—in your final presentation—within the agreed creative budget. Very long copy, informal but informative, sells much better than short copy, though most clients (and indeed far too many agencies) still remain very uneducated about this. The designer, for his part, can work on all sizes

of stock, folded in a wide variety of ways, all shapes, all types of textures, real or simulated—frequently he has any combination of colours at his disposal. Best of all, as far as challenge goes (and creativity thrives on it), he can work his wicked ways on the envelope itself, within the area okayed by Post Office regulations, which allow much broader scope than they used to. Design and copy on the outside of the envelope are intended to lure the prospect into hidden regions of promise, however, so care will be taken that recipients aren't scared off, repelled or intimidated by too much "outside" information. On occasion, the design may be three-dimensional!

6. Direct mail tells the creative man how effective his solutions to the selling problem are, in a degree impossible to the majority of press advertising, posters, point-of-sale, TV commercials or radio spots. It is the one medium to which Lord Leverhulme's plaint that he never knew which half of his budget he was wasting does not apply. With direct mail, you *know*.

7. Creative men can function in a more completely self-contained and fully-realised way in a direct mail campaign for Brand-X—it is the one *all-inclusive* selling and persuading medium; one of my private nicknames for it is the "Complete Angler"—all angles are covered since direct mail can dispense with all need for salesmen, retail outlets, distribution-centres and storage depots. It gives you the shortest distance between client and customer—which is why copywriter and designer must be on guard that they draw a straight creative line.

8. In a previous chapter I referred to reader-recall of press ads, as instanced by several tests. Well, just consider this . . . the accuracy of recall for a direct mailing piece is four or five times *greater* than recall of the same copy and design placed into a press ad. This seems to me conclusive and striking evidence, should more be needed by this time, of the power which direct mail can put into your hands. The most startling example of recent years you'll find mentioned at the end of this chapter.

THE PERSONAL TOUCH

This is very different from the "personality" touch which has to do with all the modern cant about "charisma." What value the latter quality possesses appertains to magic—the true personal touch relates to flesh-and-blood.

The copywriter and designer for direct mail have this unique opportunity of making a direct, personal approach to the customer—as many leaflets put it "in the comfort of his own home." And they never forget that even though their mailing may be slipping into a million homes, their letter and leaflet speak only to *one person* ... and they keep that one person always in mind. Charisma seeks the mass appeal. If it fails, if fails *en masse*.

Today they are greatly assisted by new printing techniques; innovations, too, like the automatic typewriter, which achieves wonders in simulating the appearance of personally-typed letters. But even if this wasn't so, the great ace up your sleeve in the medium is this quality of direct mail itself—that people *want* to be convinced of your persuasion, they desperately *want* to believe that you are talking to them alone.

In my salad days—and I was green to an advanced age—I was writing a series of sales letters to which a fictitious signature was appended. One day I accidentally discovered, from glancing at past mailings in our guard book, that this signature was being reproduced on my letters in several distinctly different scripts. Surely, I pontificated grandly to the Account Executive, if we're pretending to be personal, that we are entering into a genuine personal correspondence with our target-audience, should authenticity not at least be taken to the extent of always reproducing the pretend-signature in the same handwriting? My fears (my scruples, if you like) were pooh-poohed. No one would ever notice the discrepancy, I was assured, not even if they received two successive letters signed by different—and obviously different—hands. And no one ever did.

Nevertheless, with modern techniques of reproduction in facsimile, such a cavalier attitude is entirely needless—I do not believe that letters have to be actually signed by the ostensible sender, but I believe he should be a real individual and that it should be *his* facsimile signature, and none other, that appears under "Yours sincerely." At the lowest common denominator, it's the difference between making pigs of ourselves (or the client), and going the whole hog.

COPY IN DIRECT MAIL

In no other medium is the importance of a good copywriter more critical. Because, of course, people *read* mail—it's really as simple and basic as that, though relatively few in this country yet acknowledge the fact. And if any Brand Manager or Account Executive wonders why any copywriter worth his position below the salt appears sometimes so absurdly particular about grammar and spelling and the precise placing of words, let them ponder this quote from Donald Adams, Books Editor of the *New York Times*:

"Words have a magic and mystery. It is interesting to note how much the effect of certain words upon us can be altered by a slight change in them, and how a certain phrase can be undermined by the substitution of one word for another of almost but not quite equivalent meaning ... language is not only acted *upon*—it is an active force itself, capable of affecting our attitudes and ideas."

And I don't think I am unduly biased by the fact that this editor went to my own University, where he probably heard from the same Lecturer in Creative Writing as I did, these words: "Content can't be forced, by the writer or by anyone else. A man has got to come at what he wants to write by himself, without artificial aid. He has got to feel that this particular theme is the only thing that matters right now."

Substitute "product" or "Brand-X" for "theme" and this holds true for all advertising writing, but especially for direct mail copy. The copywriter's greatest weapon is his sincerity—which won't be a phoney "instant" sincerity, but a reflection of his ability to be interested in all things, to be "an extensive browser in all sorts of fields of information," as James Webb Young put it.

His first task will be to determine and isolate the Unique Selling Proposition involved (known throughout Adland as the U.S.P., a basic tenet first propounded by the late Rosser Reeves, one time Chairman of Ted Bates and Company in New York), that is, to settle in his own mind precisely what the prime benefit is which his sales letter will offer. Then the copywriter must convince himself that it *will* be a benefit, and if this proves difficult he must search for a creative approach which does seem to him to put a fair and honest case *for the person to whom he is writing*. He himself may never feel the need to accept a premium offer of six monogrammed plastic bags, but he must be convinced the recipient *will*, and once this conviction possesses him it is perfectly legitimate for him to manipulate his approach with every skill he knows. But an adman's insincerity will "out" like blood, every time.

DESIGN IN DIRECT MAIL

The task of the designer where the sales letter is concerned is to display the typed matter to maximum effect, making his choice between the facsimile of an apparently personally typed (or at least dictated) communication, or a blatant headline, or a tricksy new letter-heading which helps emphasise or illustrate letter-content, or paragraphs which alternate in colour or relative boldness of type, and so on. If a gift stamp is to be attached to the letter he must calculate its position so that it draws attention to itself, without distracting from the message.

Before thinking of visual, however, the designer will closely study what his colleague intends by his words, and why he has chosen those words and not alternatives. He will discover that the following copy progression usually obtains:

1. The direct involvement of the reader from the first word, leading on from the personal note of identification right into the essential selling proposition.

2. The development of that proposition, with ancillary benefits, if there are any, and some qualifying examples. In sales letters (as distinct from accompanying leaflet or brochure) the jobs of recognition and responsibility (*see* Chapter X) are both the writer's charge.

3. The exhortation to action ("Do it *now*"), followed once more by a clear explanation of how the benefit can be obtained.

After full consultation with the copywriter—and the best creative teams have much intuitive understanding, of course—the designer may decide the best help he can give the copy is no help at all, i.e. that utmost simplicity and straightforwardness of design is best. Good visual thinking is often the apparent absence of any.

The leaflet or brochure has all the objectives of the letter, and the creative responsibility will lie roughly fifty-fifty between design and copy. If there should be no letter with the leaflet then its creative presentation of Brand-X will follow the progression outlined above. If there is a letter, then the leaflet's job is to make a factual and dramatically appealing presentation of the selling proposition. The designer will pay special attention to the display of the testimonials (*see* Chapter X), which play a vital part in direct mail.

DIRECT MAIL POTENTIAL

My own belief is that the growth-potential of the medium is enormous, but it requires *agencies* to believe in it before *clients* can do so, and one remedy for this will be the regularising of fees for producing mailings. When this problem is satisfactorily solved agencies will more readily accept the creative challenge the medium offers, which is the most exciting and rewarding in all Advertising, even including television.

The annual awards given by the British Direct Mail Advertising Association are, in my opinion, as useless as any other of the various awards in Advertising (*see* Chapter XIV)—the winner in 1970 of the B.D.M.A.A.'s President's award, for example, was Wiggins Teape, even though their sales results for that period showed a remarkable down-swing! More to the point is the working party set up by the B.D.M.A.A. to study the payment problem and such initiatives as the £500 travelling scholarship donated by the Post Office (who also gave one to Lord Hall) to be awarded to the winner of a thesis-competition on the subject "The economics of export advertising by mail." Our home-grown economics need closer study first, however, in particular the "recession" in direct mail which has resulted from perennial escalation of postal charges—the cut-back may be as high as 33⅓ per cent, or £40 million—and those who cherish the potential of this medium will wish the Post Office scholarship were directed to the beam in its own eye, not to the mote off-shore.

Factors in direct mail practices which disturb the lay public, like "inertia selling" (i.e. sending items through the mail which the recipient is deemed to have "purchased" unless he returns them, even though they were never ordered) continued to come under parliamentary scrutiny, and pressure is mounting for further legislation to be introduced under this Government to be aimed at phoney "directory" firms who hawk round fictional mailing lists to naïve clients, of whom, alas, there are all too many. The Unsolicited Goods and Services Act 1971, has closed many loopholes of abuse but still leaves exploited gaps which will have to be dealt with.

I cannot subscribe to the argument that the medium is foredoomed in this country (obvious exceptions being the *Reader's Digest* promotions and most medical mailings) because of the relatively small consumer market, as compared to that available to the free-wheeling mailing giants in the United States. Entry into the Common Market has transformed the situation; even now, some direct mail operations are not only transatlantic but trans-European in scope, as instanced by the Leisure Arts Organisation, which is directed from Switzerland, maintains creative headquarters in Paris, a high-powered publicity unit in London and is under the world-wide control of Americans.

What the medium *does* need (as does all Advertising), is less "pundit" research and more study of creative techniques and principles. If fewer agencies looked down their noses at the medium such gaffes might be avoided as that perpetrated by Toronto admen a few years ago, who sent out seven thousand mailing shots inviting entries for "The Worst Advertising of the Year;" they received only seventy replies, and presumably awarded themselves the palm.

THE ALL-PRODUCT MEDIUM

It is difficult to think of any product which cannot be sold by direct mail, which again should make it appealing to all truly creative men. In recent years I too have used the medium to create promotions for cruises, charities, contraceptives, cook-books and courses in art, also coffee-tables, dog-leads, power-tools, farm-signs, rejuvenating creams, cottages in the Bahamas and hotels in Guyana, an investment journal and decimal cash-registers. One can sell most items you'd expect to buy in any decent department store ... and a few you'd only find in indecent ones!

As Bill Ambrose, Director of advertising and trade relations for the United Kingdom products division of the Beechams Group, said in a speech in May 1969 to the Direct Mail Producers Association: "Your business is as big as you want to make it." And in the United States "armchair" shopping—where your customer is literally a sitting target—is conducted on a mammoth scale. Everything from sewing-machines to sex can be bought and sold through the letter-box. So are lobsters—*live* ones! Everything for the home and family ... and the undertakers—including most of the lethal items discovered in the home of L. H. Oswald, Esq. Remember him?

This is the example I referred to earlier, in my eighth creative point, speaking of the power of direct mail. It's a sobering gloss on the meaning of responsibility (and the attendant risk) in Advertising, that one day a copywriter must have sat at his desk in a Chicago agency and planned a direct mail letter and leaflet, that a designer then must have dreamed up a good factual selling visual for the product, that one of their "converted" recipients promptly mailed back their coupon, properly signed, filled in, and ticked in the correct box as instructed, was sent the product, and with it murdered President Kennedy, that dreadful high noon in Dallas.

It is an even more sobering gloss on direct mail that the White House then possessed a signing machine for reproducing Kennedy's signature so faithfully on letters that not even friends could tell the difference, and for days after the assassination—the stunned staff having forgotten to switch it off—that machine continued to mail out "personalised" letters from a dead man, letters which no doubt became their recipients' most prized trophies.

Chapter XII

THE ADMAN'S ARSENAL—3

You will find many admen who will judge that the last chapter has dwelt at disproportionate length on direct mail. This, even though it remains the third largest medium in terms of expenditure, and in despite of the fact that it is the only medium which tends to increase its share of client appropriations in times of recession or, shall we say, blue-chip funk. Be ready for such critics to assure you with equal certainty that the moon is nothing more than the latest below-the-line gimmick for Kraft Cheese. My reason must remain that since most of my readers will have become but recently interested in Advertising as a profession, and since direct mail is almost totally ignored by texts on Advertising, I have felt urgently compelled to adjust the differential.

Now, however, in this third of the chapters devoted to the purely creative aspects of Advertising, we shall deal first with the most familiar, intimate, omni-present medium of all: commercial television. Like the concealed envelope in Edgar Allen Poe's *The Purloined Letter*, which passed unnoticed because it was clearly in view in the most obvious place in the room, or like the celebrated detective novel by Dorothy Sayers (I won't name it, for fear of spoiling the pleasure of its many new readers) which boldly proclaimed the guilty party on the very title page in certain knowledge that no one would see it there, the sheer size and influence of the commercial "presence" on the box is easily overlooked. If your television viewing averages no more than twelve hours per week, for instance, you can take if from me that you have watched at least *ten thousand* commercials during the past year. As R. P. Kelvin, in his book *Advertising and the Human Memory* pithily puts it, "people who live near railway lines cease to hear the trains."

Herein lies, of course, great opportunity and immense peril for the creative people—for such homes as Kelvin instances are scarcely likely to nurture train-spotters. They will see and hear so much, and observe nothing. The old saw about familiarity breeding contempt is all too applicable here, and one of the worst, but most insidious, errors a creative man can make (or his client, for that matter) is to conclude that soaring sales follow automatically in the wake of this familiarity. Tag-lines in TV commercials are the staple fare dished out by comedians, for whom the small-screen has provided a shortcut to non-wit,

as modern pop songs provide a shortcut to non-emotion and discotheques a short cut to non-dance. One of the most reliable "warm up"
ploys used by bingo-hall compères is getting the assembled housewives
and pensioners to belt out choruses of the latest telly-jingles. But does
anyone really contend that the resultant volume of sound bears any
sort of relationship to the volume of sales?

The answer is, alas, yes. Agencies are full of such self-deceivers. No
sensible client, however, considers himself in the business of supplying
free entertainment, and no creative department can deliver a first-
rate job in Advertising if entertainment becomes his chief aim. Thanks
to television, becoming a household name is easier than ever before
... it's much harder, however, to win a place on the household budget.
Your average housewife's head is by no means as soft as her heart
may suggest; she is more than willing to smile at a gay tune and a
lively, amusing telly-ad, but that smile freezes at the supermarket
check-out point. A point we'll return to later.

GOLDEN EGGS, OR CURATE'S EGGS?

Stanhope Shelton, former Vice-Chairman of Ogilvy & Mather
(whose creative procedures for their Egg Marketing Board commercials you can see for yourselves in the fascinating film *Sunday Breakfast*, available on free loan from the I.P.A.), has been quoted as saying
"the few seconds of an advertising commercial will fit into a pillbox
$2\frac{1}{2}$ inches in diameter," and his analogy has today even more mileage
than when he first made it ... for, just as with the Pill, we are not
sure how it works, when it works, nor what undesirable side-effects
it may produce. Many years after the first TV spot went out in Britain
the copywriters and designers for the medium are still engaged in
creating over and over again that most unwanted ingredient of any
advertising campaign—the *unknown quantity*. Which, of course, only
adds to its allure.

The heaviest douse of cold water upon their heated passions has
undoubtedly come from the Chancellor of the Exchequer. Until the
advent of I.T.V. there had been no tax of any kind on Advertising
for over one hundred years! Then in 1961 came the tax on television
advertising, and it was levied on *total net revenue before profits* ... which,
while passing without much comment in the early halcyon days of
"printing money," now raises painful and continuing howls all round
from an industry which, in 1970, needed to earn profits of £5 million
to enable it to meet the levy of a whopping £20 million. In the words
of a most embittered Aidan Crawley, then head of London Weekend
Television: "Instead, therefore, of being a goose laying an endless succession of golden eggs, independent television has become a high-risk

industry." For admen also the medium has turned into an endless, and sometimes friendless, succession of curate's eggs, good in parts, but these parts no more easy to locate precisely than they ever were.

The days when "social realism," vests, sinkfuls of dishes, provincial accents and unmown armpits gained Sydney Bernstein a peerage and several cool millions (and McLuhan calls it, after all, a "cool" medium) have given way to leaner times. Clients are on their way to the hard, but very necessary, acceptance that not even *this* alluring medium is the message. They can see escalating costs of the Independent Companies being passed on to them. All the same, a depressed period has been followed by a buoyant one. In October 1976, total advertising revenue garnered by I.T.V. companies *after tax, commissions, etc.* was nearly £27 million!

PEAK OR "PIQUE" HOURS?

There are other factors contributing to the fact that "next morning," clients simply do not "still feel the same about it," to adapt the ridiculous commercials for Cossack vodka. One involves the client–agency backlash reaction following their first rush of colour to the head, after the hue-and-cry made the scene on 15th November 1969 (as Gibbs-S.R. Toothpaste was the first black-and-white commercial, so Birds Eye Peas led the sunburst field into colour—both accounts being in the lucky Lintas fold!).

Even as most clients, who had the cash, felt it was encumbent upon them to have their ads on TV, regardless of result-uncertainties, so they were next sold on the idea that all their commercials should be in colour. Account Directors in all agencies assured Brand Managers earnestly that though these spots cost more to produce (a claim which one of the last reports from the Prices and Incomes Board effectively refuted), TV commercials without colour were as unthinkable as Laurel without Hardy or Ambridge without the Archers. In the event, a surprisingly small number of homes have bought or rented colour sets—it is still under 50 per cent even with the recent boom in sales. While it is now true that well over 90 per cent of commercials are sent out in colour, this is, of course, a very different matter from how many of those commercials are being *received* in colour ... which should be the only point that matters.

Jeremy Bullmore, Creative Director of J. Walter Thompson, reached a new high in whistling in the dark when he informed *Campaign* that he suspected many clients "have gone for colour as fast as they can for fear that their products might otherwise look drab by comparison with their rivals in the eyes of professional buyers." In *whose* eyes? For my concern is that in talking about professional buyers we forget the amateur ones, i.e. the customers at the counter. If the creative people are trying now to make both trade and consumer targets happy at the same time, they're on a losing streak before the first bets are made.

One cannot avoid the fact, however unpalatable, that the copy and design men who make the ads for the box (whether in agency TV departments or with independent producing companies) simply do not *know* what sort of picture is appearing on any of the roughly 18 million sets their ads can be seen on—all they can be sure of is that no more than 9 million viewers will see it in colour. (And it is some relief to realise that we are only, as a nation, halfway to complete addiction to *Coronation Street*.) In his book published in 1966, *Advertising Media and Campaign Planning*, Anthony Swindells reflected the prevailing euphoria when he rashly prophesied that colour would make "the impact of television advertising ... stronger than ever," one reason being "the intensified appeal to women (who are particularly sensitive to colour)." Women are even more sensitive, particularly as housewives and home-makers, to costs, not only as regards the purchase or rental of colour TV sets, but the almost double amount they would have to pay for their licence to the B.B.C.!

Besides which, monochrome commercials offer plenty of verisimilitude problems of their own (those delicious ice-creams which are mashed potatoes, for instance, or that marge which is painted wood) without additional colour problems ... such as junior's whiter-than-white shirt turning a rather bilious dirty yellow, and mother's cooking-oil turning green!

There is also the uncertainty of the audience that is being reached, no matter if your oil is green or your marge is wooden. The copywriter and designer can have a fairly clear notion of whom he is reaching in *Reveille*, the *Illustrated London News* or the *British Sugar Beet Review*, but as to whether his seven-second masterpiece is reaching a "mass" or "special interest" audience, he can have but the smallest idea. The facile assumptions that regarded "peak-time" viewing as between 7 p.m. and 10 p.m., for example, are no longer tenable; the Independent Broadcasting Authority itself has admitted in a recent report that the hours on each side of this bracket are just as "peak" as the rest. And to client as well as creative staff, this is more than a matter of pique—the cost of time in or outside of that hallowed bracket can make a difference of many thousands in the budget (and therefore in the 15 per cent commission the agency gets back from the contractors, as it does from the Press).

In terms only of buying transmission time, one second of creativity may cost as much as £150, or, as with the first colour commercial (screened at 10.05 p.m. in the Midlands) as little as twenty-seven shillings. There are innumerable permutations in between depending on the hour of transmission. There is, however, *no difference at all* in the prices as between monochrome and colour, because of the mere 50 per cent who are viewing in colour and, as Antony Thorncroft of *The Financial Times* put it, just over a year after the Birds Eye pathfinder found no path, though closely heel-trodden by Katie and Philip multi-hued for Oxo and bright alphabets exploding kaleidoscopically for Crazy Oats, in colour, alas, "the advertising impact is minimal."

TAKING THE CREATIVE PLUNGE

The creative people are only too aware, therefore, that halcyon days are over, that TV appropriations are crumbling before the secateurs of cost-effectiveness, that fewer new TV ads are being requested and more and more of the old ones repeated—during one period, the Motorail commercials being transmitted were well over a year old, for instance. No more will Players smokers go on cantering on white stallions through the bright-green "English" countryside (filmed in the United States!), for the banning of cigarette ads on TV has meant the departure of one of the top three "big spenders," the other two categories being food and drink.

On top of all this, from the creative standpoint, there remains the tantalising "open" end nature of the medium. A great deal is known about creating good commercials, and nothing is known. By which I mean there is a lot of theory, which changes from season to season, and a lot of practice, very little of which follows any theory. Even when it does, no branch of advertising promotion is more prone to the vice (or, to many clients, the virtue) of copy-catting. Supervisors in agencies have in fact gone so candidly far as to enshrine the principle in memos to their staff which, for instance, not only make viewing *Monday's Newcomers* obligatory but stress that their creative staff be on the lookout for aspects of rival commercials which can be "borrowed."

Perhaps the most unfortunate result of this "open end" character of the medium is that TV commercials are more subject to interference from client—or client's family—than any other medium used in the Brand-X campaign. Where A's opinion can be argued, for lack of sufficient data either way, as just as valid as B's, then C for client, Mrs C, or even precious-precocious little Master C seems qualified to weigh in.

Not that the little lad's opinion doesn't often come uncomfortably near the mark. It's on record (and wryly put there by the father) that the son of one American agency Vice-President, after watching a particularly absurd commercial, called his father wonderingly aside and asked him: "Dad ... am I to understand that a bunch of grown men sat around and thought up that thing? And another bunch of grown men sat around and said it was a good idea? And another bunch of grown men went to all the work to make a movie out of it?" To which his father could only shamefacedly answer in the affirmative. And his little boy, he tells us, walked away, shaking his head. This is more than a joke for creators of TV-ads for children, since these alone are worth £15 million a year to U.K. agencies.

LOOKING GOOD ENOUGH TO BUY

An excellent test of the quality of a commercial is literally a "sound" test; if the essential message cannot be communicated with the sound-knob turned off, then it's a poor example of the species. This is true, in spite of the fact that, nine times out of ten, the commercial begins in a script (for remember, it remains the copywriter who has prime *responsibility* for getting the selling message conveyed). A script is dialogue but much more than dialogue alone (as you can see by reference to Figs. 6 and 7); television is a visual medium, so the objective of the writer and designer is to produce a *visual impact* which is also a *selling impact*.

As specialisation spreads throughout Advertising the commercial is increasingly the work of an experienced scripwriter and TV director, acting in close concert with the client's Brand Manager and the agency's Creative Director ... but there are still all-round copywriters and designers who can tackle this medium with the same adaptability that they bring to any other. Where this obtains I'm inclined to favour it, since such a situation ensures the continuity of a Brand-X campaign theme, and a comfortable interrelating style that is most important. Above everything, however, it ensures that the TV ad *is* an ad, not an entertainment.

We have touched on this hazard before and it is much more to be feared when the commercial is created by people who work in no other medium. They are obsessed by the very glamour of the medium itself—by television's undoubted (if deplored by some) ranking as *the* great entertainment medium in the world today. To them, the TV ad comes in the category of a performing art; they are more interested in the vital statistics of the Turkish Nubile Delight or the Manikin's mannequin than they are in conveying the *desirability of the product*. And the only statistics which should count in TV commercials are sales statistics.

A startling example of this Achilles' heel of telly-ads occurred a few years ago in the pages of the *TV Times*, where every week a provocative damsel used to be featured in a photograph under the puzzle-

Bloxhams

Chris Radley   Bill Bloxham
Bob Madill

Bloxhams Partnership Ltd Wellington House, 6 Upper Saint Martins Lane, London, WC2H 9DR. Tel: 01-836 1237

Client:	ASKO OF FINLAND
Time:	15-sec TV Commercial
Method:	VTR
Title:	"FINNSPIRATION"
Job No:	UP 126/1
Date:	14th April, 1972

<table>
<tr><th>VISUAL</th><th>AUDIO</th></tr>
<tr><td>1. GLOBE CHAIR seen sideways on, with legs protruding. FINN lettered on back of CHAIR. Set is dark, with all lighting concentrated on CHAIR.</td><td>1½ secs. mute</td></tr>
<tr><td>2. GLOBE CHAIR revolves, revealing full word: FINNSPIRATION.</td><td></td></tr>
<tr><td>3. CHAIR continues revolving to reveal PRESENTER.</td><td>PRESENTER (with Finnish accent):
Finnspiration!</td></tr>
<tr><td>4. PRESENTER gets up from CHAIR.</td><td>Come...</td></tr>
<tr><td>5. CUT TO "Ponderosa" Bedroom Suite. MEDIUM SHOT.</td><td>Get some big ideas...</td></tr>
<tr><td>6. CUT TO PRESENTER caressing "Pulkka" chair.</td><td>Beautiful Finnish furniture designs...</td></tr>
<tr><td>7. CLOSE-UP. PULL BACK TO MEDIUM SHOT.</td><td></td></tr>
<tr><td>8. CUT TO HIGH SHOT of "Charlotta" Dining Suite. PRESENTER appears.</td><td>By Asko of Finland...</td></tr>
<tr><td>9. SUPERIMPOSE TITLE: ASKO FINNSPIRATION at J. J. ALLEN NOW!</td><td>All at J. J. Allen NOW!</td></tr>
</table>

Directors: P.S.Lane, I.J.Bloxham, C.D.Radley, R.G.Madill, A.J.Lifford, J.R.W.Huddart. Registered no. 929888 England. Registered office: Lee House, London Wall, London EC2Y 5AX.

Fig. 6.—Original script, shown for client approval, of proposed 15-sec. TV commercial, promoting "Finnspiration" line of furniture (made by Asko of Finland) for Bournemouth stockist, J. J. Allen.

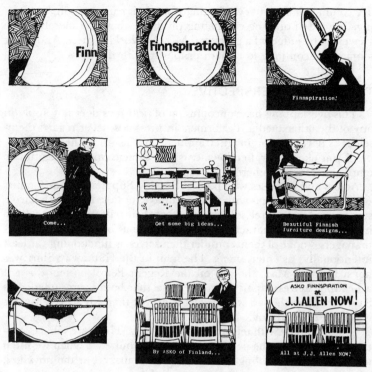

Fig. 7.—The resultant storyboard (*see* facing page).

title "Whose Adgirl?" Readers were asked to guess where they had seen her before among the commercials, checking their guess against the answer on the back page. These were among the clues on one occasion: "Mary Clubb is an established dancer, has been in three commercials ... was in the Tom Jones Show ... dances in *Oliver!* and *Oh, What a Lovely War* ... has been making a documentary for Granada about the life of a dancer in Istanbul" ... and so on. In other words, the telly-ad world was automatically included as just another medium of entertainment in her show-biz career. An issue of the *Sunday Mirror* once devoted a double-page spread, with glamour photograph, to an actress named Andrea Lawrence—but not because of her work in any film or play she had appeared in during the past fourteen years ... her celebrity status derived from her role of the bosomy barmaid "Maggie" in the thirty-second Watney's Red Barrel commercials, in which, with a wink and saucy smile, she informed the virile guzzlers: "I don't like it, but I like the men who drink it."

Until they escape from the chains of this entertainment concept

TV commercials won't even begin to find their true status in Advertising. Instead of offering competing products, they will merely invite viewers to be judges of a perennial Miss AdWorld contest. And client money will continue to remain primarily with the Press.

THE SELLING PERSPECTIVE

This overlapping haze of confusion of priorities does not apply in any of the other media. Performers in press ads never regard themselves as participating in entertainment, but as using their talents—or, if you like, natural endowments and dimensions—for legitimate employment in commerce.

Actors and actresses who pose in Sunday Supplements as families who read encyclopedias with their cornflakes or take Bach with bacon, starlets who sit in careless languor before their reflections in the dressing-table mirror, character actors who pose as bricklayers or bank-managers—none of them consider themselves as functioning (at least intentionally) as entertainers. The man in the Hathaway Shirt was not a Leading Man, the girl on the Regent Petrol posters was not a Leading Actress, apart from the sense that both were intended as Sales-Leaders; the lad whose shirt is greyer than his school-friend's is not a Principal Boy.

So it should be with television commercials. There are some exceptions which do get the perspective right, of course ... when we listen to the familiar rumbling tones urging us to marvel at the unveiling of a new Texaco station or the sizzling Findus products in the pan, we may smile to ourselves, nod wisely and say "Ah, that's the voice of Orson Welles." But we are not swayed into purchase of either product simply because Orson Welles is giving a star performance. The star, quite rightly, is the product. Did anyone buy a Vono bed because of the cultivated boudoir sneer-leer in over-familiar James Masonics on the soundtrack? One hopes not, since the voice was not that of James Mason at all and a court-case *did* ensue when Bing Crosby took legal action to prevent Shell using the voice of Michael Holliday in their "You will go well with Shell" spots, for the latter's tone was almost a carbon-copy of the Groaner's. The selling perspective had gone awry again.

Let me acknowledge at once the most famous instance of all perhaps, when George Lazenby won the right to succeed Sean Connery (inasmuch as anyone could succeed him) as the cinema's James Bond, to a large extent by virtue of the image which he presented in the Cadbury Big Fry commercials. This, however, was a fortunate by-product for Lazenby alone—the star of the commercial was still the chocolate.

The entertainment ingredient in a telly-ad should be there as a tool, not as an end in itself—for, where Advertising is concerned, that's a dead end. In far too many commercials, sales effectiveness is clearly all too often accepted as a hoped-for side-effect, and not the other way round. The right watchwords are not "Always Leave 'Em Laughing" but rather "Always Leave 'Em Buying!" It's an interesting example of how (according to admen) we see ourselves, as against how others see us, that Harry Secombe sells British Airways on our home screens, while actor Robert Morley is enlisted to do the job in the States. The only common denominators would seem to be that our national airline requires a sense of humour and that travel broadens.

As we have seen in Chapter VII, even in this mainly *visual* medium the ball is first in the writer's court, for his script must be passed by the I.T.C.A. He must ensure, by his "visual" instructions even more than by his "sound" content of dialogue and "effects," that when filmed, all the facts about Brand-X will be there on the screen to *see*, with or without the spoken word. The words (spoken by actors or by the "voice over") will guide the viewer as to what he should think about what he sees. Even the greatest of silent films required subtitles.

A good television writer thinks *visually*, as indeed does any dramatic writer, any author who is inscribing speeches, words to be performed. The plays of Aristophanes differ from Shakespeare's, Shakespeare's from Sheridan's, Sheridan's from Shaw's, and Shaw's from Osborne's not principally because of differences in time, language or thought—because the human condition never changes, only our awareness of its many aspects—but because of differences in *staging*. *These writers all worked, if you like, in a different Scene.*

The scriptwriter (which is the "hat" being worn now by the copywriter for Brand-X) will have a vivid picture of his scene in his mind while he writes. His words will delineate that picture to the designer, who is going to produce the story-board. Though the designer may eventually see the picture in quite a different way—it may well prove a better, more effective, way—he will make quite certain he understands the writer's vision before he super-imposes his own ... he will make himself satisfied that he comprehends just as much what his writing team-mate *sees* as what he *says*.

THE PICTURE IS BORN

Exactly in the same way that the picture-panels of a story-board (and thus the television picture with the sound turned off) should be effective *as to facts* without any script, so should the script be essentially meaningless without the pictures. It's easily remarked, by anyone

who cares to try the experiment, how many TV dramas can be followed without a glance at the screen. There is no more dependable
sign of poor scripting, of the author's miscalculation of his medium,
its power and its glory.

Many ground-rules have been worked out for creative people making TV commercials—such as the measure of 125 words a minute,
58 seconds of sound for every 60 seconds of picture, 1½ seconds of
picture alone at the start of each commercial—and beginners can do
no better than study *Television Advertising* by Dan Ingman, who is
no mere theory practitioner in the field, but was the man who produced this country's first TV spot of the ice-packed tube of toothpaste.
As in all Advertising, however, the detail is constantly in flux, and
no mastery simply of slide-rule aesthetics will garner sales success.

Some purely creative points are more vital to bear in mind. Many
commercials labour under over-complication of "plot"—the scriptwriter should concentrate on no more than two selling points, confining
himself to one if possible. The product should also be named on the
soundtrack (or shown on the screen) as frequently as can be managed.
Most important, writer and designer should exploit to the full their
unique advantage that, just as the bored housewife actively *wants* to
enjoy her direct mail packet, so most televiewers, slumped before the
goggle-box in expectant lethargy, are actively willing your commercial to amuse them (amuse in the broadest sense). So the TV ad
will aim to amuse them, pique their interest, arouse their curiosity,
spur their cupidity, in that order. Entertainment, I repeat, is solely
the means not the end. For your plug is of no use whatever, unless
it is a spark plug.

PUTTING SALES IN THE PICTURE

Apart from any modish visual or camera tricks he may call upon—
and television has a far wider range of these than the public appreciates—the designer's chief job, mundane as it may seem, is to show
Brand-X clearly; where feasible, without distortion of "story-line,"
he should always "fade" on a pack-shot so that this valuable identification stays in the viewer's mind, remembering that the finished print
that goes for transmission will have about ten seconds of his final frame
"frozen" for technical reasons and some possible valuable extra foot-
age may come his way as a bonus. If there is a very special selling-
point, in benefit, price or offer, it should be superimposed on the
screen as well as heard on the soundtrack.

Cinema advertising, though of course older, is used far more
clumsily than television advertising. To save money the same film is
often used in both media, which is a very mistaken economy—it will

surely fail in one and may well fail in both, falling between two stools. Some differences are perhaps more obvious than others.

The cinema is *larger* than life (hand-held cameras and all!), the TV image is *smaller* than life. Both literally and metaphorically. One medium is essentially heroic, the other domestic; one is played out on Olympus, one is on the hearth. The great minus of the cinema is that your commercial competes with far more distraction—hoots of derision, shrieks of children, back-row canoodling (and more), the sale of sweets and soft drinks and too loud and aggressive a soundtrack which alienates the audience ... in the home, after all, viewers can control volume and, at the back of their minds, always retain the comforting assurance that they *can* switch off or switch over; they are not so literally, and intimidatingly, a captive audience. The great plus of the cinema—which admen and client both frequently forget—is that you can pinpoint your target in the same way as with direct mail. You know *where* and *when* and (taking certain cinemas into consideration) what sort of audience is seeing your commercial; a splendid example of this was reported by a fish fryer in Watford, after his local cinema had shown the White Fish Authority film prepared by the Charles Barker Agency—his sales leaped by 15 per cent!

THE LIABILITY OF LIBIDO

Seeing some commercials, I often wonder if their creators aren't confusing purse-strings with G-strings in their efforts to jump aboard the permissive bandwagon. In vying with the sexy emphasis of much progressive TV drama (which is rapidly regressing us into the womb), all such telly-ads accomplish is the conversion of their potential customers into a nation of spectator "sports"—the result can only be Brain Stopped Play, for a man who doesn't think doesn't either act or react and a surfeit of striptease only breeds a nation of eunuchs.

The most supremely irrelevant offender, to my mind, which is on the current screen (and is another revival, by the way) is the Manikin Small Cigars commercial which shows a curvaceous dolly dashing along a beach, in and out of Freudian rollers in the surf, while donning some wet and clinging garments. An article in the *TV Times* has informed us, in fact, that the young lady was not a professional model at all but a hairdresser's receptionist when the Art Director met her, "clapped a hand to his forehead" and said, in ringing tones: "You are just the girl I am looking for to do an advert for me."

It is time, many feel, to stop the lunatics before they take over the asylum. The one sentence of enormous sense spoken by anyone at the Television Congress was from Stephen Frewen: "I sometimes wonder whether if in fact we have developed a business too childish to hold the interest of an adult mind."

If he's right, it devolves on the copywriters and designers of the future, with clients and agency executives backing them all the way, to drag the Manic-Manikin world of TV advertising kicking and screaming into some semblance of maturity. To remind producers of all Manikin-type commercials that the first requisite of their job is to *sell the product*, I will just quote Kipling to all Art Directors and hairdressers' receptionists who would come between me and my small cigar, "a woman is only a woman, but a good cigar is a Smoke."

ON THE AIR ... IN THE AIR

It is still, surprisingly enough, an open question what creative opportunities for promoting Brand-X on radio will be genuinely available to admen—what is agreed is that so far, if there have been opportunities, they remain un-seized. The ether is still up for grabs. One has been able for years to put out ads over Radio Luxembourg, of course, which—like the programmes—are taped in this country and merely transmitted from the Continent, but even this limited activity was once described by Herbert Morrison in the Commons (keeping up Labour's antipathy to the industry) as "sheer naked exploitation" ... what would he have thought of the Manikin TV-ad? There is also Radio Monte Carlo International, but the massive impact, desirable or not, of Radios London, Caroline and other lesser "pirates" has not been duplicated by the nineteen commercial stations (where sixty were once envisaged) that now dot-dash the nation.

Parliament and the police, raiding ships and abandoned forts, wielding the Marine Offences Act, at last made the radio-pirates walk the plank (though some survive off Continental coasts), from the end of which the air-wave buccaneers tumbled into the lap of respectable commerce. The Managing Directors of Piccadilly Radio and of Air Services respectively, Messrs. Philip Birch and Eddie Blackwell, are both reformed alumni of the one-time delightfully notorious, and romantically dashing, Radio London. And amid all the self-righteous huffing and puffing from politicians and religious leaders, it is forgotten that Harrods—before the Arabian Nights descended upon it—was sponsoring radio programmes forty-two years ago! The very first radio commercial ever made was made *fifty-four* years ago, in America, by actress Marion Davies, life-long friend of Patty Hearst's grandfather. We seem to have waited a long time to get nowhere.

Air Services and Broadcast Marketing Services are the two firms which sell radio-time on the commercial stations, or I.L.R. networks, as they are known (Independent Local Radio). Piccadilly Radio, which also harbours safely many ex-Radio Caroline D.J.s, ranks fourth in commercial listening figures. First is Capital Radio (which, even so, was only showing a profit for the first time last year), second is Clyde and third is L.B.C. The sum of commercial radio's attainment after four years—and at the beginning, a new station was hurled into operation every six weeks—is that today half the population can receive I.L.R.'s nineteen stations. The catch is, they can also receive twenty B.B.C. local radio stations and, as a whole, the sound-for-sale networks are quite a long way from truly being "sound." All the same, in areas where they directly compete, a new survey by Research Surveys of Great Britain shows that commercial stations can claim a larger percentage of "listening hours" than the B.B.C. and—this statistic is for admen the most impressive and inspiring—an average of 70 per cent of men and women in the 15–24 age group are captured for over eleven hours each week, for commercial spots.

The Annan Report called local radio "a mess," but the Noble Lord's Committee itself has produced "a dog's breakfast," according to the Tory Media Group, so we cannot confidently seek guidance from the bureaucrats.

What is clearly the surest way of increasing advertising revenue on the market-place air-waves is to make better radio ads, and I find it impossible to believe they will ever come from the strident pseudo-Americanisms and incessant choral and musical crescendos almost universally employed by those with an unhealthy love of mike. The record (or tape?) speaks for itself. Three years had to elapse before the industry could summon up the gall to give prizes for effort, with the first Radio *Campaign* Awards presented last December, sponsored by the enterprising and all-knowing journal which has driven *AdWeekly* from the field and which now reigns supreme and supremely competent over all it surveys. Perhaps a measure of the sophistication expected of radio ads was sadly implicit in a declaration by John Thompson, Director of Radio at the I.B.A., in a *Campaign* interview, that the ideal commercial should not only be funny but "an ad which was actually selling what it wanted to sell, one which met our code and one which had a United Kingdom flavour to it." Not, I think, a recipe for a devolution-battered audience whose sense of humour splits at least four ways, none of them towards Brooklynese.

It is prophetic that the winning radio ad for 1976 was about snooker? Has creativity in radio advertising snookered itself behind preconceptions derived from other media? Use of the voice alone should have liberated and inspired copywriters as the Globe liberated Shakespeare. Alas, to the contrary, and where our very own motivational research pundit, Harry Henry, prophesied four years ago that radio billings would soar to £50 million, their peak so far has been just over £14·5 million. This 1976 figure was against nearly £231 million for the I.T.V. contractors. Thus seeing remains, for the time-buying minute, more believing than hearing. Indeed, one often requires a deaf-aid to get the sales-pitch!

Undoubtedly, the two greatest beneficiaries of advertising appropriations and media schedules in relation to radio are those that batten on both broadcast media: last year, the *Radio Times* carried £7·6 million worth of advertising, while the *TV Times* carried £11·6 million.

I fear that a prophesy I made in the first edition of this book has come partly true: "My anxieties are high lest creative output for the medium goes through a similar 'dilettante' stage to TV. If copywriters aren't duly careful they will dissipate the built-in goodwill that exists, reflected in a speech by David Dutton (then President of the I.P.A.) at a Mansion House dinner—'Our satisfaction at the prospect of commercial radio flows from our conviction that it will be welcomed by the public at large.' That goodwill has been dissipated and it will take some regaining, which will start when writers of ads for radio will accept that sound and noise are not synonymous and that decibels can drown themselves, till they attain such volume that no one can hear them."

RADIO REVELS

Even as they pioneered on both the black-and-white and colour TV screens, so Lintas took early sightings on radio ads, and very wisely, too. Their creative people were encouraged to try out all sorts of ideas on tape-recorders, to cut and edit them. In the words of Ian Fawn-Meade, their creative head: "When you know all the rules, break them. Radio commercials are cheap to make and cheap to run. In radio, more than anything else, fortune favours the brave." Perhaps this is so. Clients, however, are more interested in the direct favours of the buying public. Radio is not quite such a no-holds-barred field as all that, and failure never comes cheap. I prefer the slightly different emphasis of Martin Mayer in *Madison Avenue, U.S.A.*, when he said of radio advertising: "Rules are disobeyed only at the risk of unknown perils. But ... the man who breaks the rules and gets away with it is the man who sends his client spinning away on the high road ... until the fact of his success changes the rules, and everyone gets together in the new rut."

Much of what we have discussed in regard to TV commercials will apply to radio also. Facts as to benefit will still carry the day, not mindless slogans endlessly bellowed into the mike. Nevertheless, the way in which this benefit is presented will offer almost endless, and exciting, creative scope. The writer's imagination will be as unfettered as in the days of the Globe at Blackfriars, and there seems no reason whatever why the muse of fire lurking in every creative department should not "ascend the brightest heaven of invention," while the more timorous copy boys, with run-of-the-millstone mottoes, "crouch for employment," avoiding a little touch of Harry Henry in the night.

Indeed, were Shakespeare amongst us today his fortune would without doubt be made on radio, not TV, where he could plead for his colleagues, as the chorus ...

> "Since a crooked figure may
> Attest in little space a million,
> ... let us, ciphers to this great Account,
> On your imaginary forces work."

Because radio is the supreme "word in your ear" medium of whispered confidences, as all advertising is a wooing of favours, where better to place the sweet nothings? Television comes into the hearth, radio into the heart—and without knocking! The customer lends his ear more willingly, because it does not claim the total attention demanded or imposed on the weak-willed by TV—he or she can do other things while listening: clean the house, drive the car, sail a boat, make love (or war), sunbathe, sit in class, watch a cricket-match, go for a walk—or go to bed. It has been proved that instruction can be retained and lessons remembered which are taped into the ears of persons who are sound asleep; so moralists, if you have tears for the subliminal, prepare to shed them now! Certainly the invention of the transistor has eased the path of the radio commercial into almost every conceivable place and situation, as it never did even in the richly har-vested pre-war years of the Great American Broadcast in the thirties.

THE SATURATION MEDIUM

Clients will be interested in radio because it is cheaper, of course, but also because if they have any doubts of the medium's efficacy as against the slightly soiled glamour of television, they need only be asked the question which Alfred Politz, the brilliant American researcher, once asked a sample of 5,000 people, most of whom owned TV sets: "Suppose you were at home and heard a sudden rumour that war had broken out—what would you do to find out if the rumour was true?" Turn on the radio, said most. Did the departure of B.B.C.–TV's *Grove Family* raise anything like the howls of outrage and dismay which greeted the axing of *The Dales*? The basic relevant fact, before all else, is that in 1972 an N.O.P. research team found that 95 per cent of homes have radio sets and that nearly a third of these sets are listened to for over five hours every day.

Today, when *Coronation Street* appears to clients, agencies and contractors to be nearer to Carey Street than Millionaire's Row, radio commercials—especially as "reminders" and "mileage boosters" backing an overall campaign—have plenty of mod allure. For those with ears to hear and products which stand a good chance of attracting that £570 million at the spending service of the 15–24 age group, whose little Japanese portables follow them everywhere.

We may not achieve the heights of American commercial radio where adman invented the soap opera, brought opera and symphony into every home, gave Jack Benny ("Jello again!") and Bob Hope their chance to achieve world status and wafted Bing Crosby to glory on Wrigley's Gum and Kraft Cheese, but we can have a very good try. I think it more likely that fortune favours the knave, rather than the brave, but even so I would never subscribe for a moment to the conclusion reached in November 1970 by the Local Radio (Communications) Survey: "Commercial radio will not be the bonanza which was a fair description of commercial television in the early years. Nevertheless, we believe it could be made a worthwhile investment with the correct type of programming and financial backing."

With such encouragement, who needs detractors? The arguments of the late Lord Francis Williams in regard to press ads in his book *Dangerous Estate* can equally apply to the future of commercial radio: "The daily press would never have come into existence as a force in public and social life if it had not been for the need of men of commerce to advertise. Only through the growth of advertising did the press achieve independence." It will happen in radio, too, and it will earn a prouder description than Martin Mayer's "the discout house of media."

CASH-REGISTERS THAT JINGLE

When commercial radio arrived it was inevitable that creative people would be called upon to supply even more jingles than they did for television. A good jingle is without question one of the best ways to establish your product in the public consciousness, though it by no means follows that corresponding sales will result. The first on British commercial television:

> "Murray Mints, Murray Mints,
> Too-good-to-hurry Mints!"

sung to a marching beat, was very catchy and was heard everywhere, but was not a sales success. On the other hand, possibly the world's most famous commercial jingle, also British-composed and set to a British folk-tune—though launched on the United States market—was a tremendous success from all points of view:

> "Pepsi-Cola hits the spot,
> Twelve full ounces, that's a lot,
> Twice as much for a nickel, too—
> Pepsi-Cola is the drink for you!"

which at one time was heard not only from every radio loudspeaker, but from juke-boxes, too. The tune, which took a few hearings to identify, was that square old bit of jollity "D'ye ken, John Peel."

The origins of jingles hide in many unexpected places. One wonders if Foote, Cone & Belding, much less Watneys themselves, are aware that their tune for the roaring song "Roll Out, Red Barrel!" goes back even further than the obvious source in the "Beer Barrel Polka" to a Czechoslovak composer named Jaromir Vejvoda! The longest-running jingle on British TV, "The Esso Sign means happy Motoring," was written by the ex-President of the Creative Circle, David Bernstein, Managing Director of The Creative Business Consultancy, and commercial radio may soon call on his tuneful talents again. Johnny Johnston, composer of many hit songs, switched to advertising jingles to such effect that he was forced to move to Geneva for enviable "tax reasons;" he also writes in French, German, Spanish and Italian. The story of how "Up, Up and Away" took to the air for T.W.A. was told in Chapter V, readers will remember.

Jingles have a legitimate and honourable ancestry. Byron wrote a jingle for Warren's Blacking and the *Illustrated London News* considered it was adequately advertised only by verse which extended through 128 lines. When the Reverend T. Helmore, M.A., first adapted an "ancient melody" in 1853 for a collection of *Carols for Christmastide*, he could have scarcely imagined its later flowering as:

> "Good King Wenceslas looked out
>   In his pink pyjamas;
> What do you think he hollered out?
>   'Lovely ripe bananas!'"

It wasn't long, however, before Herald Angels were singing that Beechams Pills were just the thing:

> "Peace on earth and mercy mild,
>   Two for man and one for child"

though that wasn't the only new manifestation taking place on Christmas Eve, thanks to the jinglers, for:

> "While shepherds washed their socks by night,
>   All seated round a tub,

> A bar of Sunlight Soap came down
> And they began to scrub"

which the Unilever frontiersmen at Lintas might even today not be ashamed to own.

When they came to soap, however, the Americans took a more blunt approach on radio in the thirties, with a hearty *basso profondo* rendering of

> "Singing in the bathtub, singing for joy,
> Living a Life of Lifebuoy—
> Can't help singing, 'cos I know
> That Lifebuoy really stops B.O."

the B.O. (Body Odour) being accompanied by two descending notes of a foghorn!

Perhaps in a few years the creative men of Adland will foregather in Venice or Cannes to adjudicate on the Year's Best Jingle. One thing seems fairly certain, that though old tunes will continue to be adapted, jingles will tend to correspond—and sometimes be identical with— the modern guitar-saturated pop group scene. Nimble Bread's "She Flies Through the Air" is, of course, the one-time chart-topper "I Can't Let Maggie Go" (no connection with Watney's "Maggie," needless to say). Manfred Mann has composed for commercials as well as for the pop scene, while Joan Shakespeare has written many pop tunes, including one finalist for the Eurovision Song Contest, in between concocting electronically-accompanied jingles for Shredded Wheat, B.E.A., and Bounty "Big Bounty" chocolate bars. The "It's the Real Thing" song for Coca-Cola has, of course, scooped the pool by becoming the Number One hit "I'd Like to Teach the World to Sing." Whether it has taught the world to buy more Cola is another matter.

With Elgar weighing in majestically for Wilkinson Sword, the World's Finest Blade, perhaps we can look forward to the day when William Walton turns from the seagulls at Ischia to lend some perky backing to a new shade of toothpaste or sexy bedtime drink. My own current favourite remains the hearty masculine chorus of "Double Diamond Works Wonders," even though one moment's reflection will bring the thought that, alas, there is also a "hole in my bucket." Meanwhile, the composing of jingles has, in America, become, per minute of performance, the highest paid form of writing in the world.

GETTING ANIMATED

Selling Brand-X by means of an animated discussion is bound to be considered at some time or other by the creative people. On occasion it is even suggested by the client, though for reasons more to do with prestige than inspiration; one of the client's competitors is probably using animation very successfully, and "metooism" is always endemic in Brand Managers.

By animation I mean not just cartoons, but any film-process which appears to give life and movement to inanimate objects, including the product itself! The term covers everything in the field from talking animals to dancing alphabets and low-flying cereal packets. There is always a certain proportion of animated commercials about (some have more life than the models, especially those in obscene trances over phallic flakes), but it is a "vogue" technique and comes and goes in waves of fashion. Not even the theory practitioners have come up with any solid formulations of the worth of animation *in itself* as a sales booster. The fact that many are such a joy to watch may detract from the product; animation is intended to amuse and, as long ago as 1927, in his autobiography, the great Claude Hopkins enunciated:

> "Money comes slowly and by sacrifice. Few people have enough.... Appeal for money in a lightsome way and you will never get it. ... Nobody can cite a permanent success built on frivolity. People do not buy from clowns."

David Ogilvy still incorporates that dictum in his rulebook for admen today, but I'm not so sure. Better to be laughed *with* than laughed *at*, and there are far too many commercials which inspired the latter reaction. Besides which, deplore it or not, the indisputable fact of contemporary life is that, especially amongst the enormous market of the young, money no longer "comes slowly and by sacrifice," and they're eager to spend it.

My own view is that the technique of animation, like any other tool in the adman's arsenal, should be used where it seems fitting for the subject and approach—there should be a good *selling* reason for using it, backed by sound arguments as to why this is the best method of advancing the client's claims for his product. The undoubted selling success of the Homepride Men has already been referred to; readers will also remember the "Good Night To You" TV ads for Myer's Beds, where the disembodied voices of Fred and Mabel argued the toss behind the heaving letters, and the superb Midland Bank ads (both of these in cinemas as well as the box) where captions were made to perform some astoundingly brilliant calisthenics to give graphic parallels of banking services; all of these created enormous goodwill for their products, always a good halfway step to the cash-register. Nor would I have the gloriously dotty Esso Blue delivery man vanish into oblivion.

As to animals, early 1971 saw Kennomeat's gloriously pompous

cartoon dog Albert, with his bowler-hatted little "pet" and his fawn-
ing friend Sydney, challenged by Stamina's rather more crudely
aggressive dog Stanley, whose surges of startling strength come from
the petfood much as Popeye's come from spinach (Max Fleischer's
endearing sailor, incidentally, caused single-handedly a complete
turn-around in the "image" of spinach, rocketing its sales, and must
be the most successful cartoon salesman ever, followed closely by his
bumbling friend Wimpy's efforts for hamburgers and, at one remove,
for Lyons Corner Houses). Stamina's stablemate Paws Catfood also
had the distinction of being the first commercial to be allowed to use
Walt Disney animals (from the film "The Aristocats"), although seven
years ago Disney gave an indirect boost to Volkswagens by making
one of their cars the star of *The Love Bug*. They again made this essential selling point, too—the product, your Brand-X, must *always* be
the star.

There are many weapons and ways of homing in on your sales target
for Brand-X. The adman's arsenal is always expanding, adding new
ideas and devices, discarding others for a time, only to pick them up
again and be hailed or hounded for their "newness;" those members
of the public who draw back aghast or aglee at the nude dolly in the
press ad who rises from the reeds for Cupid's Quiver would be amazed
how calmly the Victorians accepted the equally exposed young
woman who rose from her lake of Borax! *Plus ça change, plus c'est la
même chose* is always the operative slogan for Advertising itself, whatever the medium, whatever the message.

Chapter XIII

THE ADMAN'S ARSENAL—4

Now that we have styled the christening wardrobe for our Brand-X promotion, we must sew and make the garments, and activity is moving out of the hands of the creative department into the agency studio and production department. Designer and copywriter will, however, both continue their close stewardship of the artwork, if they have time (and they should demand that time, if it is denied them), since their experienced professionalism will tell them that all the blood, toil, tears and sweat of their campaign-coddling, their "campaign for the campaign," can go too easily for nothing at this stage.

It is in the studio that the advertisements, leaflets, showcards and posters are prepared for printing. The work done here will be as closely monitored by the Progress Chasers of the traffic department as by the creative people, for printers also have their tight time-schedules to meet—and if properly executed artwork doesn't reach the printer on time he has every excuse for not delivering the leaflet as promised, every alibi for not making the block or plate in time to reach the right newspaper or magazine by specified, or negotiated, copy-date (*see* Chapter VI).

The art-technicians of the studio will welcome the co-operation of their copy and design colleagues as a check to see that they are not only using the correct artwork preparation for the medium involved, but are scrupulously following design and copy instructions—to the literal letter—in such a way as to reproduce faithfully in print the intention and effect of the ad as approved. Should the creative people not have appended such instructions to the words and the visual, they must be badgered till they do.

PREPARING "FINISHED ART"

This book does not purport to be an artist's textbook nor a printer's manual. All I wish to do in these pages is indicate adequately to the student of Advertising the vital importance of this artwork stage in preparing print promotion of all kinds, from press ads to brochures and letterheads (this term refers to the name, address, slogan and other editorial matter which may be printed on a firm's business stationery).

Artwork is the blind spot on the vision of nearly every advertiser. Ask nine out of ten clients to define finished art and explain how its practitioners operate, and they will return you either the blank stare of genuine incomprehension, or the spurious stare of those who think you are "trying on" yet another fictional item to an already over-loaded bill. That the latter possibility is exactly what *is* happening in a minority of cases does not help you win their sympathetic under-standing, and they will sometimes declare in hurt, high, heated dudg-eon that their own "tame" printers (most clients have one) will manage the artwork. In which case, the likelihood is strong that they will merely succeed in compounding, indeed in abetting, the fiction they fear ... and court union trouble as well!

It is therefore crucial to the fast-budding client–agency relationship that, very early on in the "marriage," the client fully understands the "intimate hygiene" matters which lie behind full advertising fulfil-ment, and that his partner exercises a large number of needful physi-cal precautions in order to give ultimate satisfaction and maintain the "best face forward."

In W. Somerset Maugham's play *Lady Frederick*, the Lady in ques-tion (who, needless to say, is no lady) gently disabuses her too young suitor, Lord Charles Mereston, by letting him watch her at her dress-ing-table as she exercises her "artifices" of make-up and beauty-aids. Within the accepted contexts of Edwardian society and *mores*, this is a shattering blow to the youth, who has innocently taken her fetching appearance to be a bloom of natural glory. A precisely similar illusion still lives in the mind of the average Brand Manager; while being fully, nay delightfully, aware that his secretary's eyelashes and bosom are several inches out of true and that not every single one of her kiss-curls are possessed of the kiss of life, he persists in his conviction that his artist's design is somehow transposed on to the medium's printed page by osmosis. Like young Mereston he refuses to admit the reality of your agency's glamour work-bench.

ARTWORK AND TYPE-MARKUP

The "finished artist" stands to the designer as carpenter to cabinet-maker; when the door is carved and panelled he fits it to the jamb and matches it to a wide scale and variety of sills. His job is to repro-duce the designer's visual creation to a precise exactitude of dimension and colour, and he appends to his work detailed instructions for the printer and, where required, a colour-guide (which are often in streaked panels, rather like those in a paint-brochure). Each element of the artwork will be placed on a separate surface: e.g. the basic black-and-white illustration, together with the text of the body-copy, may be carefully inscribed on white Bristol "board" (a special type of cardboard whose high-gloss surface is ideal for pen-and-ink drawing), while the colour-guide panels, headlines and indicated shaded areas may be on a transparent overlay sheet which flaps over and snugly lies in position on the basic design beneath.

Let me pause at this point to emphasise that the talents of the finished artist and the designer complement each other in Advertising—the one is not necessarily inferior or superior to the other; indeed, the individuals concerned may be said to require each other's talents if they are to succeed in either department and not a few actually swap jobs and then switch back again in the course of their Advertising careers. What should never be allowed to occur is the supersession of one over the other while they have work in progress within their respective spheres.

Finished artwork consists of two main crafts: that of design-reproduction by hand, and that of "paste-up." The designer will have indicated where body-copy goes by rough squiggles, or "chinese-ing," on his drawing; when these words are actually printed on reproduction proof paper (called "repro") the paragraphs are cut out separately by the finished artist and pasted-up into their correct position on his board, to achieve the same effect in print as did the designer's squiggled lines. If the same effect is in fact *not* achieved, the designer and typographer have agreed on the wrong type-face (*see* below). In this case the choice of type-face can either be altered or the copywriter may be persuaded (and it will take very strong persuasion!) to add or subtract words or sentences so that everything *does* fit.

Similarly, if a photograph has been taken for the ad, or a wash or line-drawing executed by an outside specialist (who can be the designer himself, acting in his own time as "free-lance"), these are also cut out and pasted down into their correct position on the artboard or the overlay, always so as to match at every point the original design. For I cannot hammer home too strongly, or too often, that a designer in Advertising is responsible for designing the appearance and visual effect of the *total advertisement area*, not just the illustration, the trade-mark, the logo or the fancy lettering of the headline. His design is the sum of these parts. His overall responsibility extends into ensuring that the finished artist faithfully reproduces his original creative conception of the whole advertisement, taking no short-cuts and making no facile compromise which, while superficially attractive, may in any way lessen or even change the nature of the intended impact.

Type-casting your ad

The task of getting the copywriter's words correctly set in print on the repro before it comes into the hands of the finished artist for pasting-up into the finished artwork belongs to the typographer. With one eye on the words and the other fixed on the space which those words are meant to occupy in the design the typographer will first do a word-count, then choose type-face and type-size and proceed with "casting-off"—this has nothing to do with knitting (however much wool-pulling over people's eyes may perhaps be going on) but is the method by which, using ruled lines and numbers, he will clearly mark on the copywriter's typescript just which words are to be set on which printed line and how much space, or "leading," is to be allowed between these lines.

This is the "type-markup" which the type-setter will follow in making the printed proof, but when the ad consists entirely, or even almost entirely, of words, then the type-markup is rightly elevated in terminology to being called the "typographical design," for the appearance of the ad has now become, of course, a design in words.

Typography is therefore, as you can see, a highly-skilled craft which is frequently an art—it is, in fact, the original printer's art. Caxton was the proto-typographer, one might way! Display advertisements, i.e. large, bordered ads which consist of words alone (the appointments pages of *The Daily Telegraph* carry dozens of examples in each issue), need at best a typographical design which a wise advertiser will not leave to the unimaginative mercies of less professional printers. Here, the agency supplies to the printer the equivalent of finished artwork, which is called the typographical layout, and this is executed not by the finished artist but by the typographer. In the last century newspaper proprietors could proclaim arbitrary limitations on the type-faces they would accept—many even fought against display advertising—but pressure of demand soon eliminated such restrictions.

The incompetent typographer may sometimes feel that today he has become *too* de-restricted, with the proliferation of type-faces that has occurred since the war! However, the expert professional—though his skills are among the most under-rated of all by the lay public—once decided on a certain type-face (which means a particular shape and design of letter), can simply glance at a copywriter's submitted script and tell you almost at once how large the printed type must be if it is to fit into its allotted space on the design.

Facts about faces

New type-faces are constantly being designed (the latest crop are all in "computer"-styling) and certain faces go in and out of fashion—exactly as in the cosmetic field, as my feminine readers will be too exhaustedly aware—as clients become conscious of them, usually waiting for someone else to be sufficiently daring to utilise the new face first. Since the world's first type-set "face" came along in 1450, you won't be surprised to learn that there are over 20,000 available today. Every face is capable of reproduction in a wide range of sizes and each encompasses a complete *fount*, i.e. all the letters of the alphabet, numbers and punctuation marks in common usage, with upper and lower cases provided (though the influential *Bauhaus* school tried unsuccessfully to do away with capital letters altogether). For most needs, the size is scaled in Britain and America from 6-point (the smallest) up to 72-point (approximately an inch across), though one can go much bigger than this.

Naturally, no typographer or designer carried 20,000 or more typefaces in his or her head. There are seven main groups—Old Style Roman, Transitional, Modern Roman, Gothic, Script, Text and Decorative—and, evolved out of these, the Letraset Company make over one hundred different faces available to typographers on their instant-lettering sheets. So that we may reckon roughly that, at any one time, there are about one hundred faces to the "Typo's" hand.

Every typographer, however lowly a position he may occupy in some agency hierarchies, inherits a body of tradition closely interwoven with our history and should be proud of it. The first of his line revolutionised the world, no less, and the principles which guide the modern practitioner were laid down by none other than the great William Morris; most typos have had to be aggressive, radical lads and one famous face, the Fraktur Type, had the honourable distinction of being outlawed by Hitler! It may fairly be said that every typographer worthy of the name sets out deliberately to change the face of the earth.

The "instant" revolution

I have referred to the Letraset System in particular, because it is this company's sheets of "instant" letters (and their developments as Letrafilm, Letracolor, Letratone, etc.), which are rubbed on to the page or artboard, using exactly the same principle as a child's transfer—such transfers are now in fact produced by Letraset, though in highly sophisticated form—that are the most widely used in advertising agencies, both by the designer for his visual and the finished artist for his artwork, plus the typographer for *his* design. There are excellent competing systems, of course, such as *Magictype*, *Letterpress* and *Instaprint*, but since Letraset pioneered the method in 1956 ("wet" transfers were soon replaced by "dry" transfers) they have easily dominated the field, making the designer's task easier and halving his working-time. Letraset sheets are outstandingly important for the finished artist in preparing designs for the printer, since lithography, and the related web-offset lithography, has become by far the most popular of modern printing techniques.

"Litho" printing was always welcomed for being cheaper than letterpress printing (the raised-metal relief printing which has been standard since the Gutenberg Bible) but now, in addition, litho can give
results which are just as striking, vivid and of "luxury" quality on
a greater variety of stock (printer's term for the paper on which he
prints) than letterpress, with just as fine colour-reproduction whether
sheet-fed or web-offset.

For litho-printing, moreover, photographic plates are made
directly from the artwork, so instant lettering—which goes perfectly
on to acetate also—has become a virtual godsend for the spreading
of the "gospel" truth. Letraset does in fact carry advertising messages
in every medium; it has suggested the virtues of Murphy TV sets in
the Press and been rather more suggestive still on posters for Elliott's
"Original French Skin Boots" in the Tube, it has labelled Sainsbury's
Digestive Sweetmeal Biscuits on the packet-wrapper and "The Late
Show" on the box, you will see it on bottles of Alpine Cordials and
on equally mouth-watering display cards in the Playboy Club.

Other printing methods include gravure (again from photographic
plates) and the silkscreen process, which is a stencilling method and
particularly versatile, being as viable for flags as for catalogue-covers,
so is often used for below-the-line promotions (*see* Chapter X) and
where relatively short-run printings are required by client. Other
lettering methods, other than by hand, include photo-setting and
computer-typesetting—the second of these is at the moment of limited
adaptability, but its technology is developing with breath-taking
speed.

Taking the stage on screen

Apart from silkscreen printing, the term "screen" has another, and
much more practical day-to-day meaning for the art studio experts,
since it can dictate the *capability of communication* of the design offered
by the creative people and is entirely governed by the medium in
which the design will appear.

Every illustration (photograph or drawing) which you see in magazine and newspaper advertisements has been printed from a photo-
engraving made from the finished artwork sent to the printers by your
agency studio, that artwork having been photographed through a fine
screen of crossed diagonal lines graded as so many lines to the centi-
metre. The resultant negative thus appears as a collection of dots
which are clustered thickest where the original tone is darkest, with
shadings in between the light and dark patches.

These dots are then etched (the word means "eaten into" and it's
an acid that does the eating) on to the printing-blocks which are then
cut to size and sent to media. From the blocks (or plates, according

to printing method used by media) black-and-white photographs can be faithfully reproduced, which are familiarly known as half-tones. The medium's rate card, held by your media department, will always include in its data the screen-size required. For example, *The Times* requires a 25-screen for best results, the *Sunday People* requests a 22-screen. Where magazines are concerned the stock is of much superior quality, so finer screens can be specified—*Jazz Journal* suggests 40-screen, *Harpers and Queen*, *Vogue* and *Tatler* use 48-screen, as does *Corsetry and Underwear*, while the *Connoisseur* and *Burlington Magazine*, being art publications with correspondingly lush illustrative material, call for 54-screen and 60-screen respectively.

Titbits, however, prints in gravure, as does *TV Comic*, most women's journals and the Catholic *Universe* (which will accept from agencies "good pull artwork or photographs"). *What's On* prints in offset-litho, and photo-engraving and photo-setting methods are increasingly replacing letterpress and block-making in all kinds of media, though not by any means as fast as one might wish, for printing is notoriously one of the most conservative, not to say reactionary, of all trades (many printers actually do regard advertising design as superfluous— one even asked me once, in so many words, what it was designers did in their studios!).

Changes come, however. *Pig-Farming*, it is true, sticks in the mud at letterpress, along with *Drinks International* and the *Labour Mayor*, but more and more journals are combining both methods, with covers in offset-litho and letterpress inside, like *Birds*, or letterpress outside and offset inside, like *Fishing*. This is starting to simplify matters greatly, so that, for example, *Yachting and Boating Weekly* requests merely "photographs or original artwork" from agencies, the *Amalgamated Engineering Union Journal* needs only "artwork, layout and copy," though the *Reader's Digest* informs admen intimidatingly that *its* pages are printed by "heatset rotary letterpress," so kindly mind how you go!

Another variant which the finished artist must have at his ink-stained fingertips is the many different widths of the columns in the national press, because the space bought has its length expressed in millimetres but the width is expressed as "columns"—he must remember that a column in the *Daily Mail* is 37 millimetres wide, while in *The Financial Times* it is 44 millimetres wide and in the *Sun* it is 38 millimetres wide, and so on.

Whether the media are newspapers, journals, posters or any other kind of printed matter, enough has now been said, I think, to indicate the many aspects of production which must be as familiar to the finished artist (and ideally, the designer, too) as they are to the agency's Production Manager. Unless he has this fund of knowledge,

kept constantly up to date by personal knowledge (for even rate cards
can nod occasionally!), he cannot prepare artwork to achieve maximum effect. The client–agency marriage can stand or fall by the
"christening robes" he provides for the Brand-X promotion campaign.

And British admen in this field can draw inspiration from the fact
that not only are such innovations as Letraset all-British originals,
but for many years *The Times* led the world in newspaper printing
technology (the first, in 1814, to use a cylinder-press, the first to use
curved stereo plates and print 10,000 copies an hour!), while the
whole process of half-tone reproduction itself was invented in 1852
by an Englishman, William Talbot, though, alas, in all too familiar
pattern, it took the Americans first to put half-tones in their morning
papers. Hastily recovering our bludgeoned morale let's not forget that
the name of John Dickinson, so familiar on our notepapers and envelopes, was that of the brilliant Englishman who in 1824 invented a
machine to make cardboard—without which there would be no
finished art at all, as we know it!

Putting products in the picture

Now we come to the problem of how to illustrate Brand-X. By
photography or drawing, line, wash or scraperboard? Here also you'll
find that preference runs in fads and fashions, and much will depend
on costs—much will hinge on whether you are using the agency's
photographic facilities or a well-known outside studio, whether the
dolly-girl posing with Brand-X in her hand or under her armpit (or
wearing X, or drinking it, eating it or astounding her husband with
it) is the girl from "Vouchers" or the latest Shrimp or Twiggy. Generally speaking, the worse the newsprint (the paper your paper is
printed on), the poorer quality you'll get from photographic reproduction, and the wiser you'll be to order a drawing. Whatever the
medium, however, it is often more advisable for a drawing to be made
where the illustration just consists of showing the pack of the product.
Motor cars, for example, always show to far greater advantage in a
drawing than a photograph; without any implication of "cheating"
or distortion, significant selling details can be highlighted for immediate effect, creating paradoxically a much more *genuine* impression
than would the most expertly "touched-up" photograph.

Every designer has his favourite "outside" artists, next to himself
(though the Art Buyer will, as a rule, conduct negotiations) and many
organisations have been formed to supply them—the largest in
Europe is Artist Partners Ltd., of Ham Yard, the address being no
reflection upon their creative personalities—and these act as agents,
sending round representatives regularly to the agencies with portfolios

of current work by artists on their files. Many "big-name" artists undertake commercial assignments in this way, charging anything upwards of £25 apiece for sketched figures, so that the masterpiece hung at the Royal Academy may well have a first cousin portraying a close-up of our "under-stains." The ghost of Whistler may well have sighed for such organisations, when his celebrated *Mother* was utilised on a poster advertising War Bonds in 1917.

Irrespective, however, of whether the specialist involved is a fashion artist, a still-life expert, or a technical illustrator (an extremely skilled delineator of machinery components, tools or other industrial subjects and equipment), let us never lose sight of the essential distinction here—that it is the designer's work which has won the client's approval. It is the work of other full-time professional artists and photographers who now transpose that design into the ingredients assembled for printing by the finished artist.

THE SWINGING PHOTO-SET

The field of commercial photography—which plays such an attention-getting part in modern advertising—is very wide and superficially well known to the public through films like *Blow-Up*. Granted, it is full of phoneys and has a fair sprinkling of nymphomaniacs, but no more than most businesses, and it does produce the spice of occasional genius to provide the antidote for the unfortunate taste of the total scene.

Photographers themselves swing in and out of fashion, in both senses, often swinging their models in and out with them, their masses of equipment often in inverse ratio to their talent, making sharp contrast with the simple box camera that once gave up Cecil Beaton's finest effects.

Most of them strive to be as *unfashionable*, in the old sense, as possible—nothing, for instance, could be more in contrast with the jeans and open shirt of David Bailey, unabashed by his working-class accent and background in the top hotels and restaurants, than the overtly snobbish Baron de Meyer, with his blue racing-car, blue suits, blue beret and blue hair, yet who pioneered in the Edwardian era, in the pages of *Vogue*, many of the techniques still employed by the Baileys, Silversteins, Donovans and their peers of today. In his fascinating book *The Glass of Fashion* Beaton hails the Blue Baron as "fashion's first and most individual photographer."

Facts about more faces

The young girls who go in and come out with the fashion photographers, and get younger each year doing it (models of the pre-First

World War were blooming matrons, of the pre-Second World War were mature young women, of today are teenagers—and the Lolitas are coming!) may with literal accuracy be termed fashion "plates" since it is the camera plates which supply their characteristic *personae*; the original fashion-plates were the ninety-eight plates of contemporary dress design published 400 years ago by an Italian engraver, Enea Vico.

Most girls, and now many boys, in our schools aspire to modelling careers and quite legitimately, since their idols in *Honey* and similar publications are deliberate reflections of their callow selves—as are, of course, the fast-changing pop groups in the psychedelic discotheques. However, behind the few quite notable model agencies lurk dozens of unscrupulous outfits who charge exorbitant fees for "training" classes and then abandon their luckless raw recruits to shift for themselves.

The true working professional model in Advertising is, however, far removed from the image of *Blow-Up*, of drugs and casual couplings. She is, quite simply, far too busy for immorality; her time is too taken up with titivating for titillating and woe betide her if she confuse the two—her viewing public may, but she can't afford to do so. Any day in Mayfair or thereabouts, you can see these very hard-working girls dashing along the pavements, hunting for taxis, chasing buses, queueing for health foods (nothing fattening!), rather thin, very intent, brimming with purposeful, but oddly impersonal vitality, lugging round their make-up box, hat-box and box of whatever dresses or accessories have been requested by the advertising agency (for they usually have to provide their own wardrobe and spend more on dresses than on meals).

Their days are tightly scheduled, their faces chosen by the designer (who, as Art Director, should keep firm control of the photographic sessions) from picture-albums of themselves and their statistics, on the sole basis of their fitness for the illustration he has in mind—mother, seductress, gamine, schoolgirl, mod or dowdy housewife, filly or frump. She may well not even have been selected for her features at all, or indeed any of the more obvious vital data—only her hand or arm may appear in the ad, for she may look glamorous in gloves and tatty in tights. One model agency, New Faces, has a girl whose sole vital statistic is that she closely resembles Princess Anne. Her work is exclusively in Europe to date.

Model attitudes

There are similar face-catalogues for male models and for children, plus "picture libraries" for almost all subject matter and topics, both for colour and black and white. In making his eventual choice the designer has to be most careful not to assume that his personal bias is a shared and general one. Let me quote David Ogilvy's wry words from his *Confessions*:

> "One of the most agreeable chores in advertising is selecting pretty girls to appear in advertisements and television commercials. I used to arrogate this function to myself, but gave it up after comparing my personal taste in girls with the taste of female consumers. Men don't like the same kind of girls that girls like."

Or, if you like, there is one blonde for lagers and another for lipsticks. Whichever blonde does land the job, it's more than likely to be dull and routine; she will stand stock-still till she aches, she will twist and crane her limbs and lips into the exaggerated poses demanded by a crowd of unseen witnesses, hidden behind the curtaining glare of blinding white arc-lamps, who have gathered not to leer but to regard her as a sort of plasticine untouchable on which they can imprint the projection of their commercial (mainly) fantasies. She will earn around £35 per hour for doing it, though her fee will vary, depending on whether she is posing for a Press campaign or will only appear on posters, showcards and packaging.

Few and far between are the swimsuit ads that will take a Marilyn Rickards to Mediterranean strands and Majorcan bowers to pose in next year's Nelbarden creations; rare are the fashion assignments which will drape Shrimptons of the future over Carthaginian ruins or beneath Bermudan stalactites (looking as if she were on one of the stalagmites!) while thousands of shots take every angle and curve. One of the last memos I saw on an Account Executive's desk was a proposal to embark a veritable cavalcade of pulchritude to the Australian deserts for a new low-fat bread campaign—what the connection was to be I never knew, but the fact that the transport alone was to cost £10,000 probably cut the calories on that one.

More feasibly she will be posing for a mail-order catalogue, but payment will still be good because today's models are well organised by a determined "lady" called Alma. Actually, the name is ALMA, which stands for the Association of London Model Agencies, and it has succeeded not just in raising modelling fees but in demanding payment within *thirty days*! Magnificent darlings! In my view this admirable precept is to the world of Advertising alike in profaneness to denying the Immaculate Conception at the top of your voice in the Vatican, and it has electrically inspired the forming of the first photographer's organisation, AFAP, the Association of Fashion and Advertising Photographers, for the express purpose of getting money out of admen, who often, I regret to say, take *at least* six months to settle consultancy fees of any kind. (Advertising men are beginning

to be beset from the other direction also, by a proposal from the Newspaper Publishers' Association that a surcharge be inflicted on late-
paying agencies!)

ALMA was too late, unfortunately, to help the most famous advertising model of all time, Player's bearded sailor, whose lifebuoy-
framed robust and hearts-of-oak visage went round the world on
cigarette packets for half a century (though some may claim the title
for another sailor, Admiral Sir William James, whose apogee of child-
hood was to be the original model for "Bubbles"). It was in 1898
that Able Seaman Thomas Huntley Wood posed for the Player's portrait, but he died only as recently as 1951, having in the intervening
years been enriched for his modelling endeavours by the lavish sum
of two guineas (he beat *down* the fee from £15) plus "a bit of baccy
for myself and the boys on board." Since his brief career as a model
also cost him that wonderful beard—which he shaved off in disgust
at constantly being recognised—one can only hope that the admen
didn't keep *him* waiting for six months.

THEMES AND VARIATIONS

I have dwelt at some length, though by no means exhaustively,
on the processes and procedures of getting the agreed advertising copy
and design for your Brand-X campaign into actual print. However,
I have not done this simply because your client is almost certain
to be blissfully ignorant of the trouble, time and expense required,
but because of the vital importance of *getting it right*, for though the
copy must carry the message the fact remains that 80 per cent of our
senses are *visual* senses, and ever since the first illustration was added
to newspaper advertising copy in 1710, the *look* of an ad has been
of prime consideration.

Not that either problems or their solutions have really altered so
much through the years. The "cuts and figures" which so plagued
the block-makers of the *Daily Courant* (our very first daily paper) in
Joseph Addison's day—the day of Marlborough's great victories and
our capture of the Rock of Gibraltar which Advertising was to immor-
talise as the trade-mark of the Prudential Insurance Company—still
harass them now, when, as we have seen, the column-widths in the
London dailies alone seem almost infinitely variable. On top of these
woes, your media-schedule may call for your ad to appear as a half-
page "upright" in one paper, as a 15-cm double-column in another,
and in yet another as a full double-page spread!

"Instant" lettering, of course, is not really all that new in essence
either. In the days when Victoria was sipping Cadbury's and washing
in Hudson's Soap, letters extolling margarine were imprinted some-

how on the walls of Arctic fiords and other letters praising pills
appeared on sails along Lake Windermere—to the near apoplexy of
none other than the eminent John Ruskin, who, fresh from accusing
Whistler of "flinging a pot of paint in the public's face," could hardly
be expected to keep countenance over *this* desecration.

Lettering's most resourceful practitioner, for my money, will always
be Sir Thomas Lipton. At the turn of the century, when his cruise-
ship was stranded in the Red Sea and was forced to jettison cargo,
Sir Thomas whipped into the hold with stencil and marker and before
long the tides of Araby for miles up and downstream carried floating
bales and crates bearing the bold as brass legend "Drink Lipton's
Tea." Such enterprise was typical. Alec Waugh relates in *The Lipton
Story* how that inspired P.R. man had earlier invited Victoria to
accept a giant five-ton cheese "made from one day's milk of 8,500
cows," and even then, the Queen was not affronted: her refusal was
only because, as she wrote to him, they had not been introduced—
though whether she referred to Lipton or to the 8,500 cows was not
made clear.

Since all the space buying and media-selection is, or should be, decided upon before the artwork is put in hand for printing, one prays
that our Brand-X client won't attempt to interfere with last-minute
amendments and second-thought "improvements," emulating the
American producer who was interested in Somerset Maugham's play
Lady Frederick, already referred to in this chapter, provided the author
slipped in two dozen more epigrams, to spice things up a bit! Once
the creative work for X is approved by client the Account Executive
should *never* tolerate subsequent alterations beyond minor points of
adjustment. At the same time the copywriter and designer must keep
a hawk-eyed vigilance on proofs—which will come in first from the
block-makers and type-setters, and later from the publications themselves—though often they will have to fight tooth and nail even to
see them when their Traffic Manager is pressed for time. There are
standardised symbols by which all these proofs can be, if necessary,
marked for correction. The copywriter and designer—and all those
through whose hands the proofs pass—will append their initials to
the proof, and it is up to the Traffic Controller for his own protection
to make sure they do so promptly. Creative people, and others, can
be very elusive even in the smallest agency, and Traffic Controllers
or Managers soon develop a bloodhound nose.

I give one more caution at this point. When client is shown the
artwork for his ad, make sure he appreciates fully whether the work
is "S.S." (Same Size) or not. For better reproduction artwork is often
executed to scale larger than the size of the ad as it will eventually
appear in the media—usually it is done "half-up" which simply

means half again as large, for in this way the finished artist can fill in greater detail with more precision, and on photographing the ad is then reduced to whatever sizes are called for, or indeed enlarged if required. This versatility is obviously immensely useful, but the Brand Manager must clearly comprehend this scaling up or down when he is asked to approve artwork, otherwise his disappointment over the ad's actual look in print may lead to many rows and a refusal to accept agency charges.

PITFALLS AND PRATFALLS

So now the baby is at last in its christening robes, and the X-campaign is ready to face the world. Some of it will be exclusively addressed to the trade (*see* Chapter X) and it may undergo more preliminary tests before the full national launch.

Despite, however, all precautions and pre-launch testings, and despite the most faithful adherence to some currently "in" theory, not every pitfall can be foreseen, much less avoided—your advertising know-how will be in preventing the inevitable pitfall from turning into a pratfall. Not every second thought can be fended off, however idiotic and awkward to implement, as in the 1970 ads for Carmen Wigs, where, in *Nova* and *The Sunday Times Magazine*, a mod sophisticated lady drove her car with a smiling negro chauffeur in the passenger seat beside her (putting her one up on the Latin chauffeur of the Martini Vermouth commercials), while this same lady in the pages of *Woman's Own* drove *solo*, the chauffeur having been mysteriously wiped away.

Racial prejudice? Perish the thought! Perish the lady's wig also, if she does much more driving around in the rain with the hood down! No, let's pull ourselves together; the thought which *did* apparently seem acceptable to the Account Executive at Alexander-Butterfield & Ayer, where these variations were created and modified, was that the gratuitous inclusion of a negro chauffeur who was not employed to put his hands on the wheel (though he's grinning about *something*) was "pregnant with possibilities."

Pregnancy aside, the only racial bias which would seem involved here (though, naturally, it wasn't) was, to my mind, in putting the chauffeur there at all, not in taking him out.

FINAL CHECK-OUTS

The purely creative aspects of the agency work on Brand-X or any campaign will confront us with the innate problems and charisma of media other than the Press, of course. Nevertheless, it is right that we have highlighted here this particular medium for the excellent practical business reason that far more of your client's cash is spent on it than on any other.

This fact was always true before the coming of Independent Television, and remained so, though television made big inroads into budgets and still does. Press-expenditure still continues to dominate, however, and indeed, at time of writing, is busily *increasing* its share of the advertising loot because of the persistent fall in viewing figures for Independent Television—late in 1970, B.B.C. television programmes were making an overwhelming invasion of the Top Ten JICTAR ratings, and Independent Television's overall share of "sets viewing" had dropped to 52 per cent! Press dominance was accentuated during this period by cut-backs in overall spending, as exemplified by the fact that between June and December of 1970, J.W.T.'s clients—than whom there are none more prestigious—sliced appropriations by a cool £1 million, or 5 per cent of total billings, while some other major agencies suffered even worse withdrawal symptoms than the Brahmins of Berkeley Square, of between 8 per cent and 10 per cent. In 1975, according to I.P.A. statistics, spending on press ads was £678 million, as against £236 million for television, so the press sector of Advertising is not only retaining this major share, but increasing it to nearly an enormous 70 per cent of total ad expenditure in Britain!

Proofs, photographs, "block-pulls," all must be checked and double-checked, till finally launch-date arrives, the Brand-X campaign "breaks" across the nation, and the new offspring is proudly christened by agency and client. Christening parties, where appropriate, will be held, varying from a mutual toasting in the boardroom (where roastings may shortly follow), to a Savoy press conference, all the way up to a retailer's free-loading "girlie" spectacular, with stars and pop groups, at the Palladium, which will set your client back (at small benefit to yourself) around £150,000. Such christenings leave precious little funds to bring up the baby.

However, after the slap-happy tumult and the shouting of the odds, the hysterical excitements and incitements, things soon settle down and you watch the campaign unfold, wondering whether hunches and expertise have been right or wrong.

Chapter XIV

YOUR FUTURE IN ADVERTISING

In the novel *Kate in Advertising* by Ann Barton, one of a series for young girls, the heroine, casting career-prospects into fictional form, excitedly describes her day's work to her father:

> "We had such fun doing the coupons—there were four of them ... First we decided together what we wanted to put, and then Primrose drew out the coupons while I wrote the golden words—we always call them that ... I do love it—you've no idea how exciting it is to be a copywriter."

The enthusiasm depicted by Ann Barton's protagonist is at the opposite end of the opinion spectrum from views of Mary Whitehouse and Elizabeth Ackroyd, of the Consumer Council, who would doubtless contend that Kate's enthusiasm could well be tempered by a zeal for truth and social responsibility. But the day-to-day reality of work in Advertising lies between the two, since the enjoyment of one's career in this exciting but exacting profession should ultimately derive from the skill of selling ... but selling *responsibility*. And the knowledge that you are not selling to fools.

The British customer also has a sense of fun and poetry. He knows perfectly well that nothing is "whiter than white" and if his girlfriend's seductive smile was invariably accompanied by a shining halo round her head, he would run, not walk, to the nearest malodorous vamp. He knows his wife can sprinkle cleanser into her sink without fear of being struck by lightning, and can accept that his toothpaste is "cool as a mountain-stream," even though he has seen nothing higher than the Post Office Tower. Every mother is perfectly aware that the two men in her life are much more likely to be kept happy with a bag of sweets and a good stiff whisky than Shredded Wheat, and her daughter needs no Ombudsman to tell her that the most streamlined stereo equipment sounds better with an LP on the turntable—the manufacturer didn't wish to publicise any record company!

However, while I don't think you need fear a future blighted by censorship or government interference on the lines of the efforts made last year by the U.S. Federal Trade Commission to force Coca-Cola and Standard Oil of California to run ads confessing "we lied," you will undoubtedly be joining a profession in flux.

CHANGE AND INNOVATION

The greatest changes will undoubtedly come in the realm of media. Newspapers will be fewer, probably larger, and certainly all will be printed in colour before many years have passed. Commercial radio stations have by no means approached the possibilities envisaged for them, only nineteen having sprung up where sixty were prophesied so the air-waves are still largely virgin territory for serious professional advertising, and as television contracts come up once more for re-consideration, the whole structure of television advertising will alter in scale and scope. The largest change in this medium will occur now that we have entered the Common Market, when Eurovision Advertising is likely to become the norm. When tele-advertising expands along these lines across the world (and it will arrive sooner than many think) then we shall be seeing many more "super-colossal"—perhaps one should say souper-colossal—productions mounted for clients, like the sixty-second ad that was made in Hollywood for the new Heinz "Great American Soup." It cost £80,000 at 1972 prices. There is a very large question-mark over Europe, all the same, in the efforts being made to draw up very stringent rules for advertising in the E.E.C. A document has been issued from Brussels with the ominously long-winded title *First Preliminary Draft Directive Concerning the Approximation of the Laws of Member States on Fair Competition, Misleading and Unfair Advertising*. At the moment, this remains only a cloud, however, on a very high, wide and handsome horizon.

But there will be plenty of TV innovations on the home-viewing front as well. Apart from longer transmission periods, the rapid spread of U.H.F. coverage (there will be twenty-seven Ultra High Frequency transmitters in service in the near future, leading to a target of sixty-four right round the nation) will mean at least one more channel, and probably more (your modern set has actually the inbuilt technology now to take 40 channels!). The re-introduction of Pay-TV is extremely likely and may be particularly used for sporting events.

More imminent than either of these developments—indeed, they are already on the market—are Television Cassettes, which will be sold by three companies, E.V.R., Sony and Telefunken. These cassettes, which can be played through an ordinary TV set, have special programmes and films produced for them; the advertising tapes they incorporate give clients the equivalent of a sponsored show, as obtains today on American television. Previous "ethical and moral" objections to such sponsorship will now no longer be valid, since the potential customer can buy the cassettes or not, as he pleases.

Advertising will also take to the sky again, not, as in 1924, with the words *Daily Mail* appearing over the dome of St. Paul's, but as accompaniments to films shown in passenger aircraft on individual screens. Cold wars permitting, ads will be beamed from satellites and bounced from the Moon (perhaps from the Sea of Tranquillisers!) and Mars.

Bringing ourselves back to earth, and to more immediate media, more clients will make use of travelling exhibitions set up on custom-built rail-coaches which can travel for thousands of miles, stop any-where, for any length of time—outstanding examples include the Vono Bedding train and the "great North America Comes to Town" train, sponsored by B.O.A.C. and a number of United States travel firms. While there is nothing new in the concept itself, modern techno-logy has transformed the medium; the B.O.A.C. train has audio-visual equipment, three-dimensional colour photos, displays and models—plus a sixty-seat cinema. Last year, ex-Prime Minister Edward Heath toured the country in a special train, signing *and selling* his books and records.

Seeing will be selling

Another innovation is in the field of actual cinema advertising. Arising out of the present rather crude "localised" cinema ads, which tack on the name of the nearest retailer or distributor to a general film about, say, used cars, the Rank Organisation placed on offer their "Dick Emery Interviews" film, which showed the well-known come-dian in a number of his extremely funny impersonations of "people in the street." Fifty-two seconds of the commercial were devoted to comedy... but the final question "Which is your favourite shop? ..." was followed by eight seconds when the name of any shop can be put on the screen (traffic roar happily muffles the spoken reply). At the very reasonable cost of £25 per week, this may have made Dick Emery the most popular minute-man in the adworld.

Videotape will be used more and more, I believe, as agencies and clients make more effort to *use* the medium's limitations instead of being intimidated by them. Just as ordinary tape-recorders pick up and play back sound alone, videotapes record sound *and* vision (and provide another example, like Thermos and Hoover, of a brand-name becoming a generic one). In filming commercials, they offer the ad-vantages of speed, simplicity and economy—no "processing" is re-quired, and the film can be erased and used again and again; the disadvantage is that editing is difficult, so that (though special effects are possible) the whole commercial has to be performed "live" and *in one take*. In the field of public relations (*see* Chapter IV) they may be used as a substitute for much present promotional literature and unit-displays, since they can bring evidence of "product perform-ance" right to the executive's desk or boardroom—acting, in other words, as a film-strip but *in "live" action*. So the videotape will be an increasingly important medium for both consumer and trade advertising.

One innovation which I'm sure will come, before you have been in Advertising very long, is the use of the telephone as a promotional medium. There will be great public outcry, of course, but—as with buying or not buying cassettes—you can dial or not dial. Each region of the country will have a set number to ring, which will give you the "ads of the day." One can, after all, already pick up the phone for a prayer or a pop song, and the medium will become twice as valid when visual-phoning is generally installed, so that you can see the person speaking to you ... and see the product or service offered in the ad. You will, as customer, even be able to reply and thus place an order, if you wish, on the present "reply service" principle—much as today, in some parts of America, two-way cable-links enable TV viewers to place an immediate order for the item they have just seen advertised. Like all new media, however, this device will have to achieve a minimum 30 per cent penetration of the market before advertisers will accept it as commercially viable on a large scale.

Recruitment advertising

The fast-rising phenomenon of recruitment advertising reminds us that this branch of the profession, which now brings in approximately £70 million in total billings each year, was the mainstay of Advertising in its earliest days.

The earliest clearing-houses for ads were, in fact, essentially employment offices (of greater or less respectability), and John Houghton, the so-called "Father of Advertising," included these examples in one of the earliest issues of his *Collection*:

> "If I can meet with a sober man that has a counter-tenor voice, I can help him to a place worth £30 the year or more ..."

> "I want a complete young man that will wear a livery, to wait on a very valuable gentleman; but he must know how to play on a violin or flute ..."

> "I want a pretty boy to wait on a gentleman, who will take care of him and put him out an apprentice ..."

while the following is more in line with our notions of expanding world trade and international markets:

> "I want an Englishman that can tolerably well speak French (if Dutch too, so much the better), and that will be content to sit at home, keeping accounts, almost his whole time, and give good security for his fidelity, and he shall have a pretty good salary."

No "company car" or luncheon vouchers or mention of "holiday arrangements respected," but nevertheless anyone who could fairly answer this ad would be even more in demand today.

Whether or not recruitment advertising is riding a temporary boom, few would dare prophesy. It is not long ago that *all* classified advertising, much less the staff-ads part of it, was treated as the "poor relation" among agency accounts. The work involved was not considered sufficiently glamorous or financially rewarding to have the best Advertising brains focused on it. Things have now swung to an equally ridiculous opposite extreme, with an absurd mystique being built round the whole field. The ads themselves are certainly difficult to write properly—all classified ads are, contrary to popular notion—but the "scientific" trimmings often show Advertising at its pompous worst. For the moment, however, many big-spending clients are eating it up and *The Financial Times* (itself a good, but expensive, medium for recruitment of upper-echelon staff) estimates a steady rise of 12 per cent a year in job advertising.

The introduction of computers will no doubt attract those companies who are partial to any amount of guff, provided it is demonstrably "programmed." Some firms also see recruitment advertising as a chance to promote themselves (to themselves) and indulge in lushly-coloured prestige ads. But the big daddy medium of all in this field is the splendid *Daily Telegraph*, which invented the Box Number over a hundred years ago and thoroughly deserves its pre-eminence in staff-ads—they bring in at least half the paper's total revenue!

More entrails and auguries

One pretty safe bet is an increase in joint-promotions, with one product being offered to the customer at a premium price, provided it is bought in combination with another. The reader will have seen examples himself . . . the Nescafé people have been very active in the field, selling in harness with Kleenex, N.E.L. paperbacks and B.P. petrol, while Crosse and Blackwell have sold products tied to Ritz Crackers, Lyons Cakes and Ariel washing powder—to cite just two. Agencies will have to evolve economical methods of working on these together, or they will lose all this business to specialty premium firms. Related to this will be an increase in the practice of "generic" campaigns, whereby clients of every size and capability (and language!), who operate in the same product-area, pool their resources, either voluntarily or by a system of levy, and demand unifying campaigns from their several agencies.

The big charities, for example, already do this in the case of specific disasters. Excellent "generic" campaigns have been launched by the Milk and Egg Marketing Boards; various tour operators have combined in British Travel Promotions and, encouraged by the early success in the White Fish Authority campaign to put a bomb under the most static food industry in Britain (2,300 fishmongers went out of business in five years), our flower importers are now discussing if this is the way to take the "l" out of bloom. We have been urged to "Drinka Pinta" at a billing of £2 million per year, to "Go To Work on an Egg" at a budget of £750,000, to join the "Tea Set" at £500,000 a year. The British leather industry hopes to persuade tanners throughout Europe to pool anything up to £3 million in a corporate effort on an international scale to counter the very effective promotion of synthetics.

The last major factor I will mention is that you can expect to be increasingly asked to evolve Advertising to men and women at both extremes of the age scale. We may not follow the example of the Americans and offer bras to nine year olds, but the British Leather Institute, for instance, sees its big new market as the fifteen to twenty year olds, while admen have only recently woken up to the fact that not only are the over-sixty-fives the fastest-growing segment of our population but over two million of them belong to the top A and B categories of the socio-economic classifications (*see* Chapter VI). In the London I.T.V. area, the most avid viewers by far *are under 16 and over 55*, both segments being at least double any other age-group.

THE ROAD TO PROFESSIONALISM

In the opening chapter I made clear my belief that the salvation of all the best aspects of Advertising and the salvage of its very real achievements depends upon the business being recognised and respected as a properly organised profession. I hope that in the intervening chapters I have made equally clear the road we must follow to attain that full measure of professionalism.

One milestone on that road must be in establishing proper education for advertising and qualifications for its practice. C.A.M. award their Diplomas in Advertising, P.R. Media and Creativity, but the achievement of some sort of College of Communication (first mooted in 1968) has yet to be realised—or, indeed, the *need* for one universally accepted.

I don't advocate such grandiloquent title-mongering as exemplified by the award to Mary Wells of the accolade "Marketing Statesman of the Year." This is to kick us upstairs, out of the firing-line where Advertising belongs . . . and reminds me that Oxford was at long last moved to honour the most famous volume it ever spawned, *Alice in Wonderland*, by awarding the degree of Doctor of Letters—to Alice!

We do not need to aspire "above our station," but to make others aspire to ours. Accepting and doing our own thing is honour enough;

we should wear the dust of commercialism like a mantle of incense. Our response to pseudo-intellectual critics should be that of Rudyard Kipling, when some clever undergraduates of that same University which had "honoured" Lewis Carroll by praising the song and not the singer, on learning that the poet was paid at the rate of ten shillings a word, wired him ten bob and requested "one of his best words." Kipling was far from being in the least abashed, accepted the commission, and wired back the one word ... "Thanks."

YOUR ROAD TO PROFESSIONALISM

I'm aware, of course, that when Alice complained that she didn't want to go among mad people, the Cheshire Cat told her she had no choice, "We're all mad here. I'm mad. You're mad ... or you wouldn't have come here."

You must take this, however, not in the literal sense that a fair percentage of your fellow practitioners (starting with Charles Lamb) have been halfway round the bend, but in the sense of embracing this fascinating profession for exactly what it is, no more but certainly no less. In his *Confessions Of An Advertising Man*, Ogilvy writes the plain truth that all admen must learn to live with, that "Competing brands are becoming more and more alike. The men who make them have access to the same scientific journals; they use the same production techniques; and they are guided by the same research."

Eight years on, that truth is more evident still, and John Hobson, head of Hobson Bates, has underlined it by saying, "since with many products it is virtually impossible to have price or basic product competition, advertising is the only form of competition left, and it is far better than no competition at all."

Advertising is becoming, in other words, the last bastion of choice. And the glory of it is that the choice is a *human* one. "Advertise, or go under" was Dorothy Sayers' stark concluding sentence to *Murder Must Advertise* forty years ago ... "ADVERTISE—OR DIE" headlined *The Financial Times* on 12th November 1970. The words were right then, they are just as right now, but in a far wider context than they intended.

Rejoice that men and women *cannot* be conveniently docketed away in pigeon-holes of preference. Rejoice that colour and design of a package *can* influence our feelings towards it, that fashion gives meaning to living and style is life. If man had never hankered from the New and the Free, he would never have left his cave. Rejoice that you cannot criticise rockets to the Moon as gross materialism, if the burden of your argument is that they waste money; that the Moon is there to be shot at, just as it has always been there for poets to write at, and Von Braun had just as much right to want the Moon in his pocket as Browning did.

Rejoice that the world is *not* a "global village," that religious, national and tribal customs vary infinitely with the global customers—in a Moslem country, you cannot show a woman drinking, in East Africa you must not show her wearing earrings, in Portugal your romantic copy must not mention "rendezvous" for there it means brothel, and so on. Rejoice that every human being wears his or her "own label," but exercises the right to change labels whenever the fancy takes them, and wherever it moves them ... can we so confidently label this the "couldn't care less" generation, when in fact the phrase was coined by that apparent pillar of the between-wars Establishment, Sir Philip Albert Gustave David Sassoon, brother of the poet who lambasted the officers of the First World War, while he himself was private secretary to everyone's prototype blimp, Field-Marshal Haig?

Give a man a mask, said Wilde, and he will tell you the truth. So what we need in our world are more and better masks, not fewer and fewer in a grey conformity. "Were it not for imagination, Sir," bellowed Dr. Johnson, "a man would be as happy in the arms of a chambermaid as of a Duchess!" And imagination can likewise turn the Duchess into a chambermaid ... whatever turns you on is the vital ignition of life.

As an Advertising professional, you will hold one of the keys. You will also hold the means by which industry makes a wider choice of things available to a wider number of people ... and more and more different things, to more and more different people. Even in Soviet Russia, where the state agency Vneshtorgreklama has a staff numbering nearly four hundred people!

The key is essentially a very simple one, and without mystery or vice. As simple as that fulcrum by which Archimedes claimed he could move the world. So move it.

Chapter XV

THE NUTS AND BOLTS

As you approach the doors of your career-opening into Advertising, it seems a good time for a word of caution.

You will need to know something of the restraints upon your job, the *legal* restraints. They are there to help you, to prevent the victory going to the loudest shouter rather than to the adman who uses his technique and "proper study of mankind" to project his voice—by no means the same thing, as any actor will tell you. They are there to help you accomplish what James Benson, Vice-Chairman of Ogilvy and Mather International (who arrived via economics, journalism and writing naval history), has called "the principal function of good agency management" which is "to cause good advertising to be produced."

Your agency and client will, of course, have legal departments or retain good lawyers to make sure your ideas don't infringe any statutes or codes. All the same, you may be working on your own for small-sized clients, and some things you may discover too late. Anyway, from the very start, you should have a rough appreciation of the correct limitations awaiting you.

This is a vital part of holding on to professionalism in your work, by remembering, in the words of the Retail Trading Standards Association, that "it is quite possible to write an advertisement which is wholly truthful yet totally misleading," and avoiding what Wilfred Alman, Chairman of Co-ordinated Marketing Services, termed "a fantasy world with the kind of appeal of advertising's wild boys, the know-all young Brand Managers, and the glib Sales Promotion Consultants."

THE LEGAL ASPECTS

In January 1971 *The Sunday Times* colour magazine featured an investigation into manufacturers' "coding" on food packages, which revealed that much of what customers are offered is not as fresh as it seems. This shows clearly that the old medieval concept of *caveat emptor*, "let the buyer beware," remains still the biggest hump your advertising must surmount.

You will find a list of Acts and statutes relating to Advertising in Appendix III of this book. The sort of items they cover I shall only briefly indicate here. I hope the reader will regard these glancing comments only as a guide and will consult the laws themselves when in doubt, or one of the codes of advertising practice, which I will come to in a moment.

Of most recent interest, of course, is the Trade Descriptions Act, which lays down tight rules on such matters as precise statement of quantity, size and gauge of Brand-X, its composition and formula and its method of production, claims of testing and testimonials and of direct or implied royal patronage.

You should also know about the Pharmacy and Medicines Act, which not only prohibits the advertising of methods of abortion but any ads concerning Bright's disease, diabetes, epilepsy, cataract, glaucoma, locomotor ataxy, paralysis and tuberculosis.

Of more narrow, but alas, by no means outdated, interest is the Indecent Advertisements Act, which does *not* mean that you cannot plug rude films, "art" studies in plain wrappers, naughty books and magazines or sex-supermarkets, but that you are not allowed to advertise cures for VD! When the measure was debated in 1889, the Earl of Meath claimed that he knew of one individual who had been offered no fewer than 20,000 different leaflets advocating cures, which leaves one to large wonderments about the person so solicited! However, with venereal disease, in fact, on the increase today, the subject is no light matter.

The Protection of Depositors Act and the Advertisements (Hire-Purchase) Act have obvious applications; but if your proposed campaign for Brand-X involves any games of chance or competitions you had better take a good look at the Betting, Gaming and Lotteries Acts.

The most contentious areas of advertising, in tobacco, drink, and drugs, are now the subject of discussion and agreement for regulation between Government and the Advertising Standards Authority (which draws only half its members from the agencies) rather than legal constraint.

CODES OF PRACTICE

With the pile-up of legislation and prejudice still threatening, however, on every side, agencies and their clients, backed by the various media interests, have taken steps to put their own houses in order.

The *British Code of Advertising Practice* requires of every advertisement that it be "legal, clean, honest and truthful" and not be so constituted as to bring Advertising into contempt; that the credulity (or cupidity!) of children shall not be taken advantage of; that superstition and fear must not be exploited; that statistics must not be manipulated in such a way that they seem to suggest more than they can accurately claim; that "switch selling" is out—a technique of marketing a rather expensive product through the sale of a rather cheap one (clearly, joint-promotions have to watch this point with care).

This code pays particular attention to the marketing of medicines and medical, or pseudo-medical, treatments, and requires, among other things, (1) that no positive cure be claimed; (2) that no advertising should suggest the reader may suffer from a complaint which, in fact, he may not have; (3) that no correspondence-course of treatment be offered, even with "money back" guarantees; (4) that great care be exercised in the use of words like "doctor," "clinic," "college," "institute" and "laboratory;" (5) that no claim be implied that Brand-X can "increase virility;" (6) that no abortion methods be advertised; (7) that no other medical product be disparaged; and (8) that your product is not offered as "natural" when in fact it is nothing of the kind. You are also abjured to be very careful in the way you refer to slimming.

The *Independent Television Code of Advertising Standards and Practice* reflects, as you would expect, much of the above, but the special intimate nature of this medium makes inevitable certain additional points of emphasis, and these include the following:

1. There must be no suggestion of direct sponsorship of programmes by your client.

2. No prizes may be offered (which, for some strange reason, seems not to fetter the B.B.C.).

3. Don't try subliminal advertising.

4. You must not advertise in regard to religion, politics or trade disputes.

5. You cannot advertise money-lenders, matrimonial agencies, fortune-tellers, undertakers, unlicensed employment bureaux, betting tips or cigarettes.

6. No "special effects" technique can be used (*see* Chapter XII) which does not give a "fair and reasonable" idea of the product.

7. Extra special care must be taken with regard to advertisements concerned with medicines and children (a very touchy area).

Two further points I would like to make here, for your guidance on the threshold. I.B.A. rules at present permit *an average* of only six minutes of telly-ads per hour (yes, I agree it often seems more) and *a maximum* in any one hour by the clock of only seven minutes. Also, with certain reservations, you may not advertise charities on TV, and the whole question of ads in all media in the field is covered by the rules laid down by the Charity Commissioners, which I earnestly commend to you. The suggestion by the Annan Committee (*see* Preface to the Second Edition of this book) that 20-minute blocks of advertising be tried on the box was not received gladly by anyone, either in TV or in agencies.

You will need to have a firm grasp of all the laws, codes, restraints and sanctions, not only to produce better ads but to maintain confidence against the assailants of your profession, who are quite as prepared to undermine with as without and to let go at you the equivalent of a loud Annan Report every five years or so.

THE GUERRILLA MOVEMENTS

Like all such movements the critics of Advertising trim sails to the prevailing winds of change in a far more cynical manner than they would ever admit, and are, no doubt, in their own minds, worthy to be called "freedom fighters," though their triumph would impose a fatal diminution of choice.

In 1652, with the "liberator" Cromwell sitting on the nation with his Rump Parliament of toadies (he would soon kick out even these), Samuel Sheppard could stigmatise the adman as "a mountebank who ... drains money from the people of the nation." In 1710, with the Government about to clamp down on the Press, Richard Addison could call advertisements "instruments of ambition." In 1800, with reform and revolution in the air, William Cobbett could belabour advertising as "this species of falsehood, filth and obscenity."

The line continues, with depressing unoriginality of thought and expression, through Marie Corelli down to Richard Hoggart who, in an *AdWeekly* article of November 1965, spoke of Advertising as out to "achieve its ends by emotionally abusing its audiences," and now, echoing the lexicon of the trendy ecologists, we've even had Pat Gierth of Hobson Bates admitting—on the verge of retirement, of course—that Advertising "has its own quotas of visual, verbal and mental pollutants."

Until recently, however, doctors regarded fresh air as a "pollutant" of the sickroom, so we can take heart. As long as there is "good news" to be spread professionals will always be required to spread the gospel truth. The bad news, as always, can take care of itself.

By all means, let us admit that over the past seven years (as a J.W.T. Analysis has shown) the proportion of our Gross National Product spent on advertising has evidenced a steady, if slight, downward trend—the 1976 estimate being 1·10 per cent of G.N.P., down from 1·26 per cent. My own view of this is that much of the cause lies in mistaken agency priorities, summed up so well by David Ogilvy, as usual, when he said in a speech last December: "The most important function in advertising is the creative function. But only one in ten of the people in agencies work in the creative department." It sounds remarkably like the state of the nation—and maybe both situations are about to change.

We start here, by convincing *ourselves* we have something to sell.

Chapter XVI

LET'S DO IT

The following are a few sample projects upon which you can test your Advertising Know-how and skills—naturally, you will concentrate on your special area of interest, but you should have a "go" at every aspect of the problems they set. In the main, they were evolved for students of the Advertising Course at Rush Green Technical College, and I am most grateful to Trevor Lakin-Hall, Director of the Department of Design and Printing, for permission to reproduce them here . . . though I wrote them for Design and Copy students, they lend themselves to other Advertising Agency disciplines as well.

Consider them not only for themselves, but as models for problems you can evolve for yourself—simply choose a product or service out of the nearest magazine, colour supplement, newspaper, or television or radio commercial!

PROJECT 1

To capitalise on the rapidly-growing market for disposable garments, the big London department store, *Oxbridges*, has decided to open a new department, devoted entirely to selling so-called "paper" clothes. They will promote the launch of this department in many media, of course, and on a nationwide scale, but the agency you work for has been commissioned to handle three specific elements:

    1. a shopping-bag or carry-carton;
    2. press ads in the nationals;
    3. a letter addressed to regular customers of Oxbridges, informing them of the new department.

Shopping-bag or carry-carton

Design the bag to optional colours, to contain the following lines of copy . . .

    Name of Department: "Paper Shapes"
    Slogan: "the best *throw-away* lines in the world"

You are required to dream up a distinctive type-face design for the name and slogan, and an outstanding symbol, which may subsequently be used on other promotional material. The design may be presented to client in three-dimensional form, miniature or made-up to size, or as a perspective drawing on flat board.

Launch press advertisement

Again colours are optional, but you will design the ad to fit sizes 558 mm × 381 mm or 558 mm × 190 mm or 279 mm × 381 mm—these are for the *Daily Express* and represent full-page, half-page upright or half-page horizontal. When one ad is finished, see if it will adapt without damage to the other sizes or to other media of your choice. Try different visuals for the various sizes, if you wish, but all must of course emphasise the nature of the goods sold in this new department, and their style must be in key with your shopping-bag design. Your Press ads will use the following copy ...

Join the Paper-Chase down Oxford Street
to the great new "throw-away" lines at

PAPER
SHAPES

the world's first "paper"-made wear department
opening TODAY at OXBRIDGES

Body-copy

If we'd been in Paris, choosing a name would have been no problem. What else but "Papier Marche?" But since we're the newest— but *the* newest!—shopping idea in London, what could we do? ... "Paper Dolls" can so easily become Paper "Pieces" and even (heaven forbid!) might grow into Paper-Bags.

So we've chosen PAPER SHAPES, because this is where Oxbridges have opened the very first department in the world dealing exclusively in paper garments of all kinds! Not really "paper," of course—the material is a non-woven man-made fibre—but it's cheap, chic and chuckable.

Come in and see. The variety will amaze you! Paper-handkerchiefs have been with us a long time, of course. So have paper-pants. But under the label "Paper-Strips" you'll find swimwear, under "Paper-Hangups" are blouses and dresses, under "Paper-Strutters" are trouser-suits ... while, for those on the Unisex kick, there's "Paper Mates!"

And so on ... and so OFF! ... because you wear them and throw them away. Great for travel, for bedsit laundry problems, or weekend-guest worries, for dressing up to the latest fads and fashions week by week. And you'll see the biggest, most up-to-your-date selection of fabulous, colourful, top-style "throw-away" lines in the world *today* at

PAPER SHAPES
Oxbridges, Oxford St.

Letter to regular customers

Write a letter explaining the new department, which will go out over the signature of the managing director. In your mind, choose a person you know and adapt your writing-style to reflect *his* personality as you see it ... or as you feel *the customers see it*. Write two versions of the letter, (*a*) to the age-group 15–20 years, (*b*) to the age-group 30–60 years—and match your appeals accordingly. Your object is both to counter possible deep-seated prejudice against paper-clothes and to arouse a "buying" enthusiasm.

Research department

Go and station yourself outside the staff-exit of a large store or commercial firm, and ask the younger members of staff as they pour out for lunch-break, questions along these terms of reference:

1. Would they buy paper shirts/blouses?
2. How long would they expect "paper" garments to last?
3. If they were convinced of the practicality of paper clothes, what item of wear would they most like manufactured?
4. Would they tell their friends they were wearing clothes made of "paper?"
5. Is their present "image" of paper-wear one of Cheapness? ... Trendiness? ... "Fun"-wear ... or what?

Public relations

Think up a publicity stunt, in connection with the opening of the new department "Paper Shapes," that will focus public interest on the product, demonstrate its practicality and strength and avoid an impression of triviality.

For example, what about a way of showing that it's fireproof?

PROJECT 2

The flour combine of British Bakeries Limited have discovered a way to make bread which contains *no starch whatever*. This new slimming bread, aimed at the weight-and-health-conscious market, is to be called "Lite Bite," and your Agency has to produce a launch Press ad and an attractive wrapper for the loaf.

The wrapper

It is up to you to decide which size of loaf is most attractive and appropriate. Go out in the shops and supermarkets, take a look at the wrapper-designs and sizes of other slimming breads. Don't attempt to design "in the abstract" ... actually fold your ideas round a real loaf! You will use no more than three colours—less if possible, and familiarise yourself with the methods by which such a wrapper would be printed. The copy on the wrapper will be as follows ...

Name: LITE BITE "the light-hearted loaf"
Baseline: The only bread you can buy which contains no starch whatever!
Address: from
       British Bakeries Ltd.,
       12, Dunstan Grove,
       Tunbridge Wells,
       Kent

Though the client does not demand it, the Brand Manager would undoubtedly like to see a striking symbol for the wrapper which will also appear on the Press ad.

Press advertisement

This will be aimed at figure-conscious teenagers, to start with, and will appear in *black and white only* on a full-page of a magazine, which is 279 mm × 212 mm ... if you decide to "bleed" (i.e. have your design run to the edge of the page) the size will extend to 307 mm × 244 mm. You have your choice of setting the words (what I prefer to call "designing copy") in two versions, long or short, depending on the nature of your visual ...

Version A:
HEADLINE:

It's taken 300 years
But, at last,
the Starchless Sandwich!

Body-copy (102 words)

Who could have guessed that the nation which invented the sandwich would also one day invent the mini-skirt? Still, trust the British to produce a devilish clever compromise. Called LITE BITE ... the loaf with the lightest heart ever baked, for the first starchless sandwich in three centuries.

From British Bakeries, of course. Light-hearted because a new formula has produced a bread of high-protein content, delicious flavour and *no starch whatever*! So you can *waist* not—and *want* not, too. No more that agonising choice between wolf-whistles and tummy-grumbles when munchtime comes. You can eat to your sweetheart's content.

BASELINE:
LITE BITE   "the light-hearted loaf"
from British Bakeries

Version B:

HEADLINE:

Lite Bite
Gives Hungry Gels
A Leg to Stand On
(no thanks to Lord Sandwich)

Body-copy (200 words)

Young Lord Sandwich would never have dreamed of it, if he'd known what trouble his brain-wave would cause leg-conscious gels (and bravos) 300 years later. He was gambling all night with dice, not dollies, when he first thought of putting his red meat between two slices of bread.

But then, who would have guessed that the nation which invented the sandwich would also one day invent the mini-skirt? Deuced awkward! Still, trust the British to produce a devilish clever compromise. Called LITE BITE . . . the loaf with the lightest heart ever baked, for the first starchless sandwich in three centuries.

From British Bakeries, of course. Light-hearted, because a new formula has produced a bread of high-protein content, delicious flavour and *no starch whatever*! So you can *waist* not—and *want* not, too. No more that agonising choice between wolf-whistles and tummy-rumbles when munchtime comes.

Whenever you're peckish, forget figure-worries and eat to your sweetheart's content. Don't let your hemline dictate to your appetite any longer. LITE BITE helps you shape up to any man's expectations, and Lord Sandwich would have approved. If there had been mini-skirts in his time, who'd have needed the Hellfire Club?

BASELINE:
LITE BITE   "the light-hearted loaf"
from British Bakeries

Research department

Work out a set of questions for door-to-door interviews with housewives (don't choose a busy time of day, and offer her a free loaf of bread from a number of leading brands—but non-slimming ones!), and ask the same questions of girl students at your local technical or art college . . . along these lines:

    1. How believable to them is the "starch-free" claim?

2. When do they usually eat bread ... at breakfast? ... between-meals snacks? ... sandwich-suppers before the TV?

3. Would they pay more for a "starchless" loaf or would they resent it?

4. Do they believe that a slimming bread must have less "natural" flavour?

5. Do they slim for (*a*) beauty reasons, (*b*) health reasons or (*c*) reasons of guilt about gluttony?

6. Quite apart from what *they* believe men think, do *they* think a woman is more of a woman if ... well, if she's more of a woman?

Public relations

Prepare some Press releases for several different media—adopting your approach and style to the presumed readership (better still, ask for their rate card and readership "profiles," if available)—in which you describe interviews with doctors regarding the grave risks many young girls run in taking slimming-pills or in simply not eating enough and becoming malnourished.

PROJECT 3

Write a classified advertisement for the *Lost and Found* column of your local newspaper. The length of the ad should be between 50–100 words. You are provided with the following data by owner:

1. Dog's name is Prince.
2. He's a very valuable Alsatian.
3. Dog was lost from Rush Green Technical College.
4. A friend says she thinks she may have seen the animal near Barking Station.
5. Dog is inclined to viciousness with strangers or when frightened.
6. Reward of £15 offered.

What you must decide is the order of importance of these facts—not to the owner, but *to the reader*. Can any facts be omitted? What other facts, if any, do you need to know? Remember, you are after *prompt and optimum response*!

PROJECT 4

The International Wool Secretariat has decided to launch a campaign with this twin-objective: to promote the sale of products of all kinds which are made from wool; and to persuade manufacturers that wool should be the basic material of as many of their products as possible. There will be Press advertising, a leaflet/folder and a television commercial. Remember, all your visual designs must incorporate the famous Woolmark ... and must always have the three words "Pure New Wool" in conjunction.

Press advertisement

Since the theme to be plugged is the *universality* of wool, see if you can think of a symbol which sums it up. The theme-slogan (built round the notion of a ball of wool) could well be

"Everything On The Ball"

which emphasises the protean quality of the product, as well as its modernity.

Use the theme-slogan as your headline, or find a better one to suit your illustration to the advertisement, whose body-copy (147 words ... the typographer will want to know) is as follows and is planned to go with most visual-ideas ...

For hundreds of years, Britain has produced the finest wool products in the world. For one thing, we had to keep warm (and nothing is warmer than wool). For another, we had to keep dry (and nothing absorbs moisture, without increase of weight, better than wool). But most of all, we liked to look and *feel* our best (and nothing tailors with more style and better finish, nothing has more resilience, versatility, and comes lighter, softer to the touch, than wool).

We still feel that way about wool. And our wool products—from cardigans to cat-suits, socks to shawls, teddy-bears to tights, blankets to berets, the Inner and the Outer of every man, woman and child, for fashion and function equally—are still the world's envy. Because pure new wool is the best ever. And there's nothing that cannot be improved on by having that *Wool-Bred Look* ... there's no mistaking it!

Leaflet folder

The location of the following copy has only three specifications: front cover, centre-spread, back cover ... how the fold and spread is organised, whether or not colour is used, and how it is used, is up to the designer. The illustrative clues given in brackets guide the intention of the copy.

FRONT COVER:

Wool is Woven in the Fabric of our Lives

OPENING UP:

From the Seat of Justice ... (*Lord Chancellor's Woolsack*)

To the Seat of Learning ... (*sheepskin on academic gown*)

The Things We Play With ... (*toys or any connotation which strikes you*)

The Things We Care For ... (*garments or indeed persons in wool*)

The Things that Keep us Warm ... (*mittens, scarves, sweaters, socks, sheepskin coats, etc.*)

And Cool ... (*fashion in wool*)

The Things that come Home to us ... (*textiles in the home, from drapes and covers to oven-cloths and polishing pads*)

CENTRE-SPREAD:

Lead-in Copy

Whatever your life touches

Heading

There's No Mistaking
That Woolbred Look

Body-copy

They had that Woolbred Look in ancient Babylon. Caesar had it, too—he needed it, for that first channel-crossing! Thanks to the Normans, we've had it since 1066, when William put his furlined boot in at Hastings. Sheep-rearing monks turned Plantagenet England into a "medieval Australia." Later, Woolbred merchants got us first into Muscovy and India. The Romans put Britannia on to our coins, but it really ought to be Spinning Jenny. As a result, other nations tended to take us for sheep, when in fact we were only wool-gathering. For the man who sat on the woolsack, sat on top of the world.

For hundreds of years, Britain has produced the finest wool products. For one thing, we had to keep warm (and nothing is warmer than wool). For another, we had to keep dry (and nothing absorbs moisture, without increase of weight, better than wool). But, most of all, we always liked to look and *feel* our best in all places and situations and at all ages (and nothing tailors with more style and better finish, nothing has more resilience, versatility, and comes lighter, softer to the touch, than wool).

We still feel that way about wool. And our wool products are still the world's envy. From cardigans to cat-suits, socks to shawls, teddy-bears to tights, blankets to berets, drapes to drain-pipes, wool makes up the Inner and Outer aspect of every man, woman and child, for fashion and function. Because pure new wool is still the best ever. And there's nothing in this world that cannot be sensationally improved in appearance by having That Woolbred Look. You can't fake it. You can't mistake it.

BACK COVER:
Headline

No Need To Go
Wool-Gathering Now!

Body-copy

Find out the facts about wool. How it can affect *your* life, even more than wool affects it now.

The publications shown here are only a few of those available from us on request. We can supply films and lecturers, too, free of charge, on request.

All information and assistance, both to individuals and groups, schools and manufacturers, is easily obtainable from:

Information Department
INTERNATIONAL WOOL SECRETARIAT
6, Carlton Gardens,
London, S.W.1
Tel. 01-930 7300

Television commercial

The visual instructions given here are guides only to the shape and flow of themes and ideas in the commercial. For instance, the "cat" lead-in and finish can be done all sorts of ways ... but don't forget the Woolmark!

Sound	*Vision*
Wool is on the ball	Kitten-cat plays with big ball of wool
... like never before	it starts stringing out into
for the things you play with	toys, animals, etc. ...
the things you care for ...	actual garments or cuddly-wrapped sweethearts ...
the things that keep you warm ...	mittens, scarves, sweaters, socks, sheepskin-linings, etc.
and cool ...	fashion in wool
the things that come home to you ...	textiles in the home, or girl-friend or husband in the driving snow ...
Wool touches all our lives, because all our lives ... touch wool ...	Optional visuals ...
And there's no mistaking that Woolbred Look ... Eh, kitty ...?	Back to the kitten, ball of wool and the woolmark.

Media department

Take in hand your copy of *BRAD* (British Rate and Data, but get used to calling it *BRAD*), or consult a library copy, and plan media-schedules for the above, keeping these points in mind always ...

1. Who do you wish the Press ad to be seen by ... in which consumer or trade media will it be seen by the most at least cost?
2. What means of distribution for the leaflet/folder will you recommend? Left in showrooms? Mailed to selected manufacturers? Put through suburban letter-boxes or sent to schools and colleges? Inserted into magazines such as the Diners Club *Signature*?
3. What time of day are you most likely to catch the woman of the house with your TV ad? Will you try a test-run first ... if so, in which region?

(It is perhaps unnecessary to stress that none of the above is part of an actual campaign undertaken by the International Wool Secretariat. But I should like to acknowledge the immense help given by supplying information and previous promotional material to the students of the Advertising Course, by Raymond Keys, Education and Training Manager of I.W.S. His kind co-operation is typical of the assistance industry always stands ready to give "actuality" courses of this nature, and I and my colleagues were most grateful for his permission, and that of G. Maylett, Advertising Manager of I.W.S., to proceed with our "campaign.")

OTHER PROJECTS

There is no substitute in education for Advertising than by *doing* it ... and the above examples will, I hope, both show you ways of developing your own assignments and projects and will in themselves illustrate a number of essential points I have made in the foregoing chapters; these four projects have ranged from a small classified advertisement to a "generic" campaign for wool, and from them you can proceed (as the constables say) to planning media schedules for products you are familiar with, or shutting off the sound of the TV and writing your own script, or "masking" the illustration of an ad and thinking up your own visual for the body-copy ... with appropriate P.R. and research!

For your make-believe campaigns, you may get the willing aid of local firms or industries. For a start, however, you might concentrate on probable or possible "public service" campaigns of the future, such as the Beauty Pill, the Non-Tobacco Cigarette or Aid for Over-Developed Countries.

BIBLIOGRAPHY

Aaker, D. A. (ED.). *Advertising Management*. Prentice-Hall Inc., 1975.
Bartlett, Sir Basil. *Writing for Television*. Allen and Unwin, 1955.
Barton, A. *Kate in Advertising*. Bodley Head, 1955.
Beaton, C. *The Glass of Fashion*. Weidenfeld and Nicolson, 1954.
Bernstein, D. *Creative Advertising*. Longman, 1974.
Black, S. *Practical Public Relations*. Pitman, 1966.
Blum, D. *Pictorial History of the Silent Screen*. Spring Books, 1953.
Boorstin, D. *The Image*. Weidenfeld and Nicolson, 1963.
Boyce, N. *Business Examination Questions Answered*. Macmillan, 1975.
Brewer, R. *An Approach to Print*. Blandford Press, 1971.
Caples, J. *Making Advertisements Pay*. Dover Publications, 1966.
Caplin, R. S. *Advertising, a general introduction*. Business Publications, 1959.
Carroll, L. *Alice's Adventures in Wonderland*. Heritage Reprints, 1941.
Chandor, P. *Advertising and Publicity* (Teach Yourself Series). Teach Yourself Books, English Universities Press, 1950.
Egan, B. *The Customer and the Law*. Sphere Books, 1969.
Elliott, B. *A History of English Advertising*. Business Publications Limited & Batsford, 1962.
Ervine, St. J. *Bernard Shaw*. Constable, 1972.
Evans, W. A. *Advertising Today and Tomorrow*. Allen and Unwin, 1974.
Fairbank, A. *A Book of Scripts*. Pelican, 1968.
Della Femina, J. *From those Wonderful Folks Who Gave You Pearl Harbour*. Pitman, 1971.
Furneaux, R. *The Empty Tomb*. Panther, 1963.
Galbraith, J. K. *The Affluent Society*. Hamish Hamilton, 1958.
Gorer, G. *The Americans*. Cresset Press, 1948.
Green, A. and Laurie, J., Jr. *From Vaude to Video*. Henry Holt, 1951.
Hinwood, T. *Advertising Art*. David & Charles, 1973.
Hobson, J. *The Influence and Techniques of Modern Advertising*. IPA, 1965.
Hobson, J. W. *The Selection of Advertising Media*. Business Books Ltd., 1968.
Hopkins, C. *Scientific Advertising*. MacGibbon & Kee, 1968.
Horan, J. and Sann, P. *Pictorial History of the Wild West*. Spring Books, 1954.
Huxley, A. Essay "Advertisement", *On the Margin*. Chatto and Windus, 1948.
Ingman, D. *Television Advertising*. Business Publications, 1965.
Jefkins, F. *Advertisement Writing*. Macdonald and Evans, 1976.
McKnight Kauffer, E. *Art of the Poster*. Albert & Charles Boni, 1924.
Kempton, K. *The Short Story*. Harvard University Press, 1947.
Kleinman, P. *Advertising Inside Out*. Manton Press, 1977.
Langer, W. *An Encyclopedia of World History*. Harrap, 1973.

Leduc, R. *How to Launch a New Product*. Crosby Lockwood & Son, 1966.
Lennon, F. B. *The Life of Lewis Carroll*. Simon and Schuster, 1945.
McGinniss, J. *The Selling of the President*. André Deutsch, 1970.
McIver, C. *Marketing*. Business Publications, 1959.
McLuhan and Fiore. *The Medium is the Massage*. Penguin, 1967.
McLuhan, M. *Understanding Media*. Routledge and Kegan Paul, 1964.
Mann, C. *Market Models*. Mantec Publications Ltd., 1970.
Mann, P. *150 Careers in Advertising*. Longman, 1971.
May, L. H. (ED.). *Pocket Pal (Printing Reproduction)*. Advertising Agency Production Association, 1966.
Mayer, M. *Madison Avenue, U.S.A.* Bodley Head, 1958.
Menkes, S. *How to be a Model*. Sphere Books, 1969.
Moorehead, A. *The White Nile*. Hamish Hamilton, 1966.
Ogilvy, D. *Confessions of an Advertising Man*. Longmans Green, 1964.
Packard, V. *The Waste Makers*. Longmans Green, 1961.
Packard, V. *The Hidden Persuaders*. Penguin, 1970.
Pearson, H. *G. B. S.* Garden City, 1946.
Pearson, H. *The Life of Oscar Wilde*. Methuen, 1946.
Pigott, S. *OBM–125 years*. Ogilvy Benson & Mather, 1975.
Quiller-Couch, Sir Arthur. *On the Art of Writing*. Guild Books, 1946.
Rossi, A. *Posters*. Paul Hamlyn, 1974.
Sayers, D. *Murder Must Advertise*. Gollancz, 1971.
Spaeth, S. *A History of Popular Music in America*. Phoenix House, 1960.
Sutphen, D. *The Mad Old Ads*. W. H. Allen, 1968.
Swindells, A. *Advertising Media and Campaign Planning*. Butterworth & Co., 1966.
Turner, E. S. *The Shocking History of Advertising*. Michael Joseph, 1962.
Webster, E. *Advertising for the Advertiser*. John Murray, 1969.
Wilson, A. (ED.). *Advertising and the Community*. Manchester University Press, 1968.
Woolley, D. *Advertising Law Handbook*. Business Books Ltd., 1976.
Advertiser's Annual 1977. Admark Directories Ltd.
Art for All: London Transport Posters 1908–1949. Intro. by J. Laver, Art & Technics.
The British Code of Advertising Practice. Advertising Standards Authority, 1976 Edition.
Complete Plays of Gilbert and Sullivan. Garden City, 1938.
The Encyclopedia Britannica. 15th Edition, 1976.
The Everyman Encyclopedia 1967.
Fifty Years of Advertising—What Next? I.P.A., 1968.
Post Office Guide, 1975.
Purnell's New English Encyclopedia 1956.
What Advertising Does. I.P.A., 1966.
Why You Need an Advertising Agency. I.P.A., 1968.
Works of Bernard Shaw. Constable, 1950.
Works of Oscar Wilde. Edinburgh Society, 1911.
The Writers' and Artists' Year Book 1978. A. & C. Black.

Appendix II

AGENCIES AND ORGANISATIONS

The following are names, addresses and telephone numbers of the ten highest billing advertising agencies in the United Kingdom, as at the end of 1976. Inevitably, they are all located in London. The figure given in brackets represents the number of staff they employ and it will be seen that this does not necessarily match their billing order, though there is a clear correlation. In common with all other industries, Advertising has been subject to many mergers in recent years and a list of the twelve largest Agency Groups is given also. The leading agencies in Scotland and Wales are listed as well. Since billings are subject to constant fluctuation, as accounts come and go from agencies and media appropriations are altered, the figures are the most accurate estimate possible and were supplied to the magazine *Campaign* by the agencies themselves in almost every case. The author is indebted to the Editor of *Campaign*, Mr. Michael Chamberlain, and to Mr. Ken Viney, the compiler of these listings, for permission to reproduce them here. A fuller list is available from the offices of *Campaign* itself, which updates it annually.

This appendix also lists the principal advertising and research organisations referred to in the text.

The Top Ten

J. Walter Thompson Co., Ltd., 40 Berkeley Square, London, W1X 6AD. Tel: 01–629 9496. (751) £48·46 million

Masius Wynne-Williams & D'Arcy-MacManus, Ltd., 2 St James's Square, London, SW1Y 4JY. Tel: 01–839 3422. (480) £40·00 million

McCann-Erickson Advertising Ltd., McCann-Erickson House, 36 Howland Street, London, W1P 6BD. Tel: 01–580 6690. (485) £39·50 million

Ogilvy, Benson and Mather Ltd., Brettenham House, Lancaster Place, London, WC2E 7EZ. Tel: 01–836 2466. (403) £33·50 million

Young and Rubicam Ltd., Greater London House, Hampstead Road, London, NW1 7QP. Tel: 01–387 9366. (300) £26·60 million

Saatchi and Saatchi: Garland-Compton Ltd., 80–84 Charlotte Street, London, W1. Tel: 01–636 5060. £26·10 million

Collett, Dickenson, Pearce & Partners Ltd., 18 Howland Street, London, W1P 6AJ. Tel: 01–636 3355. (230) £25·00 million

Ted Bates Ltd., 155 Gower Street, London, WC1E 6BJ. Tel: 01–387 4313. (244) £24·50 million

Wasey Campbell-Ewald Ltd., Williams House, Eastbourne Terrace, London, W2 6DL. Tel: 01–262 3424. (257) £18·00 million

Foote, Cone & Belding Ltd., 82 Baker Street, London, W1M 2A4. Tel: 01–935 4426. (262) £16·70 million

Leading Agencies, Scotland

Hall Advertising Ltd., 11 Chester Street, Edinburgh, EH3 7RQ. Tel: 031–226 4411. (63) £3·00 million
Woolward Royds Ltd., 7 Castle Terrace, Edinburgh, EH1 2DT. Tel: 031–229 4466. (80) £3·00 million
MCS/Robertson and Scott Ltd., MCS House, 23 Park Circus, Glasgow, G3 6AS. Tel: 041–332 9733. (65) £2·64 million
Struthers Advertising and Marketing Ltd., 2 Blythswood Square, Glasgow, G2 4UB. Tel: 041–221 9927. (51) £2·10 million
R. and W. Advertising Ltd., 18 Rutland Square, Edinburgh, EH1 2BH. Tel: 031–229 7493. (54) £1·87 million
Simpson and Gemmell Ltd., 11 Royal Crescent, Glasgow, G3 7SL. Tel: 041–332 6686. (16) £0·60 million

Leading Agencies, Wales

Creighton-Griffiths Royds Ltd., 30 Cathedral Road, Cardiff, CF1 9XX. Tel: 0222 397711. (30) £1·20 million
Golley Slater & Partners Ltd., 9 & 11 The Hayes, Cardiff, CF1 1NU. Tel: 0222 388621. (38) £1·40 million
Golley Slater & Partners Ltd. (London), 125 High Holborn, London WC1. Tel: 01–242 8421. (17) £1·00 million

Agency Groups

J. Walter Thompson Group:
Main J. Walter Thompson Agency; Contract; Deltakos; Lansdowne; Recruitment, British Market Research Bureau, Lexington Public Relations.
£62·74 million
Lopex:
Interlink; Kirkwood; other general agencies in London and provinces; two specialist agencies; St. James's and Whites Recruitment, also both in London and provinces.
£42·50 million
Saatchi and Saatchi Compton:
Saatchi and Saatchi: Garland-Compton (London and provinces); Roe Downton (London and Gloucester).
£37·00 million
Charles Barker AHB International:
Ayer Barker Hegemann; City recruitment agencies; PR and film companies; Birmingham and Scottish agencies; Companies in North America and Europe.
British billings: £28·50 million
Kimpher Group:
Eighteen specialist advertising companies and agencies, including Allardyce PLN, KMP Partnership and LAP.
£24·80 million
Royds Advertising Group:
Nine agencies in Britain, Northern Ireland and Dublin, including Royds London, Stowe and Bowden, Creighton-Griffiths Royds.
£24·75 million

Chetwynd Streets (Holdings):
Rupert Chetwynd, Streets Advertising, Streets Financial, plus Chetwynd
Streets agencies in London, Leicester, Manchester and Glasgow.
£14·75 million
Brunning Group:
Nine agencies in London and provinces, public relations firms, two market-
ing companies.
£12·59 million
Rex Stewart and Associates:
Twenty-two agencies in London, provinces and Scotland, including Ste-
wart and Jefferies Associates, Forbes Keir and Riley Advertising, also P.R.
and advertising service companies.
£11·55 million
Geers Gross:
Geers Gross Ltd., Browne's Advertising.
£9·00 million
Edman Investments:
Astral Agency, plus "below-the-line" companies.
£6·20 million
National Advertising Corporation:
Six National Advertising Corporation agencies in London and provinces,
plus United Kingdom Advertising, London.
£4·72 million

(NOTES: Figure for Lopex Group does not include their marketing services and
research data activities—these totalled £3·70 million in 1976. The Brunnings
figure extends only to the company year ending 31st March 1976, and it
excludes distribution and manufacturing activities—these totalled £3·99 million in 1976.)

Organisations

Institute of Practitioners in Advertising, 44 Belgrave Square, London, SW1
8QS. Tel: 01–235 7020.
The Advertising Association, Abford House, 15 Wilton Road, London,
SW1V 1NJ. Tel: 01–828 2771.
Incorporated Advertising Management Association, Mansfield House, Bul-
strode Lane, Felden, Hemel Hempstead, Herts. Tel: 0442 58126.
Incorporated Society of British Advertisers Ltd., 2 Basil Street, Knights-
bridge, London, SW3 1AG. Tel: 01–584 5221.
Institute of Marketing, Moor Hall, Cookham, Berks. Tel: 062–85 24922.
Institute of Public Relations, 1 Great James Street, London, WC1N 3DA.
Tel: 01–405 5505.
Market Research Society, 15 Belgrave Square, London, SW1X 8PF. Tel:
01–235 4709.
Independent Television Companies Association Ltd., Knighton House, 52–
66 Mortimer Street, London, W1N 8AN. Tel: 01–636 6866.
Communication Advertising and Marketing Education Foundation Ltd.
(CAM), 1 Bell Yard, London, WC2A 2JX. Tel: 01–405 6223.
Marplan Ltd., 20 Eastbourne Terrace, London, W2 6LP. Tel: 01–723 7228.
Mass Observation (U.K.) Ltd., 229–243 Shepherds Bush Road, London W6.
Tel: 01–748 9172.
Media Expenditure Analysis Ltd. (MEAL), 110 St. Martin's Lane, London,
WC2N 4BH. Tel: 01–240 1903.

Louis Harris (Research) Ltd., 251–259 Regent Street, Oxford Circus, London, W1A 4YZ. Tel: 01–734 9611.

Audits of Great Britain Ltd. (Television Audience Research, producers of JICTAR viewing figures), Audit House, Field End Road, Eastcote, Ruislip, Middlesex. Tel: 01–868 4422.

British Direct Mail Producers Association, 34 Grand Avenue, London, N10 3EP. Tel: 01–883 7229.

British Direct Mail Advertising Association, 1 New Burlington Street, London, W1X 1FD. Tel: 01–437 4485.

The Post Office Market Development Division, Postal Headquarters, St. Martins-le-Grand, London, EC1A 1HQ. Tel: 01–432 4861.

ADVERTISING UNDER LAW

Accommodation Agencies Act 1953.
Adoption Act 1958 (section I).
Advertisements (Hire-Purchase) Act 1938 (1957).
Agriculture (Safety, Health and Welfare Provisions) Act 1956.
Betting and Loans (Infants) Act 1892.
Betting Gaming and Lotteries Act 1963 (Part III and sections 10 and 12).
Building Societies Act 1960 (sections 5, 7 and 10).
Business Names Registration Act 1916.
Cancer Act 1939 (section 4).
Children and Young Persons (Harmful Publications) Act 1955.
Children Act 1958 (section 37).
Cinematograph Films Act 1938.
Civil Aviation (Aerial Advertising) Regulations 1971.
Civil Aviation (Air Travel Organisers' Licensing) Regulations 1972.
Civil Aviation (Licensing) Act 1960.
Coinage Offences Act 1936.
Companies Act 1948 (section 38 and the fourth schedule).
Consumer Credit Act 1974.
Consumer Protection Act 1961 (section 1), as amended by Consumer Protection Act, 1971 and regulations made thereunder.
Copyright Act 1956.
Criminal Justice Act 1925 (section 38).
Criminal Justice Act 1972.
Customs and Excise Act 1952 (sections 162 and 164), as amended by Finance Acts 1964 (section 2) and 1967 (section 6) and Theatres Act 1968 (section 2).
Defamation Act 1952.
Design Copyright Act 1968.
Employment Agencies Act 1973 (in regard to recruitment advertising).
Fair Trading Act 1973.
Finance Act 1965 (section 15) (in regard to "gift" advertising).
Food and Drugs Act 1955, and Labelling of Food Order (S.I. 1953, No. 536).
Forgery Act 1913.
Geneva Convention Act 1957 (section 6).
Hire Purchase and Credit Sales Agreements (Control) Order 1960.
Indecent Advertisements Act 1889.
Independent Authority Broadcasting Act 1973.
Industrial Training Act 1964.
Labelling of Food Order 1953 (1959).

Larceny Act 1861 (section 102).
London Cab Act 1968 (as amended 1973).
Marine, etc., Broadcasting (Offences) Act 1967.
Medicines Act 1968.
Merchandise Marks Acts 1887–1953.
Misrepresentation Act 1967.
Moneylenders Act 1927 (sections 4 and 5).
Noise Abatement Act 1960.
Obscene Publications Act 1959 and 1964.
Opticians Act 1958.
Patents Act 1949 (section 92).
Pharmacy and Medicines Act 1941 (sections 8–13 and 15–17).
Pharmacy and Poisons Act 1933.
Post Office Acts 1908–1953 (sections 61 and 62).
Pre-Packed Food (Weights and Measures: Marking) Regulations 1959.
Prevention of Frauds (Investments) Act 1958 (sections 13, 14 and 17).
Protection of Depositors (Contents of Advertisements) Regulations 1963.
Protection of Depositors (Exempted Advertisements) Regulations 1963.
Race Relations Act 1968.
Registered Designs Act 1949.
Representation of the People Act 1949 (sections 63, 94 and 95).
Road Traffic Act 1960 (twelfth schedule).
Sale of Goods Act 1893.
Southern Rhodesia (United Nations) Sanctions No. 2 Order 1968.
Sunday Observance Act 1780 (section 3), Common Informer Act 1951 and
    Sunday Entertainments Act 1932.
Supply of Goods (Implied Terms) Act 1973 (in regard to "guarantees").
Television Act 1964.
Town and Country Planning Act 1947 (sections 31 and 32) and Town and
    Country Planning (Control of Advertisements) Regulations 1960 (S.I.
    1960, No. 695).
Town Police Clauses Act 1847 (section 28).
Trade Descriptions Act 1968.
Trade Descriptions Act 1972.
Trade Marks Acts 1887–1938.
Unsolicited Goods and Services Act 1971.
Vagrancy Act 1924 (section 4).
Venereal Diseases Act 1971 (sections 2 and 3).
Weights and Measures Act 1963 (schedules 4–8).

(IMPORTANT: Regulations in regard to advertising cigarettes and tobacco are
not the subject of Statute Law but are governed by a Cigarette Code of Advertising drawn up by agreement between the cigarette manufacturers and the
Code of Advertising Practice Committee, under the general supervision of
the Advertising Standards Authority. See Appendix M of the *British Code of
Advertising Practice* (1976). Regulations in regard to alcoholic beverages are
covered under Appendix N.)

INDEX